A Journey
in Search of
Korea's Beauty

Bae Yong Joon

Hollym

A Journey in Search of Korea's Beauty

Copyright © 2010 by KEYEAST

Written by Bae Yong Joon
Translated by Sora Kim-Russell
Photographed by Bae Yong Joon, Kim Ho-il, Chuu Young-ho (Studio Allstar)

First published in 2010
by Hollym International Corp., USA
Phone 908 353 1655   **Fax** 908 353 0255
http://www.hollym.com   **e-Mail** contact@hollym.com

 Hollym

Published simultaneously in Korea
by Hollym Corp., Publishers, Seoul, Korea
Phone +82 2 734 5087   **Fax** +82 2 730 8192
http://www.hollym.co.kr   **e-Mail** info@hollym.co.kr

ISBN: 978-1-56591-307-3
Library of Congress Control Number: 2010941042

Printed in Korea

*Romanization of Korean names in this book follows the Romanization System used by the Korean Government since 2000.

A Journey
in Search of
Korea's Beauty

Awakening Your Sense of Smell with Words

What does snow smell like? Probably no one has ever really smelled snow. Human beings were originally equipped to distinguish between ten thousand or more different smells, but people today have lost about eighty percent of that capacity and can only properly recognize around two thousand smells. Nevertheless, when I saw Bae Yong Joon in the television show *Winter Sonata*, I caught the scent of something pure, like a plum blossom flowering in the snow. That was not because of the wintery backdrop of *Winter Sonata* or the snow at the ski resort where the show was filmed. When it comes to actors, we all focus on the visual first. But there is more to Bae Yong Joon's acting than that. From his face to his voice, to the look in his eyes and his gestures, his performance is filled with the scent of life and the physical elegance that he carries unawares within him.

When Bae Yong Joon meets the renowned pottery expert Cheon Han-bong to talk about making pottery, I catch the earthy scent of clay. Not the coarse smell of dirt, but rather the scent of soil wafting faintly from a field in the countryside after a rain shower has passed. Hands that throw clay. Eyes that watch "flames fluttering up like butterflies" inside the kiln. This is not the Bae Yong Joon we see on the screen, but the Bae Yong Joon who smiles with satisfaction as he chooses from among the many finished items a tea bowl that he made himself. Now he says he has gone beyond being just an onlooker but studies pottery on his own and even makes bowls on a pottery wheel installed in his house. He sits before me, absorbed in making pottery, smelling faintly of the soil of my hometown and looking as poised as a white porcelain jar from the Joseon Dynasty.

When Bae Yong Joon meets Park Dong-chun, a disciple of the Venerable Choui, who revived the art of Korean tea, to talk about the culture of tea, I sense the aroma of tea leaves. Bae Yong Joon tries to identify the different smells that rise up from the tea leaves as they roast, but before he can name even one, they vanish and are quickly replaced by others. Did he soon discover the stage of tea where fire and water mingle together and heaven, earth and man become one? Bae Yong Joon's charm can only be explained through the scent of that tea.

Bae Yong Joon also studies lacquer painting with Jeon Yong-bok, a Korean lacquer artist. When I read about that experience, I catch yet another scent wafting off of him. In Korea, we use the phrase "as dark as lacquer." The darkest shade of black is compared to lacquer. The flickers of light, like stars or moonlight, glimpsed within that darkness are like mother-of-pearl. That is how black abalone shells hidden within the darkest depths of the sea sparkle. That light, which glimmers briefly like the moon's halo in the dark, gives off the mysterious scent of light and dark as they cross paths.

Bae Yong Joon told me, "I had no idea writing was this difficult. This is the first time I have ever spent so long and worked so hard on something. Now the book is done."

As soon as I heard that, I truly understood his appeal, his beauty, his good nature and his honesty. Now that he has written about studying and experiencing Korean culture firsthand, what scent might this book carry? The scent of snow falling in winter? A clay bowl fresh from the kiln? Or would it be the scent of the sea mingled with the darkness and light of lacquerware inlaid with mother-of-pearl? For those of us who have lost so much of our olfactory senses, the scent given off by Bae Yong Joon's cultural genes may be hard to detect.

This is Bae Yong Joon's aromatic endeavor, *A Journey in Search of Korea's Beauty*.

Lee O-Young
Korea's first Minister of Culture

Bae Yong Joon:
Messenger of Traditional Korean Culture

We learn togetherness through meeting, and we dream of a better world through communication. The way we meet varies in object and circumstance. But accidental meetings are all the more valuable when they happen in the process of searching for future-oriented values. I met Bae Yong Joon, one of this generation's prominent figures, for a simple reason. We were both looking in different ways for values worth sharing. Our point of overlap was traditional Korean tea.

I believe it was in early April that I got a phone call from Lee Hyo-jae, a *hanbok* designer. She said Bae Yong Joon wanted to meet with me. As we had crossed paths several times, I was happy to accept the invitation. But truth be told, I had my doubts. I could not believe that an actor was writing a book on traditional Korean culture. Not long after, Lee showed up with a young man in tow. It was the tall, handsome, world-famous star Bae Yong Joon. There was a sense of nobility about him befitting one of the leaders of this generation. The look in his eyes was clear and earnest. He simply and straightforwardly stated his goal of spreading traditional Korean culture to the rest of the world. Neither rambling nor awkward, he exhibited all the daring of a classical scholar from an earlier era. I asked him bluntly what his interest in traditional culture and his motivation for writing were; his answer was clear and assertive. I drank tea with him. Though our surroundings were noisy and distracting, he proved that he was a keen observer with plenty of focus. I was relieved. I believed he would be capable of understanding the pure essence of traditional Korean tea and the exquisite world it possesses.

Three days before the spring rain began, he hurried to the tea fields all the way down from Seoul, having heard that the first tea of the season was going to be made. I was surprised at his interest in and passion for traditional tea. His sense of awe at the first crop was impressive. The essence of first flush tea is balance, so it must be handled carefully. For the first tea of the season, Bae Yong Joon was right there, keeping pace with me through the whole process, from picking the leaves to roasting them. Very few people have experienced the inner workings of tea in that kind of detail. Through his consistent focus and insight, he learned the logic behind tea making, and we shared the profound world of tea. I am confident that through that brief moment of sharing, which connected past, present and future, he took to heart the proud tradition of tea.

For many years, tea has been consumed as medicine, as a spiritual aid and as a popular beverage. The purpose for drinking tea has changed over the generations, but it has always served as a bridge that connects people to people and people to nature. Accordingly, tea is both a part of traditional Korean culture to be shared for posterity and a part of the common heritage of humanity to be shared with the world. Only those who understand this can enjoy it and have the power to protect it. Bae Yong Joon, this generation's self-appointed messenger of traditional culture, understands the true essence of traditional tea. Through this book, his understanding of traditional culture will open the door to true communication. Furthermore, while writing this book, he demonstrated his passion for and interest in traditional culture by sparing no trouble to go off at a moment's notice in search of any place where traditional culture in all its forms could be found. I look forward to seeing his intentions to spread the message of traditional Korean culture reveal themselves even more clearly. Meanwhile, I pray that this book will be the message that he seeks to send.

Park Dong-chun
Research Institute of East Asian Tea Culture

In Celebration of Publication

At a time when culture has become a source of national competitiveness, a museum is no longer simply a cultural institution but can be called a cultural heart where the strength of a nation's history and culture is felt. That is, they are both a symbol of the national brand and a repository of cultural contents.

2009 marked the hundredth year since Korea's first modern museum, Jesil Bangmulgwan (Imperial Household Museum), was opened. In celebration of this anniversary, the National Museum of Korea is pursuing joint projects with public, private and university museums and art galleries all around the country in order to become a space that does not feel taxidermied but rather alive and familiar and joining in people's lives.

It was therefore a fortuitous time for Bae Yong Joon, one of the leading actors of the "Korean wave," to prepare this meaningful book, which is a loving tribute to Korean culture, and include a wonderful essay introducing the National Museum of Korea.

It was delightful and gratifying as a museum worker to watch as he sought out Korea's present and future in relics from the past to include in his book. Over the course of several visits to the museum, he listened to lectures, asked questions and examined the exhibits.

A magnificent performer on both the television and movie screen, Bae Yong Joon traded the stage for the museum, where he engaged in earnest conversation with artifacts and gave what may have been his most enthusiastic performance to date. I regard it as a meeting between Korea's "masterpieces" and a "master actor," and I give them my sincerest applause.

I hope that many more people will be encouraged to visit the museum, and that they will approach it as a treasure hunt, a journey of discovery to learn about our culture and understand the past.

In closing, I believe that this book will go a long way toward spreading the strength and beauty of Korean culture around the world, and I once again give my sincerest congratulations on the publication of *A Journey in Search of Korea's Beauty*.

Choe Kwang-shik
National Museum of Korea

Contents

Foreword   005

The Journey Begins   013

Staying   居

01. Home Cooking   016
02. Kimchi   044
03. *Hanbok* and Housekeeping   068

Leaving   就

04. Black Lacquer   096
05. Temple Stay   132
06. Tea   172
07. Pottery   200

Letting Go   捐

08. Hwangnyongsa and Mireuksa Temple Sites   232

Contemplating 觀

09. Hangeul and
    King Sejong the Great   260

10. Gyeongbokgung Palace and   278
    an Ancient Map of the Sky

11. National Museum of Korea   300

Returning 還

12. Wine and Song   322
13. *Hanok*   348

Leaving, Once Again 再回

14. Landscape   372

Letters from the Road   392
The Journey Ends   394

Routes & Maps

ROUTE 1.

Seoul   398

ROUTE 2.

North Gyeongsang-do Province   404

ROUTE 3.

Gyeonggi-do &   408
Gangwon-do Provinces

ROUTE 4.

South Jeolla-do Province   414

TIP   418

The Journey Begins

I believe it was a press conference in Japan. One of the many reporters there asked me a question. Were there any special destinations or tourist attractions in Korea that I wished to recommend? I remember being unable to answer right away. I thought, how much do I really know about my own culture? It was embarrassing, but I did not have an answer.

I did not become an actor because I wanted to be popular. I still feel puzzled by the popularity I have enjoyed and wonder whether I really deserve it, but I am always grateful for it. I had been looking for a way to express my gratitude and give something back when I chanced upon the idea of writing a book. I thought it could be a way for me to learn more about our culture and possibly rediscover myself in the process. I thought maybe I could uncover the hidden force that has protected me and kept me on track all these years. And I wanted to offer our beautiful, wonderful culture as a gift to all those who have cared for me. But most of all, I wanted to do it, not as Bae Yong Joon the actor, but as an individual, lonely as ever, and in search of something that I had been longing for. I wanted to return to an earlier time, back when I first started acting, when I was still young and awkward and full of passion and earnestness for life. I wanted to start fresh.

Like my family (fans) who care for me, I am just one man, still full of questions about life. Lately I have become painfully aware of the fact that if that thing inside of me, that thing that enables me to long for something, were to disappear, I would be left with a soulless existence. I wanted to find that thing, in culture, in people and in my own heart. Ultimately, this book is not meant to be a representation of Korea. In fact, part of me fears that it may even misrepresent it in some ways. Instead, I hope this book will be understood as a record of my unfledged yet earnest journey as a novice in search of that something inside all of us. I know this book is far from perfect, but I cannot help but hope that it will serve to draw people's attention to Korean culture and beyond, to the many magnificent cultures of Asia.

May this small gift bring great joy.

Bae Yong Joon
Fall 2009

居

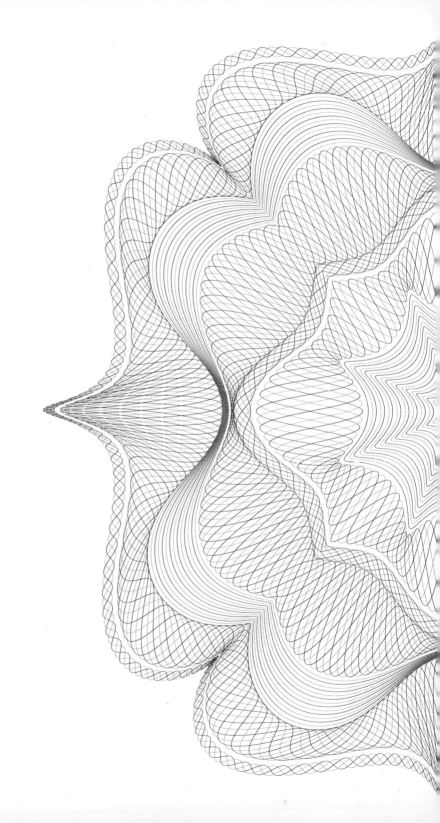

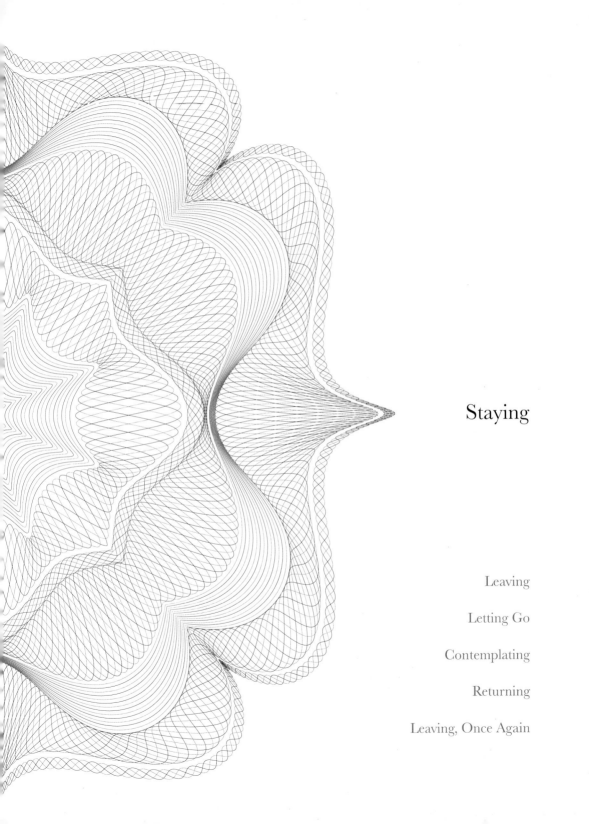

Staying

Leaving

Letting Go

Contemplating

Returning

Leaving, Once Again

Home Cooking 01

Mother's Table,
Mother's Tears

Morning

I woke up later than usual. But I was loath to get out of bed. My stomach growled, but my mouth felt like it was stuffed with cotton. On such mornings, when I worked late the night before and just want to lie around, my body as limp as a wet cloth, I wish someone would force me awake by carrying in a breakfast tray set with a lively feast, something that would fill the room with its savory mouth-watering aromas. Lying there, recalling this vain fantasy, I could not help but laugh. These mornings always end the same way: "Today... I'll eat out!"

Though I know my way around a kitchen and can make certain dishes with confidence, I have grown so accustomed to eating out that I sometimes lose interest in food. No matter how much effort a restaurant puts into its menu, it can never match the love and devotion that goes into a home-cooked meal. There is a lot to be said about the thrill of fine dining and the surprising joy of unexpected flavors. But there is also great meaning to be found in the simplicity of the everyday, and the vitality of the simple and humble home-cooked meal that people eat day in and day out. Indeed, most of my life has been filled with simple meals of rice and side dishes eaten at home.

When I was young, I was clueless about food. I only cared about my favorite foods and had no interest whatsoever in how the food made it to the table in front of me, or what the person who made the food was doing with their time. Now, a forgotten longing rushes over me.

Back then, regardless of whether times were good or bad, the moment I sat down at the family table and saw the steam rising from the food, my worries would vanish into thin air. The food gave me the strength to overcome anything. Even when I hid under my blanket and threw a tantrum, my mother would simply say, "Eat something, then go back to sleep." Urging me to eat was my mother's way of showing her love. I remember the peculiar power of food. When I was young, it bothered me to hear people say, "Food is the best medicine," as if all there was to life was eating and nothing else. But now that I have lived on my own for many years, I find myself nodding in agreement. *Mouths to feed, breaking bread*—aren't these just different words for *family*?

I left home and began living on my own in my twenties because I wanted my parents to be comfortable and to not have to look after me. But now I find myself wondering if I have been a bad son for not doing more to care for them all those years, and I find myself asking them for small favors. I whine about the things I did not get to whine about before, and my parents pretend to scold me for it. I feel fortunate that they seem to enjoy talking and bonding in this way.

Wonsan (Korea)
Elizabeth Keith, 1919,
Color woodblock print,
Collection of Song Young-dahl
(Source: *Elizabeth Keith's Korea: 1920-1940*, Chaekgwa hamkke
Publishing)

Scenes on the Way to a Country Home

In the 1920s, a British painter named Elizabeth Keith[1] produced a painting called "Morning Mists," which depicted a typical morning in the town of Wonsan in Gangwon-do Province.

> I can never hope to convince you of the beauty of Wonsan. And, with my usual good fortune, the house where I am staying has what must be one of the loveliest views from any civilized dwelling in the whole world...
>
> What enchantment there is in the land! The very stars have a new quality. As I tramp about on the look out for material I often pause and rejoice in the feeling of serenity and peace...
>
> When I look down the valley in the early morning, while the mist, or rather smoke, ascends, there rises with it a scent of burning pine. The people of the villages are cooking their breakfasts and at the same time heating their floors.
>
> From *Eastern Windows: An Artist's Notes of Travel in Japan, Hokkaido, Korea, China and the Philippines,* published by Hutchinson & Co. in 1928

It amazed me that a "blue-eyed foreigner" could so exquisitely describe a scene that seems at once so familiar, as if I saw it somewhere once when I was young, and yet so filled with heartache for some reason. This image is much harder to find nowadays, but it is the the image of Korean meals that I often think about and want to convey to others.

As I traveled the country more in search of its unique beauty, I found myself less drawn to exploring well-known regional specialties—buckwheat noodles in Gangwon-do Province, *seolleongtang* soup in Gyeonggi-do Province, cold soup with oysters in Chungcheong-do Province—and more interested in the everyday meals enjoyed in ordinary homes, the way families behave and interact around the dining table, and the unique ambience that only those homes possess. What is more, I found myself beginning to wonder where they find the ingredients they use, who does the cooking and how they do it, who they invite over for meals and how they spend their time. Images began to come to mind.

Smoke rises bluish-white from rice cooking in an old cast-iron pot.
The morning air is so clear that my eyes ache.
Suddenly, the sun pushes through a gap in the fog.
A door squeaks open then closes again.
A hearty scent wafts through the neighborhood; bowls clatter.
The sound of grandfather clearing his throat carries from the inner room.
Harried chickens run circles in the yard, chased by a playful puppy.
At last, the breakfast tray, billowing with steam, emerges from the kitchen.
The simple table bears only a few dishes, but the rice is glossy, the wild greens glow,
and the vegetables, still crisp and fresh, exude warmth and anticipation.
Sunlight and morning mist, fresh air, rocks and trees,
they each add their own spice.
At this table that delights all my senses,
my heart feels full before my stomach does.

The overcast sky threatens to spill down.
Fat flakes start to fall
as we race along the freeway.
Winter's last gift.
I crack open the window
and press the shutter
over and over.

Sower's Feast

My traveling companions and I arrived at our first destination, Seoji Village in Gangneung on the east coast of Korea, where a delightful meal awaited us. The restaurant, called Seoji Chogatteul, was named after the traditional thatched-roof cottages of the Korean countryside. Pine trees wrapped around the building like a folding screen. Flowering trees had been planted all around, and the tidy landscape gave it the relaxed air of a three-hundred-year-old house. Growing off to one side was an *eomnamu*[2] (Kalopanax tree), traditionally regarded as a "guardian tree," as its thorns are said to be sharp enough to ward off even ghosts. The tree's tender shoots that emerge in spring can be served blanched and eaten with rice—the taste is without compare. Just as we arrived, we were greeted warmly by the owner of the restaurant, Choi Yeong-gan. She had been dishing up *dongchimi*, a winter kimchi made with white radish, from a large crock outside to add to our lunch.

An unsparingly generous host, Choi offered us bowls of *tteok* (rice cake) before the meal. It was made from one of her family's own unique recipes. Made from seeds left over after sowing, the rice cake is called *ssijongji tteok*. The taste was amazing, but what I especially liked were the wooden bowls she served it in. Natives of Gangwon-do Province call these bowls *dugari*. The humble wooden bowls convey the warmth and friendliness of country folk; I was already feeling right at home.

My appetite perked up at the taste of *songjuk dugyeonju*[3], a traditional alcohol made from azalea blossoms, pine and bamboo using a secret recipe that has been passed down for hundreds of years. This home-brewed alcohol is used for holidays and ancestral memorial services. Depending on the season, chrysanthemum blossoms can be used instead of azalea, in which case the drink is called *songjuk gukhwaju*. As we drank, Choi taught me a cure for hangovers: Boil arrowroot starch in a double boiler then transfer to an ice bath. Strain the starch using a fine sieve. Add the softened starch to honeyed water or *omija* (five-flavor berry) tea. This concoction, she said, would foil even the worst hangover. In her grandfather's day, their home had seen a steady stream of guests and visitors of all stripes. These guests would stay with them overnight and thank them for their hospitality by penning small writings, bestowing names on the children or drawing pictures of tigers as tokens of their gratitude. In return, the guests would be thanked with drinks and snacks all night long. Her grandfather should have suffered considerably from frequent hangovers, but he took it all in stride thanks to their secret hangover cure.

During the labor-intensive rice planting season, women load up trays with *motbap*[4] (white rice cooked with red beans), brown seaweed soup and heaping dishes of seasoned vegetables, and rush out to deliver the food to farmhands working in the rice paddies. The farmhands are known by different titles depending on their position. The leader of the farming crew is called the *seongun*. He is followed by the *sangilkkun* and the *jilkkun*. Last but not least, men under twenty years of age are called *jeonmae*.

The men of a farming village rise before dawn to the sound of the nightingale and come together in these farming crews to help each other plant rice seedlings. This form of cooperative farm labor is called *dure* or *jil*. Accordingly, after the planting is done, they sit down together to a meal called *jilsang* and eat food called *jilbap*.

Dano, a Korean holiday that falls on the fifth day of the fifth lunar month, takes place around the end of the rice transplanting season. At that time, farmers gather on the banks of the nearby Namdaecheon Stream where they hold the annual Dano Festival and celebrate with the time-honored activities of Korean wrestling, swinging and tug-of-war. The farmers' Dano Festival has been designated as one of the Masterpieces of the Oral and Intangible Heritage of Humanity by UNESCO for its cultural originality and artistic excellence.

In the seventh month of the lunar calendar, the fields are weeded. Afterward, the farmhands get together again to pass the leisure time left before the harvest begins. Though they are called farmhands, in truth they are neighbors. Around this time, the farmers take out the rice seeds they stashed beneath clay jars at the beginning of the planting season and use them to make rice cake, adding anything and everything that could possibly be added, such as mugwort, pumpkin, kidney beans, chestnuts, jujubes and dried persimmon. This treat is called *ssijongji tteok*—sowing day rice cake.

Motbap

Songjuk dugyeonju

Ssijongji tteok

Clay jars for brewing alcohol

Choi's mother-in-law places some food
on top of my rice herself—suddenly
everything tastes even better. I eat it all,
even the enormous bowl of *motbap*.

Jilsang

The table overflowed with food. *Nudeok namul*[5] (fresh sea greens), *dolnamul*[6] (seasoned stonecrop), kimchi, stewed dried pollack, pickled radish, pancakes of every kind, meat… The table looked as if it was set for a party, but Choi explained that this spread, known as *jilsang*, is what they really serve to the farmhands during the rice planting season. Even when her family was not well off, they would scrimp and save to be able to feed the farmers well and keep them happy and strong.

Choi told me that their family once had a farmhand who was especially devoted to his parents. His mother had a stroke and had to be cared for around the clock. The farmhand was so worried about his mother that he could not bring himself to eat, even on such a joyful day. So the farm owner's daughter-in-law at that time always packed food for him to take home. Recently, in an effort to keep the beautiful tradition of *jilsang* alive, the government built *nongmak*[7], shelters in the fields where farmers could take breaks from their work, and the government has even helped farmers build extensions onto their houses. As such, *jilsang* is a tradition with a rich history in this family.

Choi asked me a question: When something good happens, whom do I think of first? I hesitated. No one sprang to mind right away. She told me: "When the farmhand was happy, he thought of his mother first. So I hope that you, too, will think of your mother when something good happens to you." When we share meals with other people, it seems we also share their joys and sorrows.

Grandmother's Diary

Choi told us that her mother-in-law had lived at Seoji Chogatteul for close to seventy years and had traveled out of town on exactly three occasions. Though her mother-in-law was almost ninety, her face was filled with warmth and her eyes sparkled with intelligence. She showed us the diary she had created for her trip to Jejudo Island—the first as well as the last trip of her life. The precise and detailed diary was filled with the thrills and wonderment of her voyage. As she read it aloud, word by word, her voice had a pleasant rhythm, and her quiet tone was comforting. I felt like I was lying down with my head on my grandmother's knee, listening to a story. Anyone else listening to the sound of her voice would have felt right at home as well.

I was amazed by her endurance, by the way she had overcome so many frustrations and all the humdrum of so many years. Yet her writing betrayed none of that. It was genuine and pure, without a single shred of gloom. Every piece of furniture in the house that her hands touched daily—even the inside of her armoire—were plastered with pieces of paper with writing on them. She said when she was first married, her father wrote down his advice for her regarding proper attitude and conduct. No doubt this father's love was the force behind his daughter's pure and honest nature.

Early Summer and the Memory of Plums

I love *umeboshi*. But instead of eating these pickled dried Japanese plums plain, I like to soak them in honey first. As luck would have it, I found a place that prepares the fruit, known as *maesil* in Korean, just the way I like it. The Cheongmaesil Plum Farm has been innovating new recipes for *maesil*, from pickling them in soy sauce to putting them in ice cream, pancakes and *gimbap* (Korean seaweed rice rolls).

The Cheongmaesil Plum Farm is located in the hills of Gwangyang, South Jeolla-do Province, where the scenic Seomjingang River flows. When spring arrives, film crews can often be found at the farm's picturesque thatched-roof cottage. There, manager and *maesil* expert Hong Ssang-ri had set out an elaborately prepared meal for us. Every single dish was made with plums, which she said she grew with the same level of care she had showered on her own children. As we ate, we enjoyed a lecture on healthy living from a real-life farmer.

Hong said that she never uses artificial seasonings when she cooks. We were impressed by the fresh, tart flavors of the side dishes, such as the plum pancakes and plums pickled in soy sauce, which I found especially hard to resist. The *maesil jeonggwa*[8] (candied plums) were sweet and sour, yet mild in flavor. No matter how many I ate, I never got tired of the taste. For dessert, there was plum ice cream. I threw caution to the wind and helped myself to two servings. So much for the assumption that healthy food must taste bad. Hong kept urging us to eat more, saying, "The food is terrible, but please help yourselves anyway." To me, though, the meal was fantastic. I could not stop reaching for more. My stomach was on the verge of bursting, but with all that wonderful food in front of us, my hand kept betraying me. As rain began to fall, we had to hurry to our next destination, but we took a quick look around nonetheless. Whenever I meet generous, warm-hearted people like Hong, I can't help but wonder if it is the result of having survived hardships. She gave everyone in our group a bundle of plums. Such was the kindness that country folk are known for. I cannot help but wonder if, generations from now, Hong's plum cuisine will be the next *Joy of Cooking*, just as *Eumsik dimibang*, the first cookbook ever written in Korean, established the canon of Korean cuisine.

Even after we left, Hong continued to send us her "terrible food" from time to time. Those meals really helped us to get through that long, hot summer.

How were people able to eat fresh vegetables in the dead of winter, back before refrigerators were invented? Around the year 1670, a *jeongbuin*[9] (noblewoman) by the name of Lady Jang wrote a cookbook, entitled *Eumsik dimibang*. It was the first cookbook ever written by a woman in East Asia. The book described in careful detail the preparation and storage of food, divided into 146 different categories. Here is one example of her instructions for food storage: "If peaches are stored in a gruel made from wheat flour, they will stay fresh and can be eaten even in winter. Eggplant should be packed in the ashes of mulberry wood. Live abalone should be packed in sesame oil."

In addition, the following was recorded in the *Joseon wangjo sillok* (*Annals of the Joseon Dynasty*): "From the winter solstice to the onset of spring, when flowers were presented to the king, he ordered that they only be placed in the Queen Mother's quarters." The fact that flowers could be offered at all in winter meant that greenhouses were already being used five hundred years ago. Oiled paper was used to let in sunlight, and an underfloor heating system was used to control temperature and humidity. Thus, even in winter, trees, fruits and vegetables could still be grown.

Home Cooking Transformed

One weekend, I received a dinner invitation from an acquaintance I had met through our shared love of wine. I visited him at his traditional Korean-style house in the neighborhood of Samcheong-dong. The objets d'art placed thoughtfully around his elegant home each asserted their own subtle beauty without competing with each other for attention. It was my ideal of interior design—a balance of simplicity and elegance that opens both your eyes and your heart at a single glance. Large clay jars stood in dignified rows in the courtyard, and instead of slippers, there was the simple comfort of traditional black rubber shoes. Strewn petals floating tranquilly in the lovely lotus pond lifted my mood.

Some conversation to catch up, and soon the lunch tray was brought out. I was excited to eat. As someone with a keen interest in globalizing Korean food, it was like seeing a ray of light in a dark cave. Everything was fresh and made using only natural seasonings. The motif was Korean cuisine, but the form embraced all eras and nationalities. The food was seasoned with a moderate hand, and nothing was in excess. Yet while the food did not shout, the flavors were sufficiently brilliant and well-matched. As I ate, they seemed to reverberate through my whole body, like an echo or the ringing of a bell.

That meal taught me the importance of the selection of a bowl, its arrangement, and the overall harmony of the table. There seemed to be a bowl from every country in the world, but the stars of the meal were the brass and clay bowls with their heavy beauty. Seeing the food and tableware in this light, I was struck by the charm of seeing Korean dishware arranged alongside that of other countries, rather than standing alone on the table as they usually do. It was as if the bowls were standing hand in hand, socializing with the diverse cultures of the world. In the midst of all that color, the simple beauty of Korean culture seemed to stand out all the more.

Bibimbap served in a *dawan* (tea bowl) fit neatly in my hands. The vegetables were arranged in order, equal in size and amount. The fillings for the *gujeolpan* were julienned very finely, making their colors even lovelier. For dessert, *songpyeon* tempted me with its bright colors, dainty portions and variety of flavors. Everything was served in just the right amount.

The meal was so delightful that I found myself asking all sorts of questions about how it was prepared. Time flew by. Soon, our hosts were bringing out tiny individual braziers and a dish that looked like Western-style steak but tasted like Korean-style galbi. I was very impressed. With their permission, I have included partial recipes for the *songpyeon* and *galbi* steak below.

Bite-Size Five-Color *Songpyeon*

The vivid colors of this rice cake represent the five points of the compass: north, south, east, west and center.

1 cup = 50g

· White: 2 cups of glutinous rice powder, ½ cup (118ml) of boiling water
· Purple: 2 cups of glutinous rice powder, ½ cup (118ml) of grape juice
· Green: 2 cups of glutinous rice powder, ½ cup (118ml) of mugwort juice
· Red: 2 cups of glutinous rice powder, ½ cup (118ml) of beet juice
· Yellow: 2 cups of glutinous rice powder, ½ cup (118ml) of gardenia juice

Do not add water to the colored rice cake. In separate bowls, mix the above proportions of juice and glutinous rice powder and knead to form a dough. Roll the dough into balls and stuff them with a filling of ground sesame seed, salt and sugar. Shape the stuffed cakes by hand into crescents and steam until done.

Bite-size five-color *songpyeon*

Galbi Steak

· For this recipe, ask the butcher to cut beef short ribs into steaks. Score the thick side of the meat.

· To prepare the braising liquid, blend 1 cup (236ml) of marinade base (see below), 1/3 cup (78ml) of soy sauce, ¼ cup (50ml) of cooking wine, ¼ cup (50ml) of rice wine, 2/3 cup (75g) of sugar, 1/3 cup (78ml) of sesame oil, a dash of black pepper and a pinch of sesame salt.

· To prepare the marinade base, blend 3.5 ounces (100g) of daikon radish, 3.5 ounces (100g) of Asian pear, 3.5 ounces (100g) of garlic, 3.5 ounces (100g) of onion and 0.35 ounces (10g) of ginger.

① Slice the daikon radish and Asian pear and blend them in a blender.
② Add finely sliced garlic, onion and ginger to the radish and pear. Strain the contents of the blender through a cheesecloth and squeeze the juice into a bowl. This marinade base can be made ahead of time and stored in the refrigerator.
③ To marinate the short ribs, first soak the meat in cold water to draw out the blood.
④ Parboil the ribs, drain and add the braising liquid. Allow them to marinate overnight.

Galbi steak

I stayed the night in Samcheong-dong,
where I slept soundly beneath a cotton quilt in a cozy,
Korean-style room with a heated floor and paper doors.
It is difficult to describe in words the softness of that quilt,
which had been stuffed with cotton and carefully stitched by hand.
It not only warmed my body, but also my heart.
To my great thanks, my host gave it to me as a parting gift.
I carry it with me still on my travels.

My Meal

I enjoy learning about and experiencing new dishes that I encounter while traveling or when meeting people. Whenever someone sends me something tasty or I discover something new, I try to recreate it on my own. Sometimes I invite friends and members of my staff over for a meal to thank them for taking such good care of me. The purpose is not to put on a big formal show, but rather to spend time with people I care about while sharing traditional food that I want them to try, or food that is good for their health. If not for such meals, how else would we be able to spend quality time together? But things do not always go as planned. A close friend of mine once told me:

"Some of the staff in your office were reluctantly eating some kind of herb and making faces, like they could barely keep it down. What was that?"
I hesitated then told him, "Just something healthy. By the way, who was making faces?"

Kimchi 02

Making an
Art of Fermentation

Weather

I had been up since dawn. Today was the day we had been planning to have fun together doing *gimjang*—putting up kimchi for the winter. I glanced out the window. The weather promised to be good. They say that if you are demanding and difficult to please, the weather will always be cold on the day of your *gimjang*. My staff had been placing bets on what the weather would be like. I cautiously opened the window and peeked out. Thank goodness!

I tried not to show it, but I was nervous. Everyone had agreed to meet at my house at eight in the morning before heading over to meet the kimchi expert who agreed to teach us *gimjang*. What kind of mood would everyone be in? Feeling good for some reason, I decided to make something special. I knew that none of them would have time to eat breakfast before they came. I sweated for close to an hour, cooking a chicken that my friend's mother raised herself at her home in Yangyang on the east coast in Gangwon-do Province, but no one showed up. Worried about my staff and anxious as our appointment with the kimchi expert drew near, and because the food I worked so hard to prepare was growing cold, I could not resist picking up the phone and calling them. Were they all sleeping in late after pulling all-nighters at the office the day before? It took several tries to get through. Eventually, they arrived, with little time to spare. I hurriedly served the chicken stew to everyone, as we really had to rush to make our appointment. Perhaps it was the homegrown chicken lovingly sent to us by my friend's mother, but everyone perked up after eating. Then, to my surprise, as we headed out, they all grumbled about how warm the weather was. I could not bring myself to chide them, for fear it would grow cold instead.

That day, I would not say a word.

We arrived at the home of Lee Hyo-jae, a famous *hanbok* designer and renowned domestic diva, who would help us prepare the winter kimchi. Though it was a little late in the season for *gimjang*, we wanted to try it for ourselves, so she had readily offered to provide the ingredients, a location and the knowhow. For three generations, Lee's family has been known for the amazing kimchi, soybean paste, chili paste and alcohol they ferment and brew at home. Lee said she is still learning the secret family recipes from her mother in her spare time. I was determined to use this experience to pick up tips on how to make really good kimchi.

Scattered Offerings

Lee's house sits at the top of a mountain—the scenery there makes it hard to believe that you are still in Seoul. Her house harmonizes perfectly with the natural surroundings. An enormous rock wall at the top of the mountain flanks the house like a folding screen, wrapping around the courtyard and serving as a natural fence for the garden. I walked up a flight of stairs next to the wall and entered the living room through the second floor terrace. Nature is at the heart of Lee's lifestyle. The living room is comfortable and minimalist with no unnecessary frills—a place where you can go to meditate, sip tea and wash away the trivial cares of daily life. Floor-to-ceiling windows invite in the sunlight.

The very first thing we did when we arrived was a custom called *gosire* (*gosure*), where you scatter food on the ground as an offering to the spirits. I filled a small earthenware bowl called *siru*, which is used for steaming food, with steamed rice cake topped with adzuki beans. The rice cake had been made in preparation for *gimjang*. I added some pork on top of the rice cake and, following Lee's directions, scrambled halfway up the slope of the mountaintop to the side of the courtyard. There, I scattered food and made a wish. Below me, I could hear my staff cackling with laughter. They were probably wondering what I was wishing for. In the cool shade of the pine trees and rocks that stood halfway up the mountain, I bashfully tossed food about and shouted, "*Gosire!*"

Dangun, the legendary founder and king of Gojoseon, the first Korean kingdom, had several officials. One of these officials, named Gosi, was put in charge of teaching the Korean people how to survive and care for themselves. He taught them how to farm, build houses and make fire. Thereafter, as a symbol of thanks, Koreans dedicated the first spoon of rice to him. This became known as *gosire*, an offering to Gosi.

When it comes to traditional culture, preserving it in its original form is important, but so too is using it in our daily lives. For that to happen, it has to become a toy—something that we use often and with pleasure. As Confucius wrote in *The Analects*, "Knowing something is not as good as liking something, and liking something is not as good as taking pleasure in something." In other words, rather than simply studying something, you should make it a part of your life and enjoy it daily. I think that even more than preserving, understanding and liking culture, we should first have fun with it.
And few are having more fun with culture in their daily lives than Lee Hyo-jae.

We took a break from making kimchi to have some tea and eat the rice cake leftover from the *gosire*. The room was furnished with little more than a folding screen, a tea set and neatly stacked floor cushions. Oddly enough, there was not a single electronic device in the room. Not even the all-too-familiar television set or air conditioner. How many people could there be who, like Lee, never watch television? And in the middle of the city at that! Keeping busy, even without the constant onslaught of media information, seems to be the trick to learning useful and substantial things and living a full life.

While I was still deep in thought, Lee brought out a rare and valuable item. It was an enormous bowl, also known as a *jwajong*¹, made from high quality brass called *bangjja*². I had never seen one before. She told me it was made by Lee Bong-ju, who has been designated as an Important Intangible Cultural Properties of Korea for his expertise in brasswork. To make the bowl, high quality brass was melted down and poured into a disk-shaped mold. The disk was then reheated and hammered into shape. This type of bowl was called *bangjja yugi*, or handforged bronzeware, and was primarily used to make metal bells or tableware. Everyone was curious to know more about the bowl. Lee instructed me to hit the bowl, so I tapped on the side. It made a clear sound that spread through the air and lingered. It was beautiful. This was no bowl; this was a musical instrument. Lee had thirty-eight of these enormous brass bowls. I pictured them spread out across the floor, being played by musicians—it would have been quite a sight. She then told me that these bowls were the last of their kind. It took six artisans to produce a single bowl. Of them, all but Lee Bong-ju had passed away.

The musical bowls had found their way to Lee's home in a funny way. Lee's husband, Lim Dong-chang, is a famous piano prodigy, known for his eccentric and ascetic ways. With his sole interest in the pursuit of the free artistic spirit of non-possession, Lim is at the forefront of culture and the arts in Korea. It is said that he has never coveted anything in his life—not even the very piano on which he plays. But he wept the first time he saw one of these brass bowls and heard the sound it made when struck.

That by itself would have made for a lovely anecdote, but there was more. A professional musician who traveled the country, was absorbed in his music, and rarely made it home, Lim showed up one day with the bowls, which he had bought on credit. From then on, Lee could no longer afford her hobby of collecting pretty dishes. Lee said she would get annoyed and nag him about the bowls, saying, "Can I make rice balls in them?" "Can I stick flowers in them?" "Can I use them to serve *bibimbap?*" By the time we were done laughing and chatting, the sun was high in the sky. Finally, it was time to move out to the courtyard and begin the main event of the day.

Preparing Ingredients for Winter Kimchi

Lee told us that her uncle lives on an island, where he periodically sends her fresh oysters that he harvests himself. She said the oysters were flavorful and delicious even without any seasoning, and that once you had a taste, it was hard not to get greedy and keep them all to yourself. I was filled with anticipation at the thought of those oysters waiting for us in the refrigerator.

Before we began working on the kimchi, Lee showed us a kimchi jar that she had prepared in advance. She had added bamboo leaf on top of the kimchi. She explained that she brought the leaves from Gongju, a few hours drive south of Seoul, and that the leaves had to be plucked while the bamboo trees were in blossom. I did not know her exact reason for this at the time, but later, while leafing through a book on trees at home, I read that bamboo leaves contain natural antibacterial and preservative properties. In the old days, people used the leaves of the Northern Bamboo (*Sasa borealis*) tree to wrap rice cake. The leaves helped to keep the rice cake from spoiling too fast.

I tied on an apron. It was a stylish garment that even came with a pocket for my cell phone. Lee had designed this special menswear apron just for me. Everyone complimented me on it, saying it suited me. Thus began my battle with the cabbage and assorted ingredients.

We were joined by Cheon Myeong-suk, daughter of the master potter Cheon Han-bong and a pottery artist in her own right. She rolled up her sleeves and dove in. The clay jars and ingredients for the kimchi were set out in clusters at the base of a large boulder. The jars were small and cute. The heads of cabbage were small and firm. The cabbage had come from a mountain farm, where produce is grown at a higher, cooler altitude. Sulfur was added to the soil, which made the cabbage crisper. The daikon radish also looked big and fresh.

Ponytail radish had been set out as well. I poured the seasonings into a large stainless steel bowl and mixed it by hand with the precut vegetables. Now I just needed to julienne the radish. It was slow going at first, but soon I caught the rhythm. My shoulders began to ache and I realized it was not so easy after all. Nevertheless, I received praise for my skill at julienning the radish. I added the julienned radish to the seasoning mixture and mixed it by hand again. I was nearly done preparing my ingredients for the kimchi. I stood up to stretch my back and took a look around at everyone else. They were all still hard at work.

The quality and amount of salt determines the taste of the kimchi. The best type of salt for kimchi is sea salt, which is dried for a long time in the sun. Once the brine evaporates, a period that takes three to five years, the salt is fermented. This creates a much higher quality salt. This type of salt, from which the brine has been evaporated, is the best for making kimchi.

However, there is one salt that is even better, though few know about it, and that is *toyeom*, or "clay salt." Almost all sea salt nowadays is produced at salt farms where the salt is spread on tile or linoleum pans to dry. *Toyeom*, however, is dried on pans that have been covered in clay soil. Impurities in the salt are leached out into the clay, which makes it far superior to sea salt in terms of purity, taste and nutrition. Only clean, high quality clay can be used. But the source of that clay has long been used up, so very little clay salt is made nowadays. As a result, it is quite expensive.

I washed the basket that I would be working with and filled it with
well-rinsed heads of cabbage. Both my hands and my mouth were busy.
I even tore off cabbage leaves, one at a time, to sneak a taste. I had been
working on my own for a while when I suddenly heard someone shout,
"What happened to all the oysters? Someone ate them all!"
I paid no attention and pretended to be absorbed in my work.

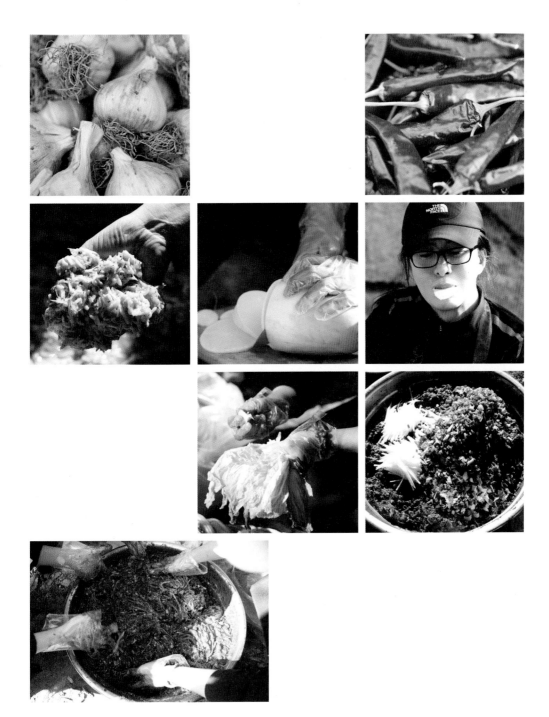

The History and Health Benefits of Kimchi

It would be impossible to recount the entire history and list all the varieties of kimchi here. Nevertheless, it is worth mentioning *baechu* kimchi. Made from napa cabbage, *baechu* kimchi is what most people think of when they hear the word kimchi. But it did not make its first documented appearance until the nineteenth century, when it was recorded in *Gyuhap chongseo*, an early nineteenth century compendium of advice for women, and *Siui jeonseo*, a cookbook from the late nineteenth century. The cabbage grown before then was not of particularly good quality, and it took many years of improvement—until the end of the Joseon Dynasty—for the heads of napa cabbage to look the way they do now. Prior to that, cucumber kimchi and daikon radish kimchi were much more common.

Other documents tell us that chili powder was first added to kimchi around the year 1689, and *jeotgal* (salted fermented seafoods) were added around 1767. When *jeotgal* is added, the salt and enzymes in the kimchi break the protein in the *jeotgal* down into peptides and amino acids. Amino acids enhance the flavor, while ammonia and carbon dioxide give the kimchi its brisk, refreshing taste. *Jeotgal* also increases the nutritional value of kimchi. In the seventeenth century, pheasant meat, boiled pork, chicken and beef were added to kimchi, and there were even some recipes that called for mixing in a soup stock made from beef bones and stew meat. But over time, these meats were gradually replaced with salted pickled shrimp and fish.

Research has shown that kimchi can aid in cancer prevention, as it helps to suppress the growth of cancer cells. Also, as the other ingredients ferment—including garlic, ginger, chili powder and chives—they provide not only anticarcinogenic but also antioxidant and anti-aging benefits.

Laboratory tests were conducted in which *Leuconostoc mesenteroides*, the main bacteria in kimchi responsible for fermentation, were harvested from seasoned vegetables that had been fermented. The harvested bacteria were then introduced to stomach cancer cells. The researchers found that these bacteria were four to ten percent more effective than unfermented vegetables at slowing the growth of cancer cells. They also discovered that capsaicin, the compound found in chili powder that gives it its spicy flavor and which had long been suspected to be a cause of stomach cancer, was in fact effective at helping to suppress cancer cells. Nowadays, researchers are even questioning whether kimchi can play a similar role in the prevention of avian influenza and the H1N1 virus.

All cultures around the world have their own fermented foods. Cheese, yogurt, *natto*—these are but a few examples. Statistically speaking, Koreans enjoy the greatest number and variety of fermented foods. Around the third century CE, a historian named Chen Shou from the Western Jin Dynasty in China compiled the *Records of Three Kingdoms*, in which it is recorded that the people of Goguryeo, an ancient Korean kingdom, enjoyed and were especially skilled at brewing alcohol, making soy sauce, and fermenting seafoods and vegetables.

Aside from such foods as rice cake, *sikhye* (a sweetened rice drink), alcohol, *doenjang* and *cheonggukjang* (fermented soybean pastes), kimchi, *jeotgal* (salted pickled seafoods), *jangajji* (vegetables pickled in soy sauce), chili paste, soy sauce, dried persimmons and vinegar, fermentation has also been put to good use in many other areas as well, such as in making the glue traditionally used on Korean paper. It is said that Koreans have a special palate for fermentation. I wonder if it would be going too far to say that we are a "fermentation people." Decomposition refers to things that are spoiled and can no longer be used, but fermentation is controlled decomposition that confers a great many benefits. Like having the wisdom to sublimate hardship and adversity with good humor. Perhaps even in our emotions we share traits in common with fermentation.

A Festival of Our Own

I stopped to catch my breath then began carefully spreading the seasoning mixture for the kimchi in between the cabbage leaves. Kimchi that is meant to be eaten over a longer period of time should not be over-seasoned. In order to get the best flavor out of the kimchi, you have to calculate how much you are making and when you plan to eat it. Snacking on the leaves that fall off the heads of cabbage with a dollop of the fresh seasoning mixture is one of the little joys of making kimchi that everyone has to try. The sight of someone pausing to wrap up a cabbage leaf and stuff it in the mouth of a person hard at work, both hands covered in chili paste, is one of the most familiar and heartwarming moments of *gimjang*.

Once all of the cabbage is seasoned, the leftover seasoning mixture can be used to make several other varieties of kimchi. Daikon radish can be diced into small cubes and seasoned to make *kkakdugi*, and ponytail radish can be seasoned whole to make *chonggak kimchi*. The crispy radish tastes fresh, even after pickling. It is interesting how each type of kimchi takes on such a distinct flavor even though they are all seasoned the same way.

Dongchimi is a radish water kimchi that is pickled before eating. Well-ripened daikon radish is first salted down. When it is ready, the radish is rinsed off and pickled again with chopped ginger, red pepper, green onion or other ingredients. Once it is fermented, the *dongchimi* broth is tastier than any beverage. *Dongchimi* truly comes into its own when it is eaten with meat, as it aids in digestion and even helps to detoxify the body. Also, it is a common sight in the middle of the winter to see Koreans eating boiled potatoes or sweet potatoes with *dongchimi* broth to help the starchy food go down easier. For those who like soup, *dongchimi* is a better choice than regular kimchi. To my surprise, Lee makes *dongchimi* without adding garlic. She said that she uses the starch from boiling grated potatoes and uses pickled sand lances to salt a stock made from *dasima (kombu)* kelp, after which the *dongchimi* water kimchi is packed and aged for two to three days. The taste is indescribable.

Meanwhile, one of the strongest members of my staff was using a pickax to dig a hole in a soft spot in the mountain soil where we could bury the clay jars of kimchi we had packed. Digging a hole is never easy, and the ground was still a little frozen, which made it even harder. He had volunteered for this heavy labor himself since he had served in the Marine Corps. Thanks to him, we were able to bury deep in the earth and send into hibernation the clay jars of napa cabbage and radish kimchi that we had worked hard to put up.

We pressed bamboo leaves firmly onto the top of the packed kimchi and closed the lids. One shovelful at a time, the soil covered the jars, and I felt a surge of pride and satisfaction. As we marked the jars with a ring of long clay roofing tiles, I completed my very first *gimjang*.

Kimchi My Way

It was late by the time I got home, but I wanted to practice making kimchi again. I took out the ingredients I had set aside in advance. Since kimchi gets its flavor from the mix of seasonings and the little tricks that go into making it, I figured I would have to try it again myself in order to put my own spin on it. It took me until dawn to finish putting up kimchi on my own. I was planning to compare it with the kimchi I had made the day before and share it with my friends and acquaintances. I also made up my mind to make kimchi again the following year and give it away as gifts.

With kimchi, nothing is thrown away. Even the kimchi brine can be used to flavor stews, and it is especially useful when making *jeon* (Korean pancakes) and *sujebi* (hand-torn noodle soup). Here, I have included my own recipe for kimchi pancakes.

Kimchijeon

Ingredients
1 cup (50g) of finely chopped kimchi, 1 cup (236ml) of kimchi brine, 1 onion,
1 squid (calamari), 1 egg, 1 cup (50g) of all-purpose flour, ¼ cup (59ml) of water,
1 teaspoon (5ml) of soy sauce, 1/3 (1.6ml) teaspoon of salt, cooking oil for the pan

1 cup = 50g

① Shake out the kimchi filling and dice the cabbage finely.
② Skin the squid and slice the body into small strips, then remove the suckers and chop the tentacles into small pieces.
③ Finely dice the onion.

④ To a large mixing bowl, add the kimchi, diced onion, squid, egg, kimchi brine, water and flour. Mix well. Season the batter with soy sauce and salt.

⑤ Over medium heat, pour a tablespoon of batter into an oiled pan and tilt the pan to spread the batter thinly, until the pancake is approximately 3 inches (8cm) in diameter. Cook until golden brown.

I would love for more people to know about the superb flavors and health advantages that kimchi has to offer. Well-ripened kimchi can revive a lost appetite and can be turned into many different kinds of charming dishes. Good food begins with good ingredients, and kimchi is nothing if not a food that requires pouring your heart and soul into preparing the ingredients. Good ingredients, good earthenware jars, secret recipes, the weather on the day of *gimjang*—all of these different factors work together in a subtle way to produce delicious kimchi.

But more than anything, what kimchi requires are people to come together, laugh and enjoy themselves as they make it. In the future, I am thinking of hosting my own small *gimjang* parties. We could take turns each year, traveling in search of the best ingredients, making cabbage soup from the leaves leftover after salting the cabbages the day before, and enjoying ourselves over glasses of homemade liquor and a plate of fresh oysters. How fun and meaningful would that be to get together once a year, put up kimchi for the winter and share the fruits of our labor amongst ourselves? I am even thinking of traveling in search of hidden kimchi experts and the ingredients they use to make their own unusual yet flavorful kimchi. I am already reeling with anticipation. I think it will shape up to be a heartwarming festival of our own.

My Mother's Recipe for *Oi Sobagi* (Stuffed Cucumber Kimchi)

Ingredients
10 cucumbers, salt, seasoning for stuffing (1 tablespoon of crushed garlic), 8 ounces (200g) of chives, 4 ounces (100g) of scallions, 4 ounces (100g) of onion, 4 tablespoons of chili powder, 2 tablespoons of anchovy sauce, 1½ tablespoons of sugar, dash of salt

① Wash the cucumbers and slice off the ends. Carefully cut the cucumber lengthwise down the middle, stopping just before you reach the end. Turn the cucumber ninety degrees and cut again without cutting all the way through.

② Sprinkle two tablespoons of salt on the scored cucumber and let it sit for two hours.

③ Place the cucumbers in a strainer and allow the water to drain out naturally.

④ While the cucumbers are draining, finely dice the chives, scallions and onion, and mix it with the garlic, chili powder, anchovy sauce, sugar and salt to create the stuffing.

⑤ Fill each of the scored cucumbers with the stuffing.

⑥ Neatly stack the cucumbers in an airtight container and leave it at room temperature (for one day in the summer, two to three days in winter). After it has aged for a day or so, store it in the refrigerator.

⑦ The seasoning mixture and salting method can all be adjusted to suit individual tastes.

Hanbok and
Housekeeping 03

Simple
Beauty

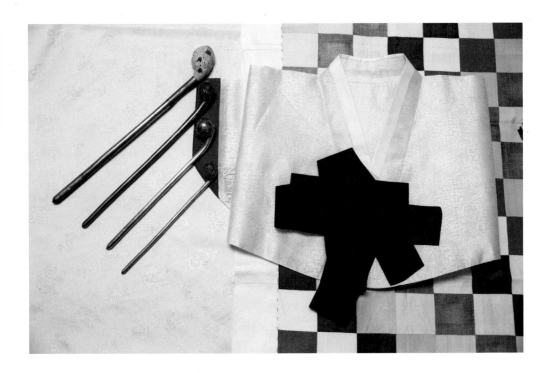

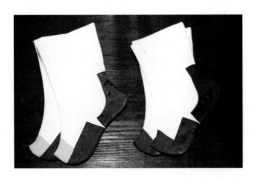

Hanbok: Traditional Korean Clothing

Sangbak hahu: sparing above, generous below. These four words describe the silhouette of women's dress, with its tight *jeogori* top and billowy skirt, in the Joseon Dynasty. In the *hanbok*, we see the natural and modest beauty that is found throughout Korean culture. The line of the traditional dress flows like water, exuding a sense of style yet without forgetting the aesthetics of comfort and practicality. For the *hanbok* that we speak of here is not the fancy dress worn just for special occasions, but the everyday dress that was worn at all times.

Hanbok can be a sensual form of dress that displays the body's curves (just look at a *hanbok* when the wind wraps it around a person's body, or when it is wet with rain!), and it can be a dignified garment that hides the wearer's physical features inside its generous embrace (who is to tell whether the wearer's limbs are thick or thin, the legs long or short, the waist heavy or slender?). This duality is also reflected in the balance of the *doryeon*[1] (hem), which curves like the eave of a Korean house, and the straight line of the *dongjeong*[2] (trim) and the *git*[3] (collar), which extends like the blade of a knife.

In winter, the fabric is lined with cotton to make cold-weather clothes: Remove the lining, and it is a summer garment. Take off the outermost garment, and you have pajamas. Tuck the long skirt up and secure it with a belt while working, and it becomes work clothes. Wash them clean and iron the wrinkles out, and you have stepping out clothes. What is more, as long as the height of the wearer does not vary greatly, each garment can be one size fits all. What more versatile garment could there be?

Safflower Dye

The secret behind the beautiful color of *hanbok* is natural dyes. For example, there is something mysterious about the deep dark blue of natural indigo that could never be expressed with an artificial dye. The splendor of red can inspire a passion that is at once subtle and strong. But in these modern times, the market for traditional dyes has mostly dried up. Nevertheless, there are those stubborn few who are willing to put up with the demands of dyeing fabric the natural way. Ahn Hwa-ja, a master dyer who lives in South Jeolla-do Province, is one who maintains the time-honored practices of natural dyes.

I visited Ahn in her studio at the foot of Mt. Jirisan. Radiant and kind, Ahn's face bore all the beauty of one who has lived in harmony with nature's rhythms. At one time, she managed a gallery in Insa-dong, an art district in Seoul, but she said that after falling in love with natural dyes, she chose to move to a place near the mountains where the water was clean. The dyed fabric fluttering in the wind was the same vibrant rose as the setting sun—I was no more able to resist its attraction.

Ahn told me we would be making red dye that day. *Honghwa*⁴ (safflower) blossoms are gathered early in the morning, between four and five a.m. The petals of the safflower are spiky, like thorns, but they are at their softest just before dawn, when they are wet with dew, which makes them easier to pluck without hurting your fingers. An hour of plucking yields only a fistful of flowers. The freshly picked blossoms are ground to a paste in a mortar and shaped into patties. After the patties are dried, they are stored in large earthenware jars. It is hard to get a pretty color from the flowers when the humidity is high, such as during the summer rainy season, so this process has to be completed before the start of summer.

Typical Method of Safflower Dyeing

→

→

① Pick the safflower blossoms just before dawn.

② Shape the ground blossoms into patties and set them out to dry.

Store the dried patties in a clay jar and allow them to ferment for 10-20 days.

→

③ The safflower blossom is yellow, which means both red and yellow pigments will go into the cloth. To use the safflower as a red dye, first extract and discard the yellow pigment by rinsing the safflower in stream water. This will also wash away any sour odors.

↓

④ When the water runs clear, rinse the safflower with lye (an alkaline solution derived from wood ash). This will draw out the red pigments. The lye must be hot.

⑤ Add a fixative or other acidic solution to neutralize the alkaline bath. This fixative is made from blackened plums that are steeped in boiling water the day before to create an extract.

↓

⑥ Add *maesil* (plum) or *omija* (five-flavor berry) extract to make the mixture a true fabric dye. After first introducing an alkaline agent to extract the pigments, followed by an acidic agent to neutralize the dye bath (PH 5.5), the liquid can be used to dye cloth.

→ 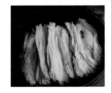 →  →

⑦ Soak the fabric to be dyed in water first to ensure that the dye will adhere evenly.

⑧ Fold the fabric into the dye bath and let it soak. Repeat the process of soaking and drying the fabric until the desired color is reached.

This process of soaking and drying can be repeated up to fourteen times, depending on the type of fabric being dyed, such as silk, hemp or ramie.

According to Ahn, the best shade of red was the one used during the Joseon Dynasty, called *hanhong*, or "Korean red." In fact, Korea's representative colors are red and blue. Since times of old, the king was robed in red, and the crown prince in blue. The colors were so important that the royal family even had special dyers who produced only these two colors. When commoners married, the brides used special rouge made from a safflower extract. Ahn explained that she began safflower dyeing after falling in love with the deep mystery and rosy beauty of "Korean red."

When natural dyes are extracted using modern methods, caution must be taken to avoid overheating the water, as this can cause the pigment to be lost. There is no such problem with the traditional method, however, even when boiling water is used to sterilize the materials. Ahn explained that people were unaware of this because they had simply never tried the traditional method, having dismissed it as too difficult and exacting. In fact, most people were mislabeling other methods, calling them traditional, but Ahn had long stopped trying to convince them otherwise and kept to herself, practicing true traditional Korean dyeing methods on her own. Her daughter, who is the spitting image of Ahn, works with her. When I met her daughter, she looked wise beyond her years. Though I do not know what Ahn's daughter's hopes and dreams are, seeing them together filled me with hope that the tradition of natural dyes would be carried on by the next generation.

Natural dyes are mainly used for special orders, such as special designs for fashion shows or for restoring antique clothes and fabrics found among relics excavated from tombs. The dyes are used to recreate the original colors of these fabrics that have faded with time.

In the old days, the royal palace employed specially appointed sericulturists to raise silkworms, master dyers to dye the silk and master sewers to make the silk into clothing. The court dyers included an expert who specialized in making blue dye, another who made red dye and another who made yellow. The court sewers produced strong, exquisite stitches that were all but impossible to imitate.

Green grass, tiled wall,
the deep blue shade of trees
and rose-colored fabric.

A warm, sunny summer day,
a cool breeze passes by now and then,
encouraging me to take it easy.

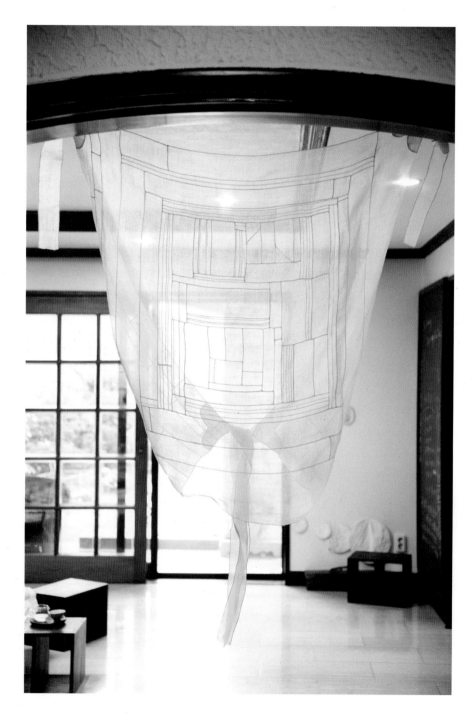

Transforming Fabric Remnants

During Korea's "Enlightenment Period" (1876-1910), when Westerners first encountered Korean culture, which image would have been the most striking to Western eyes? I imagine it must have been the garishly colorful yet pretty children's *hanbok* with its rainbow-striped sleeves. On a Christmas seal printed in 1940, two children in colorful clothes stand in the open door of a house (that appears to be at the top of a hill). Behind them, a distant mountain towers. You can almost reach out and touch it. Looking at the picture, I feel as if I am being drawn back to another era. The image on the Christmas seal was painted by none other than Elizabeth Keith, the British painter. Probably she too was mesmerized by the charms of Korean people and their traditional clothing.

Keith seemed to have been entranced by the scene that greeted her everywhere of women battling mountains of laundry on the banks of streams and rivers, struggling to clean the all-white overcoats, pants and jackets worn by men. But "still more exacting of human labour" than laundry, as Keith wrote, was ironing:

> The sound in Seoul of women ironing was of an insistent beating of hard wooden sticks on muffled metal, wood or stone. This rhythmic clink began at early dawn and was sometimes to be heard far into the night.
>
> (From *Old Korea: The Land of Morning Calm*, published by Hutchinson & Co. in 1946)

Top **Embroidery**, 1921, color woodblock print
Bottom **Woman Sewing**, Collection of Song Young-dahl
(Source: *Elizabeth Keith's Korea: 1920-1940*, Chaekgwa haṃkke Publishing)

For me, the clack-clack of ironing sticks was a familiar, cozy sound from my childhood. When the sticks rang out against the ironing block, the whole house would be at peace. But I came to learn that it caused my mother's wrists to swell and her fingers to cramp out of shape, and that she never stopped ironing despite the pain. People used to speak of the Three Happy Sounds: the voice of someone reading aloud, the crying of a newborn baby and the sound of ironing. It took me until now to understand that, of the three, ironing is the sound of pain and hard labor. That sound told the story of women, Korean mothers from a time gone by and yet only as far off as my grandmother's generation, who endured the difficulties of housekeeping. They had to be tough and strong for their children and for their families, despite being frail themselves. Housekeeping means keeping a house alive. It means maintaining it with the proper tools and tasks. From all those women's sacrifices, we grew up healthy and strong.

I sometimes wonder what I should mention first when I want to explain
what Korea is like to people who are unfamiliar with the culture.
What comes to mind when I think of China?
The Shaolin Temple? Qipao?
What about Japan?
Picturesque gardens? Sushi? Kimono?
I think about other countries in Asia, like Vietnam and Thailand,
as well as several countries in Europe.

Then I try listing the things that come to mind when I think of Korea.
Kimchi, bulgogi, *hanok*, hangeul…

and

hanbok.

Hanbok: the traditional dress of Korea. With its own unique aesthetic, it is beyond perfection. But *hanbok* cannot be explained solely through clothing. It is more than that. It is also about the Korean home, household goods, food, even the country itself. If we fail to convey a more complete or holistic image of our culture, then other people will not be able to recognize Korean things as Korean. That is why I am determined to find a way to bring together all of the elements of real life in Korea—food, clothing, shelter—and portray them in their natural, everyday state. Because the image of someone wearing colorful *hanbok*, eating bulgogi and doing taekwondo in the courtyard of an old traditional house just seems so awkward and contrived.

I was able to solve this dilemma with the help of Lee Hyo-jae, the *hanbok* designer. If the United States has Tasha Tudor and Martha Stewart, and Japan has Harumi Kurihara, then Korea has Lee Hyo-jae. In Lee's hands, even a scrap of tattered cloth can become the winged robe of a fairy; a coarse meal of herb roots and tree bark turns into a sumptuous feast. What is more, Lee's home is like a showcase of Korean culture. The first time I had the pleasure of visiting Lee at her home was December 2008, in the depths of winter.

Few couples live like Lee and her husband Lim Dong-chang, the eccentric piano prodigy. They exude culture, constantly generating new and wonderful ideas.

The first time I saw their traditional Korean home in the Seongbuk-dong neighborhood of Seoul, after being introduced to them by a shared acquaintance, my first impression was that it was a captivating combination of simplicity and splendor. All around me were countless numbers of wrapping cloths in every color; I felt as if I were standing in a field of flowers. The works of artisans, chosen with Lee's sharp sense for beauty, were casually scattered about. This was no dull exhibition— the items in her home gleamed from daily use.

She had an unusual way of entertaining guests. Small tea tables and cushions were set on the floor, one for each guest. The tables all differed in size and shape, and we were told to seat ourselves before whichever one appealed to us. She described the different plates and dishes by comparing them to fabrics; we could practically feel the cloth beneath our fingers and see them right before our eyes. White porcelain became finely woven ramie, a simple bluish-green pottery called *buncheong*[5] became hemp and Western china with a tiny pattern resembled delicate lace.

The Yonsama Blouse

As luck would have it, Lee had a garment in her house that she had named
"Yonsama," after the nickname bestowed on me by my Japanese fans.
She said she had been calling it that since before meeting me.
The garment was made using scraps of fabric leftover after making a *hanbok*.
Each remnant was a different size, which lent the garment a very geometric look.
It reminded me of a Mondrian painting.
I took a closer look. Some of the pieces were no bigger than a fingernail.
Lee told me she hoped the blouse would one day—maybe a couple hundred
years in the future—be known as a traditional Korean garment called Yonsama.
I would just like to make it clear, for posterity, that this was entirely her idea and
not mine.

A Woman in *Hanbok*

Lee came downstairs with a rock in her hand. The natural patterns in the rock appeared to resemble a woman beautifully dressed in *hanbok*. The mysterious rock had found its way to her house in an unusual way. One rainy day, one of her friends had a guest who stumbled across it in his yard. When Lee visited the friend later, he showed her the rock. Struck by the strange, chilly energy of the rock and the story of its appearance at his house, Lee exclaimed in wonder. Suddenly, her friend's wife pressed it into Lee's hands and urged her to take it with her as a gift. As it turned out, her friend had cherished that rock bearing the image of a woman a little too much and had stared at it and stroked it whenever he drank.

The woman in the rock bore a striking resemblance to a Joseon Dynasty *gisaeng*, otherwise known as Korean geishas. It was hard to believe that the image had occurred naturally. It was no less superb than Shin Yun-bok's famous painting, "Portrait of a Beauty." The tilt of the woman's head looked vivid and bewitching. She appeared to be wearing a full skirt and even the grand wig of a *gisaeng*. The wig was ornamented with a flower, and on her chest hung a *norigae*, a decorative pendant worn by women. Of course, that was just my impression, whereas Lee said most people just saw a simple silhouette of a woman. I had not been so delighted by an object in some time. A lot of the objects in Lee's house came with interesting stories.

Putting Old Things to Modern Uses—What I Learned from Lee

Hwaetdae (traditional clothes hanger)
These hangers were once used for clothes that were taken out of storage and aired out before being worn. Use *hwaetdae* as a wall decoration to display seasonal embroidery.

Tteokpan (rice cake mortar)
In the past, every house had one; now, a *tteokpan* can be used as a tea table. Fill the basin with fresh water every day to humidify a room, or add ivy for freshness. When guests come over, hang the ivy from the ceiling to add a touch of clean elegance to the room.

Seonbi chaekgwe (scholar's book chest)
In the Joseon Dynasty, *seonbi* (Confucian scholars) built *chaekgwe* (book chests) for carrying books around with them, in case they wanted something to read in their bedchambers or for when they were going to Seoul to take the state examination. By shrinking the size of the chests and preserving the original design, these *chaekgwe* can be stacked like boxes and used to beautify an unattractive wall or simply used as a desk.

Hyang (incense)
Burn incense before guests arrive. If incense is burning while drinking tea, the smell will block the flavor of the tea.

***Hanji* (traditional Korean paper)**
Use *hanji* to cover windows. The paper can be torn by hand to cover or reveal the window as desired, creating a "peek-a-boo window."

A Journey in Search of Korea's Beauty

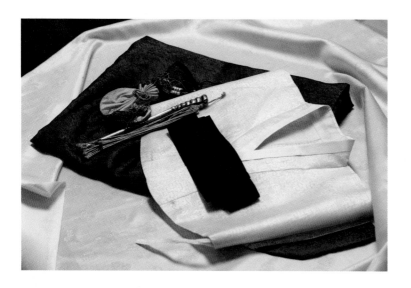

Father-in-Law and Daughter-in-Law

In the old days, many parents arranged marriages for their children in advance by pairing them with their friends' children. When that happened, the daughter of a man's friend became his daughter-in-law. The bride would present her in-laws with the wedding gift of a set of *bapjubal*[6] (brass rice bowls) to express her intent to care for her husband and his parents and live happily together for the rest of their lives. However, there was one such bride who found herself widowed early, while her parents-in-law were still in their prime. For the sake of his daughter-in-law who was bereaved at far too young an age—for the daughter of his dear friend—the father-in-law prepared to marry her off again. He looked around for a suitable match, and after a month he found a scholar who was living alone, some distance from the village. One day, the daughter-in-law was presented with a more elaborate meal than usual; she knew at once what her father-in-law's intent was. She bowed deeply to her father-in-law and clutched the wrapping cloth filled with wedding gifts that he had prepared for her to her bosom—a new dress, a pin for her hair. What was she feeling, this married woman who found herself having to accept wedding gifts and leave her late husband's family to be married again? What was he feeling, this father-in-law who wrote a letter, wishing happiness for his friend's daughter, and stashed it deep inside the wrapping cloth? Their feelings seem to have been passed down through the ages.

Lee said that she wanted to share this story about wedding gifts— so modest compared to these affluent times we live in, yet heartfelt nonetheless. In the end, she said, wedding gifts are gifts of the heart.

Hyo-jae's Tricks to Housekeeping

Housekeeping means the work of maintaining a household. It can also refer to the condition the household is in or indicate the items used in that house. The mood of the household depends upon the person in charge of the housekeeping. Housekeeping can move us and bring us joy. It is an extremely selfless job, because it is one of sharing. For that reason, I wish that everyone would take housekeeping seriously and work hard at it, even if they live alone.

Lee's housekeeping tricks do not require extraordinary effort but simply apply to daily life itself. When serving even a single cup of tea, for example, she gives it a great deal of thought and chooses a teacup suited to that person's unique background and sensibility. Lee told me that she was preparing to move deep into the mountains in order to live as close to nature as she could. She was deciding which varieties of plants to take with her to plant in the mountains, as well as the dishes she would use there. She had already packed over three hundred dishtowels embroidered with all sorts of Korean flowers, including Chinese pinks, azaleas, cigar flowers, pepper flowers and pumpkin flowers. She was even knitting a thick scarf to wear when she met the head of the village. If anyone should want to find her in the mountains, they should just look for the person wearing a full pink skirt shaped like a clay jar. Of all of her clothes, those skirts, which call to mind the line of those old clay jars, are the ones I like best.

就

Staying

Leaving

Letting Go

Contemplating

Returning

Leaving, Once Again

Black Lacquer 04

A Passion
to Last through the Ages

Meeting

The ties that bind us can be so coincidental sometimes. I came to know the lacquer expert, Jeon Yong-bok, because of a single blurb in a newspaper article one day. According to the article, Jeon, a master of traditional Korean lacquer arts, had designed a special wristwatch in collaboration with Seiko, the Japanese watch company. Despite the extremely high price, all of the watches had sold out. To me, masterpieces are those that keep old traditions alive while modernizing them in the spirit of craftsmanship, and that contain their own stories, thus becoming items anyone would want to own. However, design is not just about preserving tradition but innovating it, which I believe most traditional artisans are capable of doing. But commercial success is something else entirely. There are not many cases of a watch designed using an industrial art like black lacquer or inlay—and not even diamond-studded—selling for a high price in the fiercely competitive marketplace.

I met Jeon Yong-bok at Lee Hyo-jae's home in Seongbuk-dong. Tall with big, bright eyes, Jeon is a man of many talents: master artisan, modern designer and a businessman who blazes his own trails. Thanks to his easy-going and open-minded personality, we immediately broke the ice, and I earned the rare opportunity to see firsthand one of the watches that were mentioned in the newspaper article which had left such an impression on me. The black lacquer looked as mysterious as the night sky, while the red lacquer captivated me with its intense beauty. This was not a watch but a work of art. As I peered closer at the small watch face, where every exquisite lacquer painting technique had been brought together, it seemed to grow into a giant masterpiece, like a landscape of the universe.

The story of Jeon's life was no less dramatic than his artwork. After finishing his military service, he was hired by a woodworking company where he made armoires. Then, a few years after establishing the Yerin Lacquer Research Center in Busan, he had a fateful meeting with the Meguro Gajoen in Japan. Though he was by then already the leading authority on lacquer, both in fact and in name, things did not go easily for Jeon. After two whole years of careful preparation, he had sought out Seiko only to have the door slammed in his face. But in the end, thanks to his characteristic perseverance and confidence, he was able to win over the executives. His passion, which compelled him to take risks and explore new territories for himself, was proudly apparent in his artwork as well.

Lacquer refers to the craft of painting wood with the sap of the lacquer tree to prevent rot and enhance color and shine. Most of the traditional Korean furniture that has been passed down through the generations was inlaid with mother-of-pearl and finished with lacquer. Black-lacquered wood has a clean and deeply refined look that is indescribable. It is said that a lacquered item will remain in pristine condition for a thousand years—in some cases even as long as ten thousand.

In recent years, it was discovered that black lacquer can block electromagnetic waves, which has led to its use in electronics like cell phones and laptop computers. It was also developed into a paint finish and is used in place of regular paint for ships that require strong resistance to corrosion. Furthermore, musical instruments varnished with lacquer are said to produce a superior sound, and a decoction made from the wood of the lacquer tree has been shown to improve blood circulation and stomach disorders, as well as being effective in the treatment of cancer.

True lacquer, extracted from the lacquer tree, sells for a high price due to the extremely low rate of production, and eighty percent of the lacquer produced worldwide is consumed in Japan. In fact, *japan* with a lower-case *j* means "lacquer." Perhaps it is for that reason that wooden lacquerware is such a common sight in Japan. Just as china has come to signify Chinese pottery, perhaps japan reflects the soul of Japanese lacquerware in the Western world.

Are traditional crafts to be relegated to museum exhibits? Is there any way for them to survive in the dog-eat-dog marketplace for cutting-edge technology? As I looked at this man who was waging a solitary battle while searching for answers to these questions with his whole being, I caught a glimpse of where the future of traditional arts and crafts needed to be headed. No doubt there are others like him, countless artisans waging their own battles, toiling away to the indifference of the general public. I do not believe that tradition is unconditionally superior and must be preserved and used at all costs. But I do believe that the value of tradition should be appraised and reappraised from time to time to examine whether it is really understood and whether it merits a little more of our love and attention.

Intrigued by Jeon, I wound up making a difficult pledge: I would learn the art of lacquer painting from him. Though circumstances were not quite on my side, I was able to live up to that pledge with the help of many others. One of the things I never want to hear is that I am a man who does not keep his word, whether it is a promise to my family (fans) a promise to myself or a promise to anyone else. Sticking to my word at least that much is my one desire.

Korean lacquer has been recognized worldwide for its superior quality, and over seventy percent of it is exported annually. This is because of several factors that contribute to lacquer production: amount of sunshine, soil quality and a favorable climate for growing lacquer trees. Korean lacquer, which is high in urushiol, the molecule that causes lacquer to harden, is most preferred in Japan as it dries thick and has a clear, luminous quality. Currently, most lacquer trees are grown in Wonju, Gangwon-do Province; Okcheon, North Chungcheong-do Province; and Namwon, North Jeolla-do Province.

The watch on the left is unadorned with any gems and was made using traditional Korean techniques. In 2008, when the watch was produced, it was valued at 52,500,000 yen, or 900,000,000 won. The watch on the right was the first one ever made. It is valued at approximately 1,500,000 yen.

Iwayama Lacquer Art Museum

A few months after meeting Jeon, I traveled to Japan to visit the Iwayama Lacquer Arts Museum in Iwate, Morioka Prefecture. My plan was to make the trip quietly so as not to inconvenience people. At the same time, I also just wanted to quietly immerse myself in learning.

We landed at Sendai Airport and drove for an hour. After a friendly welcome from Jeon's family, we unpacked our bags and took a look around the museum. The museum was located at the foot of a mountain; the surrounding forest and the fallen snow were refreshing. The first thing we saw when we stepped inside was one of Jeon's lacquer paintings exhibited on the ground floor. Lacquer of every color, mother-of-pearl, and gold, as well as other media unfurled in an exquisite and splendid harmony across an enormous black panel. I realized I was standing in the largest lacquer art museum in the world.

Jeon Yong-bok's early works are on display here.

Trying My Hand at Lacquer Painting

March 3, 2009
12:12 a.m.

Jeon gave me a few words of warning then hurried out of the studio. Without so much as a moment to ready my mind, he had given me "until sunrise" to finish. I was a bit thrown when Jeon told me to paint something on the canvas, with no instructions whatsoever, but that was his personal approach to teaching: "Practice is less important than overcoming fear." Later, I would find out that he came back to the studio before first light to see what I had painted.

At first, the brush felt strange in my hand and did not move readily. I paused to get some fresh air, calm my nerves and share ideas for the painting with my staff members who had traveled with me. I cleaned a brush, shook off the dust and steadied my mind. Nearly two hours passed before I could bring myself to stand in front of the canvas. I dipped a new brush in cobalt lacquer and let it drop onto the pitch-black canvas. I caught my breath, then laid the brush at a forty-five degree angle and pressed into it. I recalled how Jeon said you should keep one hand behind your back and stand up straight in order to put your whole body into your brushwork. My mouth was dry. I looked up from the brush strokes on the panel that I had been staring at for some time. My staff were watching and waiting. They were practically holding their breath. "You guys, it's okay if you talk..." Finally they all seemed to exhale at once. Cobalt sky, a kaleidoscopic field of wheat, and above it all, a bird in flight... that was what I wanted to paint. But there was no trace on the canvas of the image in my mind. I blushed with embarrassment and mortification; my head spun.

The sense of pressure did not let up. The black canvas leered up at me, as if it would not accept even the slightest mistake, making me all the more tense. I closed my eyes and pictured my father and myself when I was little. Whenever my father taught me something for the first time, I would stumble, intimidated to have him standing there, watching. But I realized later that he did not mean to scare me, that it was a father's overpowering love for his son that I felt back then. I concentrated on my fingertips, drawing forth the quiet echo of that memory.

During my first attempt at lacquer painting, my hand had crept forward, haltingly, then retreated, over and over. The second time, my arm moved easily. I readied myself and chose a color. Before, I had brought the brush down and pulled it back three times; this time, I thought first about where to place the brush then began. I felt like I was getting a little more confident.

Finally, I completed my first painting. I had fun trying, but I wondered what Jeon would say. The lines were dull, and it was obvious that it had been painted over and touched up again. The staff offered their opinions, saying it was not bad for a beginner, but I was not reassured.

After hesitating for what seemed like a whole hour, I took out another panel and began my second painting. I made a rough sketch in my head first and planned out my moves. This time, I was not afraid. When there is no one there to help you, you have to make every decision on your own, from start to finish, based on choice and faith, and then begin drawing. I spent an hour painting the background then another thirty minutes debating. Suddenly, I could hear Jeon's voice in my ears, reminding me, "You have to know when to stop." In a single breath, I drew two curving lines and stopped.

The second painting was nothing to be proud of, but I felt better than I did after the first attempt. Or perhaps I just felt attached to it because it was something I had created all on my own. I felt an urgent desire to create my own style. Something with sharp, crisp lines that don't spread yet linger in the viewer's mind. But I have a long way to go before I can create a true work of art, something truly satisfying. All I can do to hurry that day along is practice, then practice some more.

"If your goal is not to be the best in the world, then you do not belong here."

Playing the drums for the first time, to blow off steam.
I may look like I was enjoying myself,
but it sounded like I was beating two trashcan lids together.

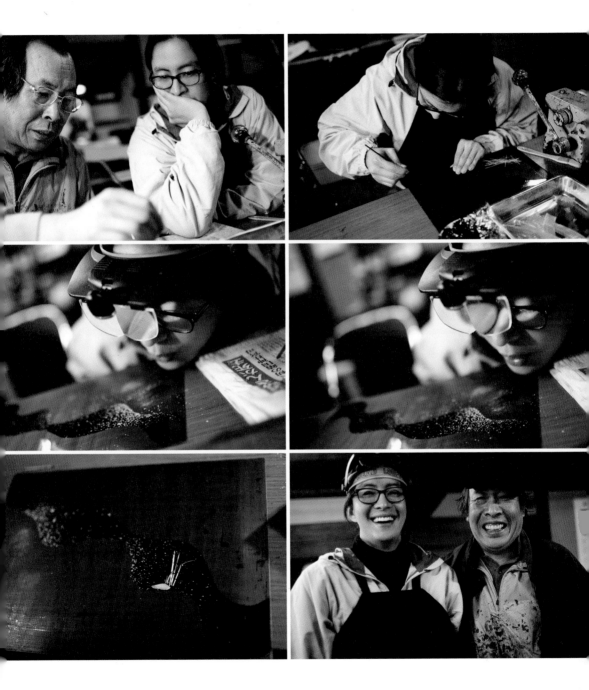

Travel

This is the first time I have ever tried writing a book. I have had my hand in every part of it, from preliminary research, field trips and photo shoots, to organizing the materials, preparing the manuscript and selecting the final photos. This project, with its tiny crew, feels completely different from the enormous production of a movie or television show. We pull over to take pictures wherever we feel like it, sleep crowded together in one room and help each other in the kitchen. We have become so close that we can tell what the other person wants just by the look in his eye, even with the staff members we hardly knew before the trip.

And for every little bump along the road, there have been just as many beautiful moments. To travel truly is to take a journey—of getting to know yourself, of getting to know each other.

Morning Stroll

A field white with snow.
Cedar forest stretching to the horizon.
Sky turning pale over the city.
Swan floating leisurely on a lake.
People diligently sweeping the sidewalks
in front of their houses.
A high school student riding his bicycle to school.
Elementary school students running with backpacks.
With my camera, I capture the small details of
everyday life in Morioka.
A long-awaited serenity.
These days, the fresh air at dawn
has eluded me.
Too many late nights, lying awake,
turned to habit.

The Fish Market and the Yellow Coffee Truck

Jeon offered to make us sushi. We all cheered and followed
him to the market. He picked out the freshest looking fish:
snapper, rockfish, abalone. Excited at getting our first glimpse
of a Japanese fish market, each one of us had a camera out.
Everything looked different: rather than the chaotic dynamism
of Jagalchi Fish Market in Busan, we were greeted by the
clean calm that typifies Japan. And of course, no trip to the
market would be complete without stopping for snacks.
We shared traditional Japanese cookies and strong espresso
from a yellow minivan in the parking lot.
Everyone had a satisfied look on their face.

Lacquer Chicken

Jeon raises chickens in the yard behind the museum. When they are chicks, he mixes their feed with a 200-times dilution of lacquer sap. As they mature, he adds ground-up lacquer bark. Lacquer bark is so effective at killing toxins and bacteria that most chickens raised without being fed the lacquer sap will die if they eat the bark. All plants contain some measure of poison. So it is a given that lacquer, which can last for ten thousand years, will be more toxic than other plants. As a result, it must be handled carefully and administered appropriately, no matter how medicinal it is. Jeon reminded me several times that the toxic bark of the lacquer tree should not be boiled together with the lacquer chicken. His trick is a long aging period and a long cooking time. He strips bark from the middle of a hundred-year-old lacquer tree and allows it to age for several years. Then he boils it for a minimum of eight hours before he adds the chicken. Only then can it be eaten. It took forever to cook, but everyone exclaimed over the taste. Bursting with flavor and healthy to boot, it was a meal made straight from a father's heart.

Walking around downtown Morioka,
I could not resist stopping for a snack.

Chusonji, a Traditional Buddhist Temple

Chusonji, a Buddhist temple in Iwate Prefecture and Japan's number one national treasure, is famous for the Konjikido, or "Golden Hall." Inside the Golden Hall, elements of traditional Korean architecture can be found, including the rafters and foundation stone, and all of the wood is covered in gold leaf, which uses one of the techniques of lacquer varnish. Traces of cultural exchange between Korea and Japan are still evident; this exchange would have taken place in the late eleventh century, or the Goryeo Dynasty in Korea.

In the tearoom of the temple, I was treated to *matcha*, a powdered green tea. I cradled the tea bowl in both hands and slowly turned it around to admire the design. I sipped carefully, once, twice, three times. The flavor was superior to any other tea I had ever tasted. The tea was an intense shade of green—it even *tasted* green. The soft foam and delicate scent grew stronger as the vivid green of the tea seemed to spread inside me.

All of my senses were awakened and my mind was cleared. The door to the tearoom was so small that you had to bow to enter. In accordance with the wishes of Senno Rikyu, the Zen tea master from Japan's feudal era who valued restraint, simplicity and natural beauty, samurai had to remove their swords and armor in order to pass through the tiny two-foot-square (60 × 60cm) door. I only had to remove my hat. More surprising than the tiny door though was the tea master's explanation:

"The spirit of this tearoom is Korean."

Our journey to Morioka complete, we returned to our
lodgings for our last dinner together in Japan. Jeon
entertained us with a charming song. One of my staff
followed with some energetic dance music, and Jeon did the
"dog leg dance," waggling his legs for us. His impassioned
performance put all the young people to shame.

To Meet Again

It was a nine-hour drive from Morioka to Tokyo. We decided to take the bullet train to save time and energy. After dinner, we went to the station and waited on the platform. Jeon gave us drinks and snacks for the trip then turned his back to hide the fact that he was sorry to see us go. Despite our short stay, he must have developed great affection for us. With his back turned, he looked so fatherly that I felt my heart skip and my eyes sting with tears. The whole way to Tokyo, I thought about everything he had taught me and the kindness he had showed us. He had opened the door to a whole new world for me, and I would never forget my gratitude to him for that.

Later, Jeon visited Seoul several times and showed me his latest artworks. I was particularly impressed by one painted on a large sheet of *hanji*, traditional Korean paper. The vivid colors of his artwork looked especially posh against the elegance and the subtle textures of *hanji*. It was intriguing to consider the idea of painting *hanji*, which can last for thousands of years, with lacquer, which can last for ten thousands of years. That day, my fascination with *hanji* began.

The Paper Mulberry Tree's Dream of a Thousand Years:
The Story of *Hanji*

For something with such an insubstantial name as "paper," *hanji* has tremendous vitality. By vitality, I mean that it is strong and durable. It is thanks to that vitality that so many old Korean books still exist today. It is also the reason the *Mugu jeonggwang daedarani gyeong*[1] (*Pure Light Dharani Sutra*), the world's oldest printed book (printed in 751 CE) still exists. Even now, government documents and other texts that require preservation are printed on *hanji* made using only the most traditional methods. This traditional *hanji* is extremely expensive, so it is only produced for special orders.

The secret behind the long life of *hanji* is the paper mulberry tree from which it is made. The bark is so strong that it could sit in water for a year and the fibers would remain unharmed; even the strongest hand would struggle to tear it in two. To make high quality *hanji*, a one-year-old paper mulberry tree must be used. Normally, twenty to thirty-year-old trees, at least two arm spans in circumference, are used for making paper, but *hanji* is made from young trees that are harvested each year.

The characteristic durability of *hanji* is due to the *oebal* (single frame) method of papermaking. The frame is made from bamboo splints woven together with thread. The single frame method is unique to Korea. The frame, which can be moved in all directions, is dipped both vertically and horizontally, which distributes the paper fibers into a 井-shaped formation. But because this process is done by hand, it is difficult to distribute the fibers evenly from top to bottom. To create paper of even thickness, the wet sheets are layered on top of each other, alternating top to bottom, then separated by means of a thread laid between every two layers. This traditional technique, known as *hapji*, creates one sheet of paper for every two layers, resulting in a thick, strong, durable paper. However, the downside to this technique is that it is difficult to learn and does not produce high volumes of paper. Meanwhile, there is a similar form of papermaking practiced in Japan, known as *yangbal* (double frame). In contrast to the single frame method, the double frame is dipped in only one direction, and a single sheet of paper is made for every layer. The paper is not as strong, but more sheets can be produced even by a single craftsman working alone. When paper was first invented in China, the method used was the double frame. The single frame method was developed independently in Korea for *hanji*. Because of the superior quality of *hanji*, it became one of the leading exports during the Three Kingdoms era.

In order to learn more about *hanji*, I went to Jangjibang, a traditional paper mill. There, Jang Yong-hun and his two sons make high quality *hanji* in keeping with traditional methods. The family-run company has been handed down for three generations. Jang told me that his great-grandfather started papermaking as a side business, using the best soil on his land to grow rice and the remaining soil to plant paper mulberry trees. He farmed in the spring, summer and fall, and made paper in the winter,

Lacquered *hanji* at Jangjibang, a traditional paper mill

gradually increasing his land one field at a time. When Jang's father took over, he began making paper full-time. Even though the family business first began in Jeonju, Jang, out of a desire to leave behind the years of difficult financial circumstances in Jeonju, relocated to Gapyeong in Gyeonggi-do Province, where he knew no one.

Jangjibang is the biggest paper mill in Korea, and Jang also owns a shop in Insa-dong, an art district in Seoul. Nevertheless, the facilities at his mill seemed, even at first glance, quite poor. I took that to mean that the conditions at other *hanji* paper mills in other parts of the country are even worse off. I suppose that is why people used to say, "I'd rather eat sand than see my son become a papermaker." Traditional papermaking is difficult, exhausting work, but thanks to the efforts of many artisans, it is being held back from extinction. They say that the traditional technology for making the frames used in *hanji* production could vanish into obscurity at any moment, so the burden on Korea's *hanji* artisans seems to be growing heavier by the day.

Meanwhile, handmade paper, which was once dismissed as poorly made, is now popular and regarded as a work of sophisticated design. Paper is crumpled and smoothed back out to create different patterns and colors, and the concept of using natural dyes, much like dyeing fabric, has also been introduced to the craft. Demand for *hanji* intended for use in interior design has grown, leading to the creation of *hanji* of all shapes and sizes suited to different purposes. Prices, as well, can vary considerably according to the materials and processes used to make *hanji*, regardless of whether the design is identical.

With *hanji*, nothing is thrown away. Leftover lye can be used in fertilizer. Leftover scraps can be used to make *hanji* wallpaper. Larger scraps can be mixed with glue and molded like clay to make baskets and bowls. Damaged sheets can be dissolved in water and the pulp reused. Finished sheets can be cut into cords and strips and reused to make various household goods. They can also be boiled in lye and remade into fresh sheets of paper. For this reason, *hanji* has been gaining attention as an eco-friendly art.

The following is a brief overview of how *hanji* is made.

The first step in making *hanji* is to steam the wood of the paper mulberry tree in a cast-iron pot. After it is steamed, the bark is peeled off and dried. Normally it is impossible to peel the mulberry bark by hand, but once it is fully steamed, it can be separated by hand, revealing the fibers. The pattern found inside natural mulberry bark resembles extremely fine netting and is quite beautiful. As the cells in the fibers are still alive, it makes for very durable paper. The wood must be stored somewhere cool as it can rot in warm weather, but chemically treated wood will not rot regardless of temperature. However, the color of chemically treated wood will change after a while, which means it cannot be stored for long. Such paper does not merit being called "paper that lasts a thousand years."

The dried mulberry is soaked in water and the outer layers of bark are scraped away to reveal the innermost white layer. This inner bark is dried again, washed thoroughly and boiled in lye. During this process, the mulberry fibers can be softened and separated. Natural lye produces a more beautiful color in the paper. However, with the exception of special orders or high quality *hanji*, a chemical lye is normally used, due to its lower cost. Lowering the cost helps to ensure that *hanji* reaches a wider market.

The advantages of natural lye show in the quality of the paper. This type of *hanji* has a superior gloss and texture. And unlike chemical lye, natural lye is not toxic. In fact, it can even be beneficial, as it improves blood circulation—in the old days, when a criminal was sentenced to death by poisoning, the poison was mixed with natural lye to speed its effect. Natural lye is made from a variety of ingredients, including beans, chilis, buckwheat, rice straw and cotton. Paper made from this lye burns down to a white ash; chemically treated paper leaves black ash.

After the white inner bark is dried and bleached in the sun, it is ground mechanically to make the pure paper pulp. Traditionally, the bark would be placed on a stone and beaten with a club to soften the fibers. But that is only done for special orders because nearly two hours of beating yields only a very small amount of pulp.

The mulberry fibers are heavier than water, which causes them to sink or clump together, so an additional agent must be added to help disperse the fibers. For this purpose, a variety of hibiscus plant, *Hibiscus manihot*, discovered long ago by Koreans, is used. According to the *Dongui bogam (Mirror of Eastern Medicine)*, published in 1613, *Hibiscus manihot* was used to treat gynecological disorders and stomach problems. When dipped in water, *Hibiscus manihot* gives off a viscous liquid, much like aloe.

Koreans have always been fond of anthropomorphizing objects. *Hanji*, a daily necessity for the nobility, was frequently described as having human qualities. They even used the term *inmul*, referring to a person's appearance, in describing the grooming effect *Hibiscus manihot* has on *hanji*. Also, when the paper is being dipped and layered, the thread used to separate the layers is called the "pillow." It amused me to learn that they named it that because it is where the "head" of the paper falls.

Once the sheets are dried, the *hanji* is complete. One final step, known as *dochim*, helps to improve the texture and durability of the paper even more—this step entails smoothing the paper by beating it on a fulling block, as with ironing *hanbok* fabric.

Lacquer painting on *hanji*

A Passion for the Ages

Recently, I set up a lacquer painting studio in my home and have begun painting objects with *saengchil²*, the fresh sap of the lacquer tree. Not only does the fresh sap make wood strong and watertight, but the colors are beautiful. I thought it would be a nice way to give gifts to people I know.

The eighteenth century philosopher Edmund Burke wrote, "The next property constantly observable in [beautiful] objects is *smoothness*. A quality so essential to beauty, that I do not now recollect anything beautiful that is not smooth." [From *A Philosophical Enquiry into the Origin of Our Ideas of the Sublime and Beautiful* (1757)] Of the crafts that have bridged tradition and modernity, probably few have achieved such a high level of aesthetics as lacquer painting.

I made up my mind that, from now on, any important letters or notes that I wished to save would be written on *hanji*. Barring the possibility of fire, they would survive for a thousand years. Perhaps even ten thousand years if the paper were lacquered. The beauty of *hanji* and lacquer were unknown to me not long ago, and now, in such a short time, they have become so deeply embedded in my life. I resolved once more to figure out what I could do to shed light on the works of artisans who have endeavored over the millennia to cast the glow of traditional culture down to those of us living in the modern world.

Temple Stay

05

A Thousand-Year-Old
Community Living in Tranquility

Baekheungam Hermitage

"Do not stay at the same inn twice.
Choose a blanket that has not yet been warmed.
Do not kill living things.
Keep nothing more than the clothes and daily necessities you
cannot do without.
Eat no meat, no matter whether it has scales or wings or fur.
Do not become attached to any particular food or flavor.
If your meals are simple, you can do anything.
Do not reveal that you are writing a poem when the other person
has not asked you to.
But when you are asked to, do not refuse them.
Avoid any noisy places.
Do not put on airs and ignore others.
Always keep an eye on yourself.
Meditate in the evening, and meditate in the morning.
Do not covet other people's things, not even a single needle or leaf.
Do not cause other people trouble.
If you do, remember that you are pushing them away.
Be thankful to those who teach you things, even if it is just a single letter.
If you do not understand thoroughly, do not teach.
Never take for granted the person who gives you a meal and
a place to sleep for a night.
Do not fawn over others."

- Matsuo Basho

Basho's rules for wandering, which pierce to the heart of the human condition, were grown from Buddhist soil. I could not help but wonder whether my own temple experience approached the essence of Zen. "Learn about pine trees from pine trees, and learn about bamboo from bamboo," said Matsuo Basho (1644-1694), the haiku poet who lived during the Edo period in Japan. This quote was the inspiration for me to seek out a temple in the mountains in order to gain a deeper understanding of Buddhism, which forms one of the pillars of traditional Korean culture, along with Confucianism.

Though I am not a Buddhist, I always wondered how Korean temples were able to maintain their communities and produce so much cultural heritage over so many generations. Excluding Buddhism from a discussion of Korean culture would be like leaving out the core and discussing only the remainder. After much thought, I decided to knock on the door of the Baekheungam Hermitage at Eunhaesa Temple

in Yeongcheon, North Gyeongsang-do Province. Baekheungam Hermitage is unique in that it is only open to the public on Buddha's Birthday. But after explaining the purpose of my visit, I was allowed to enter.

As soon as we reached Mt. Palgongsan, which is regarded as the spiritual heart of North Gyeongsang-do Province, we felt refreshed by the rows of pine trees and the fast-moving stream. We had been following a winding path for quite a while, moving up the mountain and past a reservoir, when the elegant Baekheungam Hermitage appeared before our eyes. Baekheungam was built in the ninth century during the reign of King Gyeongmun of Silla. First named Songjisa (Pine Branch Temple) after the many pine trees that surround it, it was renamed Baekheungam in 1546, during the reign of King Myeongjong of Joseon. Though the suffix *am* refers to small temples, Baekheungam is quite large in size.

The nuns at Baekheungam spend two seasons out of the year cloistered inside the temple. During those times, they do not go out at all. This meditation retreat, called *gyeoljae* (Tight Dharma), takes place from mid-April to mid-July and from mid-October to mid-January, by the lunar calendar. Of the three types of hermitages—Yurwon for studying religious precepts, Gangwon for studying Buddhist scriptures, and Seonwon for Zen meditation—Baekheungam focuses on Zen meditation. The writer Shin Young-bok described Baekheungam as "a home away from the world," "where nothing is preached," "tranquility and idleness," and "the teachings of an unlettered silence." And indeed, the ambience there did seem dignified and removed from worldly affairs.

Sumidan Altar[1], Baekheungam

Altar portrait of Buddha, Hall of Paradise

When you zoom in on people's faces and focus on just eyes, noses and mouths, these features can all look more or less the same. But when you take a step back and look at faces as a whole, their differences become clear. Likewise, the countries within the East Asian cultural sphere have much in common up close but are clearly different in the long view. This is true, too, of the natural environment. Things may look alike, but seen as a whole, we find clear distinctions. Therefore, it makes sense that houses will differ depending on the landscape around them, as will the interiors of those houses. Then, just as houses and living spaces naturally take on distinct styles to suit their contexts, so the people who live inside of them differ as well. Culture seems to spring forth into the world as human beings mirror the landscape in themselves and in the things they create for themselves and for others. Perhaps culture is born out of the things we pour our hearts into and from how we treat others.

A tightly built stone and tile wall is beautiful to behold. I had grown so used to the bright colors and sounds of the city that the sight of a stone wall and the distant sound of birds struck me as fresh and pure. As I entered the temple grounds, the nuns, who looked very young, greeted me with shy smiles. Their clumsy and awkward welcomes and the heartfelt sincerity in their properly folded hands told me that this truly was a place where few outsiders ventured.

On my way across the grounds of the temple to the main room where the nuns practice meditation, I saw that they had guard dogs. The *jigaek*, who was in charge of showing guests around, said that security was a problem for them, as the temple was home to several important items. Things had improved considerably with the recent installation of closed circuit cameras, but the altar portrait of Buddha had actually been stolen once. She said, with an embarrassed smile, that their temple had been labeled as unfriendly because of their stern restrictions on outside visitors.

Zen Room:
Where Meditation is Practiced

I was led into a simple, unfurnished room filled with light. The only items in the room were the *hanji* wallpaper, clay-colored linoleum, bamboo rods on the walls for hanging *gasa*[2] ("saffron" robes) and *jangsam*[3] (monastic garments), and floor cushions folded in neat rows.

My eyes were drawn to the *yongsangbang*, a placard posted on the wall showing the division of roles at the temple. The *yuna* oversees everything; the *jijeon* keeps the meditation room clean; the *dagak* prepares the tea; and the *gongyangju* cooks the food. The placard contained twenty such titles. I wondered whether the secret to maintaining a community of monks or nuns over so many generations was the strict adherence to rules and loyalty to such subdivided roles. I studied it carefully, as I thought it might help me to realize my dream of living in the countryside some day. When people have to depend on each other more, as they do in the countryside, it is difficult to avoid conflict.

The seats marked *cheongsan* (green mountain) were for those who resided at the temple permanently: This signified that they were "as immovable as mountains." The seats marked *baegun* (white cloud) were for those who were only there for Zen meditation; in other words, *unsu napja*[4] (cloud and water monks), or itinerant monks and nuns who move from temple to temple, "drifting like clouds." When they were not attending to their duties, they all gathered here to meditate together.

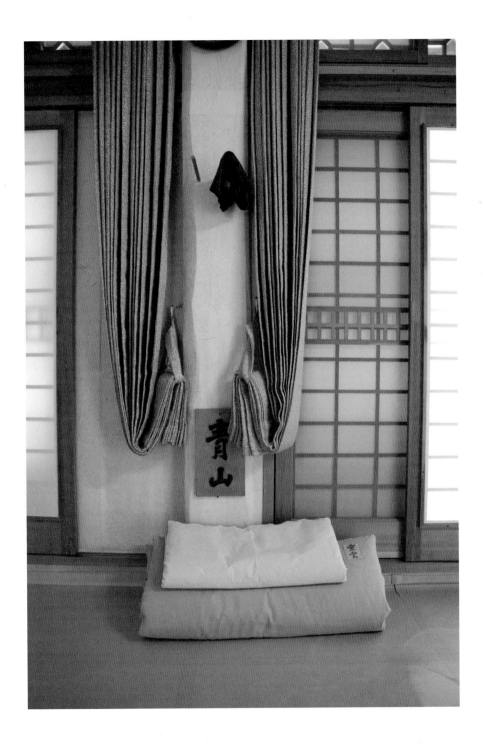

I took a look around the temple grounds and returned to find all of the nuns busily preparing food for us gatecrashers. Inside the high-ceilinged temple kitchen was an enormous cast-iron pot. A young nun with bright-red cheeks—either from the heat of the flames or from shyness—diligently attended to the fire. She explained that it was not easy to cook so much rice in such a large pot without burning or undercooking it. Feeling guilty, I paced around for a while instead of heading straight to where the food would be served.

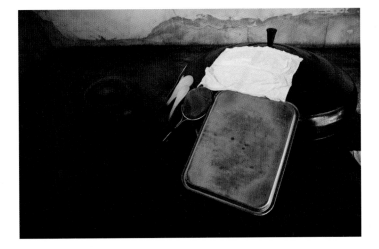

Shoes neatly arranged,
umbrellas stored by order of name,
straw hats hanging on an old wall like an art installation,
a cat drowsing on a porch,
its body curled tight like a ball...

On the terrace where the clay jars of fermented foods and sauces are stored, each jar is labeled with the contents and packing date for the benefit of nuns who will stay at the temple on future meditation retreats.

Out of curiosity, I open
several lids and peer inside.
I wish I could eat food made
from scratch everyday!
I quickly put the lids back,
for fear of getting caught.

Temple Food

I returned to the back garden to find the nuns moving even faster to finish up. Aside from fresh vegetables that they grow and put up themselves; seasonings made from all-natural ingredients like fermented soybean paste, chili paste, soy sauce, cinnamon and Chinese pepper; and salt, there are no other additives. You hear a lot of talk nowadays about the slow food movement and well-being, but I cannot help but think that temple food, in which only moderate amounts of seasonal produce and grains are eaten with an attitude of respect and thankfulness, is the true health food. In Japan, *shojin ryori* (temple food) filtered down to the general population a long time ago, but in Korea this has only happened recently.

For today's stew, radish greens were first dried in the sun then blanched in one of the cast-iron pots, chopped and mixed by hand with fermented soybean paste and chili paste. They were then added back into the pot and pan-fried in a few drops of oil. Finally, a mushroom and tangleweed broth was added to the pot and boiled. I was astonished to learn that, even in growing the vegetables, they do not use any chemicals, and insects are picked off the plants one by one with tongs and moved away from the garden.

Finally, a table was brought out and I enjoyed a long-awaited meal.

According to the *Jaba hamgyeong*[5], there are four types of food that should be consumed by Buddhists: *dansik* (material food), which is the food we eat to nourish our bodies; *choksik* (contact food), which is the energy we absorb from contact with the world around us; *sasik* (thought food), which is the strength we gain from ideas and ideals; and *siksik* (consciousness food), which gives us energy through thought and cognition.

The purpose of temple food is to achieve a clean and even balance of all four of these, from preparing and cooking the ingredients, to eating and cleaning up afterwards. Buddhism emphasizes constant gratitude and humility by flavoring your food with devotion and consuming it in a humble way, rather than with loads of spice.

While listening to the cooking instructions for pan-fried tofu, *majeon* (Korean yam pancake) and scorched rice soup, I found my hands reaching for the food of their own accord. I was scolded for stuffing my mouth too much, and blushed in embarrassment. But I cannot help my fondness for coriander. Others may wave it away, saying the pungent scent makes it hard to eat, but I love the aroma and the way it perks up my appetite.

I remarked that customers would line up if a restaurant like this were to open in Seoul. The nun smiled happily and asked me to be her first regular.

Scorched rice from the cast-iron pot
was cut into evenly sized pieces
for a fantastic snack.

After the meal, I had tea with the oldest nun at the temple, who was currently in charge of the Seonwon (Zen meditation center), and the chief nun, who had struggled for many years to cultivate and maintain it. I could sense the strong faith and friendship of these two women who had persevered and sacrificed to reclaim a temple that had been on the verge of ruin.
After the tea was done, I was sorry I had to leave,
but I turned my steps to the neighboring Unbuam Hermitage.

Sharing pleasant conversation with
good people in a mountain temple
left me feeling fully awakened.

Haeuso: Where You Go to Resolve Your Worries

The Unbuam Hermitage had the classic yet rustic air of an old temple. Its beauty was different from that of Baekheungam. We ate sweet potatoes from a wooden bowl and shared small talk. Soon, it was evening. From out of the deep stillness, I heard the *tok-tok-tok* of the *moktak*, or the "wooden fish" beaten by monks. The evening service drew to a close. Time flew by as we listened while the head monk of the Seonwon at Unbuam regaled us with stories. I cannot remember how long it has been since I lay with my head on my grandmother's knees and listened to old tales. Perhaps that is why the opportunity to listen to this older monk seemed all the more precious and heartwarming.

Did I drink too much tea, or was I just giddy? The sound of insects in the grass kept me awake. I had slept so soundly at Baekdamsa Temple during my visit to Mt. Seoraksan before… Of course, if this were a place where sleep came easily, the monks would never get through their Zen meditation. Better to be an insomniac. Their shoulders would get no rest from the *thwack-thwack* of the monk's bamboo stick.

The monk who tended to the heating must have been particularly concerned that the guests from Seoul might get cold. The clay floor in the big room sizzled all night. In the early dawn, I opened the windows to let in some air and looked out at the temple courtyard, unable to sleep. As my companions began to awaken one by one, I passed around handfuls of chestnuts, and for fun I even stuffed a few in the mouths of those still groggy with sleep. They ate the chestnuts readily, as if waiting for them with their eyes closed, and I could tell they had not slept well either. Then I remembered that the word for "staying up all night" was the same as the word for "raw chestnuts," or *nalbam*. I pictured women sitting up all night peeling chestnuts before a holiday or ancestral memorial service.

The hermitage still has an old-fashioned outhouse, called *haeuso*, a colloquial term meaning, "where you go to resolve your worries." Though they can easily become smelly or messy, the old-style squat toilet was neat and well-maintained. Ashes from the fireplace are spread to keep the smell down. But as even the faintest of embers can cause of fire, sawdust is sometimes used instead to the same effect. After a while, the contents can be scooped out and dried then sprinkled in the fields as an excellent fertilizer.

To my surprise, I learned that waste from the outhouse used by the general public was kept separate from the monks' and simply discarded. This was because it was too toxic and lacked nutrients, probably from eating too much instant food, which made it unsuitable for use as fertilizer. I could not help but think of the phrase, "You are what you eat."

Very few places are left in the world where people collect their own manure for farming. As even the most remote mountainous spots have roads now, it is difficult to turn one's back on the conveniences of civilization. I pray that the strong-willed head monk gets his wish for the classic grace and age-old beauty of the temple to remain safe and untouched. I also earnestly hope that the mirror-like pond out front and the gingko trees that glow like gold in the morning light will last a long, long time.

Woljeongsa Temple, Mt. Odaesan

In the car on the way to Mt. Odaesan for a temple stay program, I found myself growing anxious. After being warmly and genuinely welcomed by the nuns at Baekheungam and cared for by the earthy, easy-going monks of Unbuam, I was anticipating something more intense and regimented, which had me a little scared. Our choices were Mihwangsa, a picturesque temple in distant Haenam at the southernmost end of the country; Baekdamsa near Mt. Seoraksan, where the memory of Manhae Han Yong-un, a Buddhist reformer and poet, is kept alive; and Woljeongsa in Mt. Odaesan, the most propitious land in South Korea. This time, I chose Woljeongsa.

The thick forests and deep sea of Gangwon-do Province have a strong effect on travelers. Someone once said, "Gather the vital force of nature in the mountains, and cast your deepest sorrow into the sea." Rather than a light stroll, the serene yet majestically rolling waves of the East Sea call for deep contemplation and a sense of awe. I love Gangwon-do Province. I love the power of deep contemplation and the sense of awe that this land inspires in me.

Mt. Seoraksan and Mt. Odaesan are two of the most celebrated mountains in Korea. If Mt. Seoraksan is an imposing edifice of strange rock formations and deep ravines in the same mountain range as Mt. Geumgangsan in North Korea, which has the most magnificent views in the peninsula, then rather than sharp peaks, Mt. Odaesan is memorable for its soft and gradual yet brawny, boulder-like ridgelines. The two best views in Korea are the path at the entrance to Naesosa Temple in Buan, Byeonsanbando National Park, which is said to be the most beautiful place for a stroll, and the forest path at Woljeongsa, where large fir trees soar out of the ground.

As we approached Mt. Odaesan and stepped into the shadow of the mountain, we were gripped by a cold breath of fresh air. We walked for some time in high spirits along a forest path thick with trees before reaching the temple. Many of the buildings had been recently built, which gave the place a more modern feeling than the other temples I had seen thus far.

No sooner had we received our room assignments and unpacked than our temple stay experience began. We were given instructions on basic rules and etiquette and ate dinner. Then, before the evening service began, I took a stroll around the temple grounds. The sound of the drum reverberated throughout the mountains and deep into my cells. It seemed to wipe away all of my complicated thoughts and emotions and enabled me to concentrate on the service. The first day consisted of drinking tea and doing the traditional one hundred and eight bows. Because of a knee injury from filming a television show, I was unable to join in the bowing, much to my disappointment.

Mt. Odaesan is famous for its many legends and for Sangwonsa Temple, where the True Body of Buddha is housed. A humble cave once used by Naong Seonsa, a high priest from the Goryeo Dynasty, is still used for meditation by monks, and Sejo, the seventh king of the Joseon Dynasty made up for the indelible guilt of a tragic history through countless good works at Mt. Odaesan. For example, the Gyeongju Emille bell and the Silla Beomjong bell (National Treasure No.36) were the only two of their kind in the whole country, so King Sejo searched high and low and brought the Silla Beomjong to Mt. Odaesan.

Mt. Odaesan was also home to one of the five temples where a copy of *The Annals of the Joseon Dynasty* were stored for safekeeping, following the Japanese invasions of Korea in the sixteenth century. In the modern era, Mt. Odaesan became famous for its great Zen master Hanam, who looked after Sangwonsa completely on his own in order to protect the temple from fire during the Korean War. To this day, Mt. Odaesan is still alive with intriguing stories, like the monk Tanheo who was famous for predicting the future, and many others.

Dawn not yet risen, in a silence so hushed as to be frightening, half in and out of a dream, we performed the rites in perfect lockstep. Just as we were fully awakening, my companions and I ate breakfast: *baru gongyang*[6], the monastic Buddhist meal eaten from four wooden bowls. Each step in this precise and methodical way of eating is rich with meaning, which makes the *baru gongyang* a truly joyful experience. My awkward companions watched each other out of the corners of their eyes as they stumbled through the process, but having received detailed instruction in the past, I was slightly more at ease. Good preparation seems to be key to relaxation.

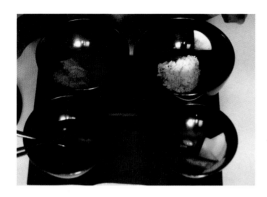

Eating this way made me strangely ravenous.

I looked at the fistful of rice inside that large wooden bowl, and it was like I was looking at someone that I knew and saw every day but was suddenly seeing in a new light. I poured water into the bowl to rinse it and swallowed every last drop. With *baru gongyang*, not a single grain of rice is wasted. The person next to me carelessly poured too much water into his bowl and struggled to drink it all.

I thought to myself, if only this spirit of valuing the act of eating and not wasting food could take root in every home, regardless of religion. It might help make up for the fact that Korean food tends to produce a lot of leftovers.

After the meal, it was time to clean.

For the first time in my life, I took up a large broom and swept the grounds of a temple in silence. This is called *ullyeok*, or communal chores. Unaccustomed to this kind of work, I felt drowsy and struggled to get through it, but soon my complaints vanished into thin air. Beads of sweat broke out on my face, and a passing breeze cooled my skin.

The *ssak-ssak* sound of the broom rang pleasantly in my ears.

The next part of our itinerary was not the easy stroll along a forest trail I had anticipated, but rather a difficult climb up the side of the mountain. Having shown up for the hike in comfortable shoes and casually carrying large bags, we took one look at our guide's light clothing and sturdy hiking boots and cocked our heads in alarm. Sure enough, our expectations of peacefully taking in a woodland path were shattered. We clambered up that mountain as if engaged in a desperate battle, and then we clambered some more. My knees ached, but I tried not to show it. Nevertheless, the moment I saw the cool mountain stream, my heart opened up. I could feel the power of the mountain in its rushing streams, the runoff steady despite the nationwide drought. Our hike up Mt. Odaesan was unlike any other.

After returning from our hike, we finished our brief temple stay experience in the museum by taking rubbings of stone inscriptions. When I think about it, it seems regrettable that the virtue of passing things down from one generation to the next is disappearing. Heritage passed down from father to son, from mother to daughter, from teacher to student—there is so much tradition and culture that should not be lost. In Buddhism, these traditions seem to be surviving through the generations. The spiritual world of Buddhism is one that strives for the beauty of nature, for quietude, for something loftier than mere buildings. It is these things that make people's hearts a little more open and a little bit fuller.

Tea and Talk with a Great Monk

By the time the solitary landscape of the mountain temple was but a faint glimmer before my eyes, we had reached Seokjongsa Temple in Chungju. Chungjuho Lake is the second biggest lake in Korea, after Soyangho Lake in Chuncheon. It is quite huge and has a strange feel to it. Though the scenery there is strikingly beautiful, there is something strange and unnatural about the way the landscape stops abruptly at the waterline, perhaps owing to the fact that it is a manmade lake, created when the valley was dammed.

Seokjongsa Temple dates back to the Goryeo Dynasty, but the temple itself was recently built. Nevertheless, it was built with great care and attention to detail, making it a traditional Korean temple worthy of being passed down to future generations as part of our cultural heritage. Despite its size, the meticulous work that went into each pillar and every brick was apparent. Though I am no expert, I closely examined the joints of every building I looked at. The places where different building shapes or materials meet require an especially high degree of skill and concentration. You can tell how well something was built by examining the joints. This is true not only of architecture but of other objects as well.

The head monk of Seokjongsa Temple had a fatherly look about him— like a strong, stubborn father. At first, I was quite nervous, having heard that he had undergone an unbelievably difficult training. But the more time I spent with him, the more I found myself relaxing and opening up.

The monk's right hand had been burned, leaving only the thumb unscathed. In Buddhism, there is a saying: *sosin gongyang*, to set yourself on fire as an offering to Buddha. Prepared and determined to carry out this ritual immolation without fail, he had set his fingers on fire as an offering—no ordinary man could hope to follow suit. Though back in school I had read Kim Dong-ni's book, *Deungsinbul*, about a monk who immolates himself, I did not remember being that moved by it. But when I saw the monk's scarred hand right before my eyes and heard his superhuman tales about teachers he had met in a previous life and about dying and coming back to life while meditating alone in the mountains, I felt my head begin to spin, as if I had stepped inside a fable. Then, when he told me that happiness was only possible if our spiritual lives take the lead over our economic or material lives, I found myself deep in thought. It seems that temples are not merely repositories for ancient relics that inspire curiosity and are designated as national treasures. They also contain the tools we need to make us better, more talented people. Living people are the ones who breathe life into buildings and sculptures that could just as easily be dead. How depressing would it be if we had only stores that sell pottery and no master craftsmen at the wheel? The great monk repeatedly urged me to become a man of culture before becoming a man of fame. I took his advice to heart.

I was treated to a nice cup of tea and then went for a short walk alone. Temples offer relaxation, time to look closely at your life, and the asceticism of self-admonishment. Temples have culture and tradition, tea and food, architecture and relics. Most of all, temples have stories. They are not hushed but alive and kicking. This is called *jeongjungdong*, a movement in the midst of silence.

A life without stories, an object without stories, a house without stories—that is not life. Though our stories may not be as big as renouncing the world and living in a temple as monks do, we make our own stories every day. In fact, I believe that as we move through life, we each make our own myths.

One of the monks I met on my journey wrote down a poem for me in a letter. I wondered whether it was a Zen poem that had been passed along from monk to monk. Maybe it was his way of telling me to live a kind and generous life.

I prefer walking alongside someone to sitting above them.
Sometimes we have to roll up our sleeves and get to work,
but even those times are joyful.
Shouldering other people's burdens is a foolish thing to do,
but a beautiful day with a cool breeze is reward enough.
Embracing our fates, too, can be a beautiful thing.
We do not have to share things that are difficult and perilous.
A single small tear can be sufficient.
If you were to become the tears of the world, I would gladly become a drop.

Tea

Sky and Earth and People
Becoming One

My First Encounters with Tea

Once, while staying somewhere in the mountains when I was around twenty years old, someone offered me a hot, fragrant cup of tea. Back then, everyone preferred instant coffee, so drinking tea was quite a new experience for me. The tiny cup looked like it held barely a mouthful. The aroma and flavor of that first sip of tea had me so spellbound that I later sought out similar teas. Most were Chinese. Eventually, I found some Korean teas. But each time I steeped the leaves in hot water, the flavor turned bitter and astringent. That stopped my infatuation with tea. I found out later that the teas I drank at the time were all *jeungjecha*, made from steamed tea leaves, which must be steeped in water warmed to 140-176°F (60-80°C) in order to taste right. Since the water I used was too hot, there was no way it could have tasted good.

Then, while visiting a Buddhist temple several years ago, one of the monks offered me a cup of tea. The tea was hot but not bitter, and the flavor and aroma stayed the same despite steeping the leaves multiple times. Astonished, I asked what kind of tea it was. He told me it was wild tea that he had roasted himself. It was perfect for someone like me who likes to drink his tea hot, around 203°F (95°C). To this day, I make time once or twice a day to drink this hand-roasted tea. Other times, I opt for *puer* tea when I want to relax and unwind, green tea when I am reading a book or talking with friends, and a cup of *matcha* (finely ground Japanese green tea) before making pottery.

Teas are categorized into four groups based on how much the leaves have "fermented," or oxidized: unfermented, half-fermented, fermented and post-fermented. Green tea is unfermented (0-10% oxidation), *oolong* tea is half-fermented (50-55% oxidation), and black tea is fermented (85-100% oxidation). *Puer* tea differs from naturally fermented black tea in that it undergoes a secondary oxidation and fermentation caused by microbes that grow in the tea. This method of classifying tea began in China but is now used around the world.

Green tea is the most common tea consumed in Korea, China and Japan. The leaves may be either roasted or steamed, which stops the leaves from oxidizing after they are picked. "Roasting" refers to heating leaves that are still a little bit moist, but not to the point of burning them. "Baking" refers to heating dried leaves. With "steaming," the leaves are either blanched or steamed.

Korean teas are traditionally roasted. The tea leaves are rubbed by hand to soften them, and then they are roasted in a large cast-iron pot, shaped like a wok, which is heated to 662-752°F (350-400°C). Roasted green tea is known for its clear, refreshing aroma. The leaves turn a soft and mysterious shade of pale celadon. *Jeungjecha* is made by either blanching the leaves or cooking them in a high-pressure steam cooker at 212°F (100°C).

On the Way to the Tea Fields

The tradition of Korean tea began with the Venerable Choui (1786-1866), who is credited with reviving the art of tea making in Korea. It continued with the Buddhist monks Beomhae Gagan (1820-1896) and Eungsong (1893-1990), and is now being carried on by Park Dong-chun, the head of the Research Institute of East Asian Tea Culture. I visited Park's tea plantation to learn more about the two-hundred-year-old history of tea and to find out how it gets from the field to the cup. Visitors are normally prohibited from entering the tea fields when the delicate first flush leaves are being harvested and processed, but Park graciously allowed me to watch and learn how it is done.

Around the ninth century, Seon (Zen) Buddhism[1] came to Korea along with monks who were traveling in search of Buddhistic truth. Zen temples were built, including Silsangsa, Borimsa and Taeansa. Zen monks drank tea as a form of meditation, and temples in the southern part of the peninsula, like Ssanggyesa Temple near Mt. Jirisan, cultivated their own tea fields. Up until approximately four hundred years ago, there was a Zen temple named Daegwangsa in Suncheon, South Jeolla-do Province. It was a very large temple, said to contain twenty-seven hermitages, which means the tea fields must have been endless. Park Dong-chun discovered the fields, which had gone fallow, and recultivated the soil. A good thirty minutes from the nearest house and well-preserved in their natural state, the fields grow wild tea.

I could not tell at first that I was standing in a field of wild tea. A mix of bamboo and tea plants, Park's fields were full of life.

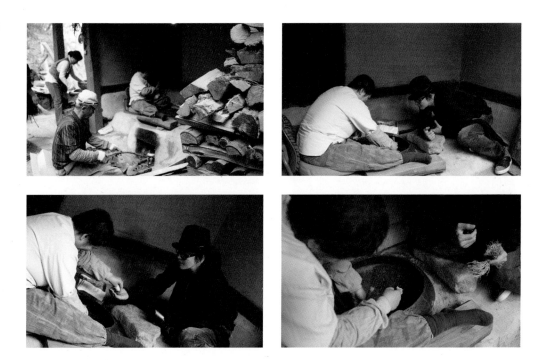

I had a feeling that once I saw
how it was made,
tea would never taste
the same to me again.

Tea Making

My first time watching tea being roasted: it was strange yet exciting to see how everyone took on different roles, rubbing, roasting and drying the tea. I looked around, eager to jump in and give roasting a try myself. Park Dong-chun looked very comfortable sitting on top of the hearth. An elderly man from the village sat motionless in front of the fire, like a stone Buddha. He had worked with Park for twenty-five years, tending to the fire. Park's apprentices were all hard at work. One woman rubbed tea leaves carefully between her hands; another transferred the rubbed leaves into the cast-iron pot; and another dried the roasted tea. When Park began roasting the tea, everyone crowded together in front of the hearth, reluctant to miss even a single detail: from the deft way she used her hands, to the timing of the fire, to the subtle changes in her expression. Park glanced around briefly and seemed to notice the look on my face. I could barely contain my curiosity. She motioned for me to sit closer, and I blushed at how obvious I must have been.

I sat across from Park with the cast-iron pot between us. From there, I could easily observe the changes in the shape and scent of the leaves, as well as Park's energy.

When the tea began to roast, the color and aroma changed so quickly and in so short a time that it was impossible to tell whether the leaves were first releasing their aroma then changing color, or changing color then releasing their aroma. The scent was heavy at first but soon became light and pleasant. It was refreshing to the nose. The color, too, turned from dark to light. The scent and color mixed together, growing heavy then light, sinking then rising, over and over. No sooner did I smell seawater and something sour than it disappeared, followed by a bitter note that soon disappeared as well. Sweet, bitter, salty, sour, tart—every smell in the world rose from the pot then just as soon vanished. Park asked me what the leaves smelled like. But before I could even begin to answer, the scent was already gone and the next one was rising. I figured this must be what it meant to make tea—putting these many smells and energies in order and condensing them. You have to start with topnotch materials, but no less important is the process of balancing out the various properties already present in the tea leaves. The mouth of the cast-iron pot was so wide that it seemed all of the aroma and flavor would escape, but Park's hands cast an invisible net to trap them into the leaves.

The cast-iron pot is heated to 662-752°F (350-400°C).
Temperature is very important in cooking,
but even more important is preserving
the natural flavor of the ingredients.

With tea, temperature is critical.
Bringing out the true aroma of the tea regardless of the temperature of the water
used to steep the leaves depends on controlling the heat
so that it can penetrate deep into the leaves,
and roasting it all at once so that the temperature stays the same both inside and out.
A tea maker must understand every minute change in the flame and
seize the right moments.

Park does not use gloves.
The only protection she wore was cotton finger cots.
She told me that gloves make it impossible for her to gauge
the heat of the fire and the doneness of the leaves.

Drinking Tea

After roasting the leaves, we all gathered in a small room to taste the first flush tea. Park took a sip then said, "This tea has to be served hot." She explained that *dancha*, tea that has been compressed into bricks or disks, is prepared by adding small amounts of cold water to hot water as it reaches a boil, but this process is unnecessary for loose leaf tea. The secret to tea that does not turn bitter even in hot water lies in the roasting method. Because the leaves are heated to over 662°F (350°C) during roasting, the tea retains its properties and can produce a fine taste even in very hot water. The hand-roasted tea that I tasted so long ago was likewise a high quality tea made using the same method.

Most people say that you can only steep tea leaves the same number of times they were first roasted. But Park's tea leaves smelled and tasted the same after steeping them four or five times, despite the fact that she had only roasted them twice. I was reminded anew that it is not the number of times the leaves are roasted that matters but the proper care with which it is done. Likewise, with ginseng, the *gujeung gupo* ("nine steam, nine dry") method of steaming and drying ginseng roots nine times does not actually mean that they must literally be steamed and dried nine times; rather, it means handling ginseng carefully and being mindful. "Tea leaves are so precise that if you handle them too much, the flavor may lose subtlety." Park's theory is that a good tea is one that balances flavor, aroma, color and energy.

A month after my tea roasting experience, I had tea with Park. She told me that she went all the way to a Buddhist temple called Cheongamsa in Gimcheon to get the water for our tea. She explained that the type of water you use to steep tea is important. Tea aficionados devote a great deal of time to selecting water, as it can change the flavor, aroma and vitality of the tea. Fortunately, the water all over Korea is very good, and the Hangang River in Seoul is clean enough. She said that tap water can be left at room temperature for up to four to six hours and still be good for tea. Some believe that tea tastes better when it is steeped in water that comes from the same region where the tea is grown. Lee Jae-jong, whose family grows tea in Gurye, tries as a rule to only make tea with the same water used to grow the tea, as it is believed that the tea will taste better if the tea and the water share the same source. The importance of finding the right water to match a good quality tea must have been a big part of the daily life of tea aficionados in the old days.

Tea leaves are not usually picked on cloudy days or right after it has rained. The tea farmer must wait three days. Right after it rains, the flavor and aroma of the tea can decline in quality and become heavy and cloudy in flavor. Park said that they had missed the right window for "third flush" tea due to the heavy rain, but the tea had come out well anyway. Since I had tasted the first flush tea right there in the tea field, I was very curious to know what third flush tea would be like. As soon as the hot water was poured into the teapot, the room filled with the scent of tea, just like when we roasted the leaves a month earlier. The third flush tea had a clear, cool energy. If first flush tea has a clean, fresh and delicate flavor, then third flush is a bit more rich, mature and complex.

Korean Tea Culture

Tea must be grown from seeds, not seedlings. The plant has a strong axial taproot that can penetrate rocks and grow to three times the size of the trunk. Transplanted seedlings, however, do not develop this taproot and have trouble surviving. Even if they do survive, they never fully develop as tea plants.

According to an old, long-vanished custom, tea seeds were placed in a pouch and slipped into the hands of newlywed brides leaving for their in-laws' house. Tea plants have unusually strong roots and do not grow well if they are moved, so the seeds were a symbolic message to young brides to put down roots in their husbands' homes and remain faithful to their husbands even if they became widowed. The message contained in the custom was stern, but it had a more sentimental meaning as well. Even if two seeds are planted in the same hole, they will grow only one root. So the tradition was also a reminder that a husband and wife "become one in mind and body."

At first glance, most people would mistake a wild tea field for just an overgrown meadow because tea plants naturally grow right alongside weeds. By having to compete with weeds, only the strongest tea plants survive. Also, in the summer months, insects eat the softer weeds next to the stiff, older tea plants, which eliminates the need for insecticides. Lee Jae-jong calls the weeds his "selfless back-up troops." The weeds martyr themselves to the insects to protect the tea. At the end of August, the weeds are cut down and spread around the plants to nourish the soil and provide warmth until winter. The weeds are then covered with sawdust or fallen leaves, which likewise help fertilize the plants. In mid-March, the weeds are removed to make it easier to pick the tea leaves that survived the winter, and the first harvest takes place before mid-April, when the spring rains come. Growing tea without the use of pesticides and chemical fertilizers is mandatory

for producing high quality tea.

The reason tea farmers do not use pesticides and chemical fertilizers is simple. Tea leaves are not supposed to be washed before they are roasted. Also, tea grown with artificial fertilizers does not smell good. Naturally, the taste suffers as well. As stated before, insects prefer weeds to wild tea leaves. But chemical fertilizers sweeten the leaves, which attracts insects, which in turn means adding herbicides and insecticides. Therefore, wild tea and organic tea are much higher in quality.

There are still many nameless tea growers who pick and roast wild tea at dawn. They do not only adhere to traditional methods but also combine tradition with modern science and technology to help develop the tea industry. After witnessing the process multiple times myself, I feel strongly that more people should seek out hand-roasted teas that have been made with such care.

> Was this clear scented tea picked in April?
> First you sent ripe persimmons
> touched with frost,
> then sparrow's tongue tea
> roasted in spring.
> They say a monk never forgets old friends,
> but I blush at the undeserved kindness.

The poem was written by Ikje Yi Je-hyeon, a brilliant writer from the late Goryeo Dynasty. It is said to be the first appearance of the term "sparrow's tongue tea," or *jakseolcha*, coined by Ikje in a letter sent to a monk named Bangjang of Songgwangsa Temple upon receiving a gift of tea leaves. The Korean word for the tea, *jakseol*, literally means "sparrow's tongue," so named because of the tea leaves' resemblance to the same. That he would think of that teeny-tiny tongue inside the bill of a cute little sparrow is amazing. He is certainly deserving of the title "Greatest Master in Joseon's Three-Thousand-Year History." Up until the 1980s, most people were still using the name *jakseolcha* (sparrow's tongue tea) instead of *nokcha* (green tea). *Jakseol* was synonymous with "precious tea." I believe this was because it is the freshest, highest quality tea made from the first shoots that appear, when the plum trees are first in blossom and spring is on its way.

Images of tea drinking during the Three Kingdoms era that appear in old literature show that there were many different customs and types of tea. "Tea" did not just refer to the green tea that is most common now. According to these records, *yudancha* was a fancy brick tea that was ground to a fine powder, passed through a sieve, mixed with hot water and frothed with a bamboo whisk before drinking. Powdered tea is usually thought of as Japanese, and fermented tea as Chinese, but all of these different teas were found in Korea, China and Japan alike. Also, there are still tea producers in Korea making powdered and fermented teas.

This once-diverse Korean tea culture went into decline following the policy of *Sungyu eokbul*[2] ("Promote Confucianism, Suppress Buddhism") implemented during the Joseon Dynasty. This was no doubt because tea culture had grown alongside Buddhism. It went through a period of chaos then seemed to all but disappear. However, Park Dong-chun had this to say on the subject: Korean tea culture did not disappear. It went through a difficult period but survived thanks to people who understood the essence of tea, and it has blossomed again today. Korean tea culture continues to evolve and develop. And not just roasted teas, but fermented teas and powdered teas are also being tried.

In addition, other traditional herbal teas made from petals and leaves, such as mulberry leaf tea, persimmon leaf tea, chrysanthemum tea, white lotus tea, Chinese matrimony vine tea, mugwort tea, lotus leaf tea and amrita tea, are an extension of this revival. Such hidden efforts to uncover old traditions and keep them alive are helping to create new teas suited to Korea's climate and to diversify our tea culture.

Jakseolcha (sparrow's tongue tea)

Roasted teas are grouped into three grades based on when they are harvested: *sejak* or *ujeon* (second flush), *jungjak* (third flush) and *daejak* (everything after the first three harvests). *Sejak* tea is made from very young leaves picked before mid-April. *Jungjak* tea is made from slightly matured leaves picked between mid-April and early-to-mid-May. *Daejak* tea comes from the coarser leaves picked between mid-May and early June.

The words *sejak*, *jungjak* and *daejak* are all derived from Chinese, but I prefer the native Korean equivalents: *cheonmulcha*, *dumulcha* and *semulcha*, which mean literally first, second and third-crop tea. So for tea made from leaves picked after July, I like to call it *kkeunmulcha*, or "last-crop tea."

With tea, the harvest period is the most important factor; however, that period can vary slightly depending on local climates. At the time that I wrote this, for example, some tea farms were already harvesting their second flush, while other farms had barely begun their first flush. So, depending on region and climate, the quality of the tea comes down to how closely the farmer is in communion with her or his tea fields.

Lively yet flexible, familiar yet never vulgar—
what if the spirit of the classical Korean scholar
could be propagated along with tea?

2009 was an unusually dry year for wild tea. As a result, production was down, but the taste and aroma of the first flush tea were even better as a result of the drought. The poor soil and low moisture turned out to be very good for the strength and fragrance of the leaves. To compare it with wine, this case was similar to the 2003 Bordeaux from the Medoc region, which had a particularly hot summer that year. But the adverse combination of lower-than-average rainfall and higher-than-average days of sunshine made the grapes more resilient.

In the climactic episode of *Kami no Shizuku* (*Drops of the Gods*), a recent Japanese television adaptation of the comic book about a man who must identify thirteen mystery wines described in his deceased father's will, the final wine turns out to be a 2003 Chateau Le Puy. Though the 2000 Chateau Le Puy is generally more highly appraised, the authors, who go by the pseudonym of Tadashi Agi, valued the 2003 more highly as it had blossomed beautifully despite the adverse conditions. The Chateau Le Puy winery has been growing its grapes without any pesticides or fertilizer for eight generations. They say that the roots of their grape plants extend eighty meters below ground. I wonder if the fact that tea tasting is said to be an extension of wine tasting is because of the similarities between tea and grape plants. It seems that tea and wine enthusiasts share nearly all the same questions.

I began to wonder whether the flavor of a tea could be enhanced by the type of cup you drink it from, just as wine drinkers use different glasses for different wines. As it turned out, I got my answer the very same day: indeed, the teacup can affect the flavor. Some of the people in our group drank from a Song Dynasty blanc de Chine clay cup, while others drank from a *cheonghwa baekja* porcelain cup.

The Song Dynasty cup was a bit large. If it had a handle, it would look like a Western-style teacup. I thought about the story of the British queen who tried to drink tea from a Chinese teacup. She said black tea made the cup too hot to be held in both hands, so she requested that a handle be attached. Since then, black tea has been served in teacups with handles. The Song Dynasty cup places more emphasis on the last sip than the first, allowing the tea to linger on the palate. In contrast, the porcelain cup enables you to taste the first sip in more detail. We all drank the same tea, but we experienced different flavors depending on which cup we held. As fun as that was, I couldn't help but think, "Great, now I have to find the right *cups* for my tea as well," and I worried about my growing china collection.

Since tea is harvested annually, most people drink *haetcha*, "new harvest tea," on principle. But even newly harvested teas need time to mature. Teas that have just been processed need time to cool and stabilize their aroma, flavor and energy. There is no rule against drinking tea that is over a year old. However, if the tea was not processed properly in the first place, it can spoil or turn stale before the summer is out. Spoiled tea turns light brown then later black and white. Tea that has turned will taint the steeping water and lose its flavor, and it can even be harmful to your health. On the other hand, properly processed tea can be stored for six to seven years without going stale. Stored correctly, tea can acquire a new grace. The freshness of a new harvest tea does not last, but the character and body stay the same while new flavors can emerge. The flavor of a tea can grow more beautiful with age.

The date on the tea package read "May 2001." I could not believe my eyes. Park scooped some tea from the package, placed it in a cup and poured water over it. What would it taste like? I hurriedly took a sip, too impatient to wait for the water to cool. In a word, it was different. To begin with, it had a sweet aroma. The energy of the tea had mellowed. The flavor was slightly similar to that of a fermented tea, but it tasted clear and fresh for the most part. The color was quite different from a new harvest tea, but it had a hint of gold. Warmth spread from my stomach to my arms and legs. I felt that the tea had departed somewhat from the character of a roasted tea and was closer to a half-fermented tea.

Seonamsa Temple's tea fields

A Journey in Search of Tea

I fell in love with hand-roasted teas during my visit with Park Dong-chun.
"I know I could make money selling tea," she said, "but my mission is not
to sell tea but to pass on the spirit it contains." In keeping with her goal of
preserving cultural integrity, Park's teas cannot be purchased, and her yearly
output is very small. She offers them like Buddhist alms to those she loves.
She does so to preserve the spirit of traditional tea that cannot be bought
through material means.

I wanted to find a tea that approached the quality of Park's teas. I had
been inspired to learn more about tea from her. In the meantime, I had to
take a trip to Gwangyang in South Jeolla-do Province. As luck would have
it, one of my travel companions told me about a tea plantation run by a
Buddhist temple called Seonamsa in nearby Suncheon.

Seonamsa Temple's stone basins

It rained on the day of our visit to Seonamsa Temple, located on the slopes of Mt. Jogyesan. There we saw the temple's hidden tea fields and a stone water fountain made from four *dolhwak*³ (stone basins). The shape of the basins gradually change from square to round, signifying the Buddhist ideal of refining one's character—as if rounding off one's hard edges—through meditation. The water in the first and largest basin is considered sacred and used only as an offering to Buddha, and the second is used for steeping tea. The third is water for cooking rice, and the last one is all-purpose water for washing one's face or doing laundry. The water in this fountain continues to be used for *darye*, the traditional tea ceremony, which is observed daily at Seonamsa. The term *charye*, which refers to the ancestral memorial services traditionally observed on holidays, was originally synonymous with *darye*. Both share the same Chinese characters and mean literally "tea etiquette"; only the pronunciation varies, depending on the context in which the word is used. Though alcohol is now used for ancestral memorial services, tea was the original beverage served to ancestors, hence the name. I imagine how nice it would be to hold a tea ceremony or make offerings to God and Buddha every morning while thinking about my family, my ancestors and those who have passed away and to whom I am grateful. I would start each day with a clear cup of tea and a thankful heart.

Shin Kwang-soo, a tea expert in Suncheon, used to cultivate the tea fields now run by Seonamsa from 1966 to 1989. In 1989, he transferred the fields back to Seonamsa and is now cultivating more fields on higher land. Shin explained the differences between native and improved varieties of tea.

As tea became scarce in Korea, improved seeds were brought in from Japan. The seeds were a variety called Yabukita, developed to produce a high output of tea. Yabukita tea plants mainly grow by absorbing fertilizer, so the roots develop laterally rather than axially, which means that the roots do not penetrate as far into the ground as the native variety. The plants are said to live for no more than twenty-five to thirty years. Currently, over ninety percent of the tea plants in Korea are grown from Yabukita seeds, making the deep-rooted native variety a rare species. The tea plant native to Korea can survive with little care for three hundred to seven hundred years. Though the output is not as great, it is hands-down superior in terms of taste and quality.

The top three teas in the world are generally considered to be Chinese *oolong*, Indian Darjeeling and Sri Lankan Uva. All three are grown in highland regions. Shin's tea fields, as well, are located in the highlands at an altitude of 2,296 feet (700 meters). The tea is priced at 1,200,000 won for fifty grams (approximately 1,000 US dollars for just under two ounces). Though some may consider this very expensive, the sight of those tiny, delicate tea leaves resting in a cup draws a clear picture of the scrupulous and demanding process they went through, which makes the price seem justified. The flavor—a blend of gentleness, strength and brilliance—also leaves no doubt that this is a very high quality tea. Currently, Shin grows twenty-four acres of wild tea and eight acres of native tea, but he receives no support from the government for his efforts. In fact, his tea is more highly esteemed in Europe and Japan than at home.

If a person whose senses are not fully alive and engaged handles tea, it will not be high quality. Shin told me that he received the following message from a Czech man who tasted his tea: "When I drink your tea, I hear the sound of a waterfall. I feel the immense power of nature. And the flavor stays strong, even after the leaves have been steeped multiple times."

"Most trees do not send down roots that are longer
than their trunks. But Korean tea plants have deep
roots, up to three times the length of the trunk, so
they can draw in energy from the earth as they grow.
That is why the tea has such a deep flavor."

Tea and Daily Life

First and foremost, tea must be a part of our daily lives. When I try to convince others of the appeal of tea and suggest that they make it a daily habit, the response I usually get is that tea is expensive and difficult. But if you really look at it, that is not the case. There are many inexpensive teacups to be found, and in my own case, I have used my set for over ten years. With care, I will be able to continue using it indefinitely. When you consider that ceramics can last for hundreds of years, then they are not so expensive. It is the same with the cost of tea. Generally, a high-quality hand-roasted tea will cost around 50-200,000 won for eighty grams (approximately 43-170 US dollars for just under three ounces). I go through an eighty-gram canister of tea a month, at a cost of around 80,000 won (68 USD). I entertain guests often, so I drink a lot of tea. The amount can vary, but a person drinking alone will use around two grams of tea at a time. If you drink tea every day, that comes out to around 2,000 won (1.70 USD) per day. When you consider all that tea does—provides mental rest, has anti-aging properties, helps fight cancer and other diseases—then it really is not such a great expense.

If you know the basics about tea equipment and can boil water, then you can enjoy tea in any fashion you please. You do not need a tea tray; a simple cloth can suffice. Korean tea can be drunk from a Chinese cup, and likewise Chinese tea can be drunk from a traditional Korean cup.

You can wait until you have begun to enjoy tea and want to explore it on a deeper level to study the philosophy and proper etiquette. I think the more important question is who you drink tea with.

The Venerable Choui, the Korean "sage of tea," wrote in *Dongdasong*[4] (*Ode to the Tea of the East*) that drinking tea alone was *sin* (godly), as it was the realm of the divine and the profound. Two people drinking tea was *seung* (victorious), as it was refined and tranquil. Three or four people were *chwi* (pursuing), as it was the realm of mirth and enjoyment. Five or six people were *beom* (wide), and more than that were *si* (giving), as it signified the sharing of food.

According to Park Dong-chun, "Tea reveals its essence in silence, so you reach the realm of the divine by emptying your heart and drinking alone in peace."

I prefer to drink tea with at least one other person, a like-minded companion preferably. When I do drink alone, I do not go to great effort. But if I have at least one person with me, I am motivated to put more care into conveying the flavor and aroma of the tea to that person. I think that one person drinking tea can achieve meditation; two people, communication; three, shared sympathy; and four, harmony.

Lu Yu, a Tang Dynasty writer and China's own "sage of tea," wrote in *The Classic of Tea*: "Birds of the air, beasts of the earth and human beings who move among them have always planted, hunted and drunk their food. People drink water to quench their thirst and alcohol to quell their anger. And they drink tea to dispel the darkness inside them." In other words, what elevates us beyond water and alcohol is the enjoyment of tea.

The desire to make tea a part of daily life also leads to the creation of new teas. Lee Jae-jong created his own fermented tea after being inspired by an acquaintance who preferred the warmth of wine to the coolness of tea. While the tea leaves were drying, Lee sprinkled the leaves with homemade rice wine and aged them for about two years. He said they needed to ferment a little longer to develop the right flavor, but he let me sneak a taste to appease my curiosity.

Before taking a sip, I breathed in the aroma. The rich bouquet had floral and chocolate notes. Enjoying a tea at every stage of its transformation even before it is complete seems to be part of the appeal of a fermented tea. One of my traveling companions suggested we raise our glasses in a toast—since they did contain some alcohol after all—and we all happily agreed. The tea, which was beautiful in color, fragrant and clean on the palate, showed great potential. It made me realize there were more possibilities for Korean tea. A sudden idea occurred to me: what if, every spring, families could make an event of picking and roasting their own tea for the year? I think people nowadays are looking for something more than simply trying new things. They want experiences that impact their lives. We get together for drinks for a friend's birthday, or we meet with our family to celebrate a birthday over a meal and then go our separate ways. But how much nicer would it be if we used these times to make memories with each other, engaging in the culture that surrounds us, sharing a healthful meal? We could also get together with friends once a year to pick tea, roast the leaves and divide it up afterward. Or we could brew our own alcohol and get together again two months later to partake of it together. Isn't that culture, after all? Spending time together with good people, naturally, as part of our daily lives? I am confident that the fun we would have together would transform into something powerful and tangible for us.

I am coming to understand that nature is the new cultural heritage we will bequeath to our descendants. Only by leaving the abundant natural environment cleaner than how we found it can we better cultivate our senses in the process. The mountains and rivers of this country are very healthy, and they produce healthy fields and foods. What the country lacks in land area, it makes up for in natural resources. The plant life of Korea is amazingly diverse, from lowland plants to the alpine flora of our many mountains, from subtropical plants to the polar plants that follow the four distinct seasons, and from not only the many *yeomsaeng singmul*[5] (salt plants) that have adapted to the broad salt flats of the south and west coasts but to the aquatic plants and plants that grow in marshy land. Korea is home to 4,597 species of native plants, comparable to the variety found in Europe, which is fifty times larger in area than Korea. Furthermore, the natural environment of Korea that supports so many plant species imbues those plants with outstanding medicinal qualities. Even when they are of the same species, plants can very dramatically in their medicinal properties depending on climate, region and soil quality, but Korean medicinal plants have long been known throughout China and Japan for their medicinal effects.

(Source: Korea Biodiversity Information System, National Arboretum Service)

I hope Korea will become more widely recognized as a country with lots of healthy food. Because it is true. When we were little, we were told all the time by our mothers and grandmothers, "Eat it. It's good for you." Korean food *is* medicine. If someone were to ask me, "What do you think is Korean food's competitive edge?" I would say, "It brings us closer to nature." If we could create an image of Korea as a place where good ingredients and good food, healthful ingredients and healthful food, can be found anywhere, not only would our own lives improve, but more people from other countries would want to visit Korea to experience and learn about it for themselves.

Pottery 07

A Noble Simplicity
Speaks to Me

Mungyeongyo Kilns

In the early autumn of 2008, I went in search of Docheon Cheon Han-bong, who lives in Mungyeong, a city in North Gyeongsang-do Province. He had managed to recreate the Joseon *dawan*[1] (or *Ido dawan* as it is known in Japan), a style of tea bowl that had all but disappeared from Korea after the sixteenth century. His early attempts, which were not stamped with his signature, were such accurate recreations that some people even mistook them for "three-hundred-year-old Joseon *dawan*" excavated from archaeological sites. But such is the talent of this renowned master.

Around ten years ago, I stopped in at a pottery shop on my way somewhere and purchased a tea set. I did not give much thought to where the bowls came from but just picked the first one that looked right to me. Later on, I began to wonder about the man whose name was stamped on the teaware that I had been using every day for the last decade. I probably should have asked that question a long time ago. Luckily, I had some time off and decided to ask around to see if I could find this man named Cheon Han-bong. This time, the bowl in the pottery shop that had extended its hand in greeting and spoken to me was also leading me to him.

Mungyeong was new to me. To get to Cheon's house in Dangpo-ri Village, we drove along the main street and turned off onto a narrow, unpaved path surrounded by rice paddies. One of my companions shouted in wonder, and I rolled down the window. The whole world had turned gold. Against the folding screen of the mountains, the yellow stalks of rice were nodding their heads as they ripened in the sun. The paddies stretched wide on each side of the road. Halfway across, we pulled over on the side of the bumpy road and could not stop taking pictures. In the distance, the rocky mountains were dotted with autumnal bursts of red. All around the village, tree branches visibly sagged from the weight of the apples hanging from them. Mungyeong and Yecheon are famous for their apples, both for the ideal growing conditions and for the flavor. Mungyeong has also been known for its good soil, which is why it has long been home to many kilns where pottery is made.

As recently as the seventeenth century, the only countries in the world that produced their own pottery were China and Korea. China had been making celadon porcelain since the latter half of the tenth century, and in the eleventh century, Korea succeeded in creating green celadon using its own inlay technique at the Gangjin Yongunni kilns and the Gochang Yonggyeji kilns. Japan began making its own pottery as well in 1616 with the creation of white porcelain at the Arita kiln, while Europe began producing pottery in the eighteenth century. Yet while the word "china" is used all over the world to signify both the country and the porcelain, and the Japanese brand-name pottery Noritake has conquered the global market, the culture of Korean pottery has walked the path of obscurity.

Cheon Han-bong

"Come right in."

We were meeting for the first time, yet it felt like we were old friends. My traveling companions and I had crept in carefully, expecting the air of a great master whom no ordinary mortal dare approach. But the impression he gave off was very similar to the humble tea bowls I had been using for so long. I stole a quick glance at his hands as he ran them shyly over his hair. 'Ah, so those are the hands. Those small but strong square hands made such free shapes.'

Cheon's creations were on display in his studio. There, he threw clay on the wheel with a masculine flourish and churned out all kinds of Joseon Dynasty-era tea bowls, such as *duduok dawan*[2], *bunin dawan*[3], and Gimhae *dawan*[4], then set his creations out so that visitors could handle them freely, letting their hands and hearts reach for whatever called to them. I carefully wrapped my hands around a bowl. The fluttering sensation in my fingertips made me shiver. I have always liked that feeling. Koreans use many colloquial expressions that refer to *gi* (known as *qi* in Chinese), such as *giun naeda*, "to draw strength," or *giun charida*, "to gather strength," perhaps because we are sensitive to *gi*, the strength or energy that moves through all things. I paced around a bit, enjoying the feeling. Cheon laughed and waited for me to sit back down. One wall was covered with plaques, letters of appreciation and badges of honor. He said he kept them on display even though they made the room look cluttered because he did not want any of the people who had given him these awards to feel bad if they came back and saw that they were missing. Those words said a lot about the kind of person he is.

Cheon was as busy as a little bumblebee. He appeared to be lost in thought, but each time I asked him a question, he looked me right in the eye and gave me a thoughtful answer. The wrinkles on his perpetually smiling face were as beautiful as he was. When eating or drinking, he looked comfortable and composed. But even when devoid of desire, he always seemed to be focused on something. Pottery must be empty so that it can be filled. As I watched Cheon, who always seemed to be emptying himself out completely, I realized, albeit faintly, that to mold pottery is to mold yourself.

The Italian philosopher Luigi Pareyson had the following to say about artistic mediums in his book *Estetica*: "If the artist is to control his medium, he must question himself, and if he is to tame it, he must analyze why. He must submit to the medium in order to make the medium submit. At the same time, he must study his subject deeply to uncover the latent possibilities that suit his purpose... Art is nothing more than the expression and formation of the medium. But that medium takes shape solely according to that which forms the mind of the artist, whose style is complete, and nothing else."

Breathing Life into Pottery

Making Potter's Clay

Finding good clay is the first step to making pottery. This is why pottery kilns are located wherever there is good clay to be found. Around sixty years ago, Cheon Han-bong selected Mungyeong, where the soil is weathered by the elements. He also collects good clay dust from regions around the country. To prepare potter's clay, grind the clay dust and soak it in water to remove impurities. Sponge off the water that floats to the top, and sift out the fine particles of dust that sink to the bottom. This process is called *tonmul batki*, or *subi* in Korean. As the water separates out, the fine potter's clay emerges. Clay can be reused over and over before it is fired in a kiln simply by grinding it up, soaking it in water, and sifting it again. Not even a single lump of clay is wasted.

Wedging the Clay

Drain the prepared potter's clay, gather it into one large mass and carefully walk on it barefooted to compress the clay and press out any trapped pockets of air. When the *jilbapgi*, or "treading the clay" is complete, shape the clay into blocks of manageable size and thickness and wedge them by hand. Wedging, or *kkobak milgi* as it is known in Korean, gives the clay the right texture and eliminates air bubbles that can expand in the heat of the kiln and cause the pottery to explode.

Throwing a Bowl

Center a ball of clay on the potter's wheel. To make a bowl, press your thumb down into the center of the clay ball to create the mouth of the bowl and use your fingers to shape the sides. Finish the bowl by using a tool to even out the bottom and smooth out the sides. Dry the bowl slowly on a heated floor. If the clay dries out too much, it will be difficult to trim the hardened clay from the foot of the bowl. Control the drying process by progressively moving the pottery from a warm room to a cooler room.

Shaping the Foot

Carefully place the bowl upside down on the wheel and turn it slowly. Use a loop tool to carve out the rim of the foot. The height and thickness of the foot must be even for the bowl to balance properly when it is set upright.

I kept my eyes wide open the whole time,
but I still felt like I was missing something.
It seemed like it took tremendous concentration
and total effort just to make one bowl.
The timing of the wheel, the delicate handiwork,
the feel of the clay as it turned beneath my hands—
how long before I would be able to say
I was familiar with these things?
The clay was cold at first
but soon relaxed and warmed to my hands,
making it hard to tear myself away from
this captivating routine.

Is that how he fell in love with it?
He told me that back when he was making pottery for a living,
he had to make three to four hundred jars and bowls a day.
I suppose that is why it took him all of fifteen seconds to throw clay on the wheel
and churn out a finished bowl.
I snuck another glance at his hands.
This time, I looked more closely at the insides of his fingers.

Not a single fingerprint left.

In the valley, the master artisan sat with his back to the cold wind,
staying awake to keep the fire alive.
If I had not come, he would have spent the whole night with only the flames to talk to.
A wordless conversation between fire and artisan.
I was granted the simple pleasure of being allowed to intrude however briefly.
What was he looking at?
I followed his gaze, and my eyes filled with the dancing flames.

"Now the soot begins to crumble," he said gravely.
For him it was routine, but for me, everything was strange and unfamiliar.
At his words, the pine firewood vanished. Having burned itself down,
it had completed its duty and waited to be dismissed.
After witnessing how the kiln was fired, I felt changed somehow.

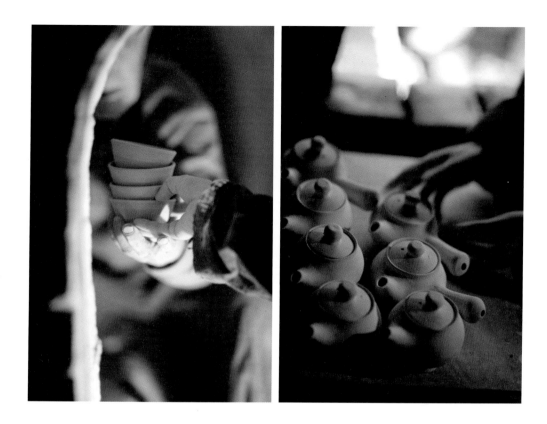

After the biscuit firing was complete, the pottery was left in the kiln to cool for a day.
At dawn, the clay seal on the opening of the kiln was removed.

All of the pottery had to be dusted off before glazing.

Biscuit Firing

Before glazing the greenware (dried, unfired pottery), fire it at 1292-1652°F (700-900°C). Use firewood for the first firing, which is called biscuit firing. The process takes six to seven hours and uses one ton of firewood.

Making and Applying Glaze

Traditional Korean glaze is made from ash and water. There are many different types of glaze, but in Mungyeong it is mostly made from applewood. The color varies with the type of glaze. In Korean, glazing is called *jaenmul chigi*, or *yuyak chigi*. Likewise, the method in which the glaze is applied varies depending on the specific qualities of the pottery.

Into the Kiln

When firing the pottery a second time, stack the bowls on top of each other to maximize the space inside the kiln. Attach small balls of clay to the bottoms of the bowls to keep them from fusing together as the glaze melts. The small pieces of clay will leave a mark inside the bowls, giving each tea bowl a unique look when the tea soaks into it.

It was not easy to transfer all of that pottery, stacked in groups of four or five, into the kiln. Cheon decided where everything would go based on the characteristics of the pottery. Tea bowls were placed furthest from the opening of the kiln to keep them from being directly affected by the fire and ash.

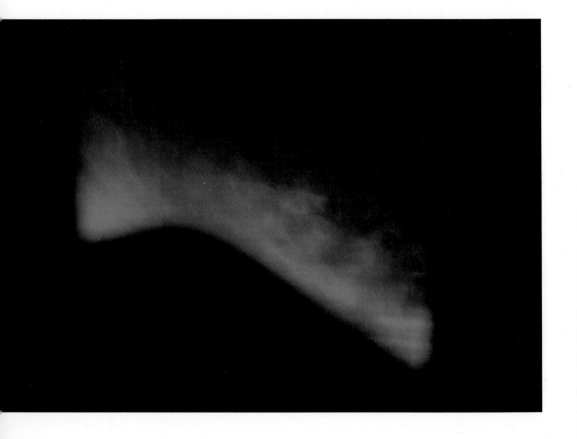

Glaze Firing

Early morning, a low thump followed by a rattle, then something rustling. My traveling companions and I listened to the sound of Cheon, who had risen before everyone else, as he opened the door, crossed the courtyard, and headed to the kilns. We rushed to get dressed and follow him. Cheon did all of the cleaning and organizing of the glazing room himself, then idly watched the morning news before emerging. He zipped his jacket all the way to the top and quickly entered the kiln. I hurriedly readied some wooden boards to receive the fired pottery. Unsure of my steps and fearful of breaking something, I trailed behind Mr. Kim, who worked for Cheon. Every muscle in my body was tensed. That might have been the tensest moment of my entire life. Each time Mr. Kim handed me a bowl, he let out a little rhythmic shout of "*Eucha!*" As we headed toward the final stage of the pottery making, everything came to center on the master.

The chambered kiln was built to exactly Cheon's height. A silly thought occurred to me: if I built my own kiln, the door would have to be one and a half times as tall. Cheon told me that, out of a total of five to six tons of firewood, two tons of pine alone goes into the *bongtong*[5], the large furnace at the front of the kiln, during the glaze firing. Considering that it produces over three hundred kilograms of ash, the nickname that people used in the old days to refer to kilns makes sense: *aguri*, a mouth that devours everything in sight.

I had never sat and watched a fire that long in my life. The flames seemed to flutter up like butterflies, like something I saw once as a child in the throes of a fever. The fire was breathing life into the bowls. Cheon looked extremely peaceful as he sat in front of the kiln and watched the fire. He studied the fire calmly then tossed in more firewood. Even without a thermometer or clock, he seemed to understand the fire with his body and heart. If it were my kiln, I would have been on pins and needles the whole time.

I watched Cheon's restrained movements as he stoked the fire for the thousandth time, and all of my worldly thoughts vanished. The cold morning air and the hot air of the kiln made me feel simultaneously awake and drowsy. They say that pottery has a life of its own and is sensitive to the seasons, so pieces made in spring and autumn tend to look more polished and fresh.

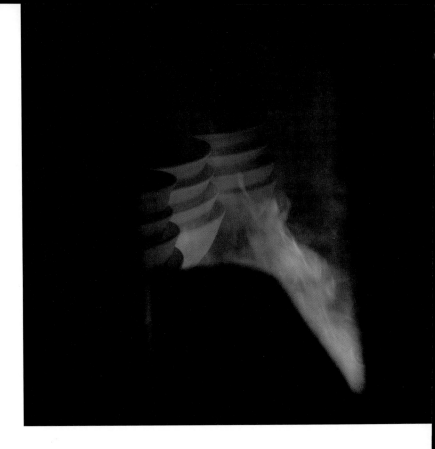

The fire had to reach 2372°F (1300°C) for the glaze to melt, covering the surface of the pottery, forming an even glassy coat, and strengthening the clay. Flickering into view between the flames, the pottery looked tranquil and happy. I helped Cheon pick out large and small pieces of firewood.

One of these days, I will learn how to look cool while throwing wood into a fire, an indifferent look on my face like there's nothing to it, just like Cheon.

The flames that had slowly reached 2372°F began to die down and flicker out. That was the critical moment. The success or failure of the firing depended on whether or not he should add one more stick of firewood when the fire went out. The pressure Cheon must have felt as he completed this last step was unfathomable to me.

The soot devoured the pottery, and the fire burned off the soot.
Then the flames rose again and created more soot.

The soot swallowed the pottery, and the fire erased the soot.
The flames rose again and carved out the soot.

Having stoked these kilns for
over sixty years, Cheon looked
like he had become one with
the fire and the clay.
Tiny blue sparks
flew out of the kiln.

Standing Crane Tea Bowl

Cheon hurried into the kiln while it was still hot, as if eager to check the bowls without a moment's delay. I was surprised to see how the colors, none of which were identical, had transformed. He told us that of the nearly eight hundred items, only fifty were to his liking. I was a little more relaxed while carrying the still-warm pottery, but my steps felt heavier than before. The pottery seemed to have grown heavier as it moved through the different stages of its making—the weight of time and effort, perhaps.

Cheon waved me over. "Pick one." He wanted to give me one of the *Iphak dawan*[6] as a gift and motioned for me to choose the one I wanted. I felt honored that he would allow me to select a bowl still warm from the kilns even before he had a chance to sort through them. I wondered how he would react to my choice.

I examined forty-eight bowls and pared them down to six, then two. Of the remaining two, one seemed to tug at me. With several people watching, I reached out my hand and picked it up. As I set it down before Cheon, my hand trembled slightly.

"I'll never top that one," he said. Finally, I exhaled.

A Cultural History of Pottery

Understanding pottery is one of the best ways to understand culture. For one thing, the amount of pottery outnumbers paintings and sculptures. It makes up the largest number of existing cultural artifacts. To this day we are still uncovering new information from the 1,500 kiln sites scattered across every part of the peninsula.

By examining the development of pottery, we can understand the culture of different eras and find traces of exchange with other countries. A piece of pottery is a container. It is an important item that holds both food and alcohol and contains people's daily lives. Understanding a bowl is the means to understanding the life, spirit and dreams of the people who used it.

Since ancient times, bowls have been made from different materials, including silver, earthenware, porcelain, wood and lacquerware. Iron, however, was difficult to find and hard to keep from corroding. Lacquerware was expensive and difficult to make, so not everyone was able to use it. In contrast, clay was relatively easy to find and to handle. It did not rot, it resisted corrosion, and it could be made in all different sizes. Furthermore, since it could be made in large quantities at one time, more people were able to use it.

The Korean word for pottery, *dojagi*, is a combination of *dogi* (earthenware) and *jagi* (porcelain). In general, sturdier bowls, made from *jato*[7], glazed and fired at a high temperature of 2372°F (1300°C) are called *jagi*, while bowls made from *doto*[8] and fired between 1832 and 2192°F (1000-1200°C) are called

dogi. Earthenware can collapse if heated over 2192°F. Porcelain, on the other hand, is divided into soft-paste and hard-paste porcelain, based on whether it is fired above or below 1832°F. Soft porcelain fired between 1292 and 1652°F (700-900°C) is used for cookware that can be set over an open flame, like steamer pots. Hard porcelain fired above 1832°F (1000°C) was mostly used for storing and transporting food.

Earthenware is sometimes called *jilgeureut* in Korean. The word is derived from the native Korean word for clay or mud, and it refers to unglazed pottery. *Oji geureut* is a dark brown pottery that is glazed before firing. Both *jil geureut* and *oji geureut* are collectively referred to as *onggi*.

A row of *onggi*, also known as *hangari* and *dok*, has always been both an indispensable feature in virtually every Korean home, except apartments, and a fine form of decoration. Nowadays they are becoming harder to find, but when I was a child, they could be found in practically every home. Fermented foods like kimchi, soybean paste, chili paste and soy sauce, were stored inside the *onggi* year-round. These large clay jars in the backyard held the joys and sorrows of Korean women and are one of the most classic household items that have been passed down through the generations.

Once, when I was a little boy, the grown-ups all went out to enjoy the spring sunshine.

Since the weather was good, they did not bother to put the lids back on the *onggi* before they left. I was home alone when it suddenly began to rain. I was very young, not even in school yet, so I don't know what went through my mind, but I ran out into the rain and lifted dozens of those heavy *onggi* lids back into place. Probably I was doing what I had seen my mother do before. That day, I earned a lot of praise from the grown-ups and got to drink a cupful of honeyed water as my reward. The sweet refreshment and the pride that welled up inside me are my earliest memory of *onggi*.

Since both climate and lifestyle vary among the different regions of Korea, *onggi* as well can take on many different shapes and appearances. Even the royal palace had a *janggo* (storeroom for preserved foods) where numerous *onggi* were kept. The palace lady in charge of the *janggo* was called by the honorific title of *Janggo mama* (roughly, "Her Royal Highness of the Storeroom"). The *Janggo mama* was said to be so imposing that even the well-connected government officials showed her respect. Even in Korean television shows like *Jewel in the Palace*, which depict palace life in the past, the *Janggo mama* are depicted as frosty authority figures. The palace had three *janggo*, one in the east, one in the west and one in the south. The sight of hundreds of these large clay jars all lined up can be seen in the large painted screen *Donggwoldo* (*Painting of the Eastern Palaces*, National Treasure No. 249), which offers a panoramic view of Changdeokgung Palace and Changgyeonggung Palace, both located to the east of Gyeongbokgung Palace.

The type of *onggi* that was directly handled the most by Koreans at home was *dongi*, a

Buncheong stoneware

clay jar with handles on each side. These were used for carrying water and other items. They were featured often in the genre paintings of Joseon Dynasty-era painters, like Kim Hong-do and Shin Yun-bok, who depicted such familiar scenes as women gathered at the side of a well.

There were many other forms of pottery that once played important roles in daily life in Korea as well. *Janggun* were jars designed to fit on wooden A-frame carriers to transport alcohol, water and night soil. *Danji* were small condiment jars that can still be found on tables in Korean restaurants today. All of these were types of *onggi* that were put to good use since the early days of Korean history. In the winters, snakes would follow the mice that snuck into the storerooms in search of grain. Wanting to keep the abhorred and sometimes treacherous snakes in easy view, people in those days would carefully place a *danji* in one corner. These *eopdanji* (spirit jars), as they were known, were where the snakes lived.

One item that has always been of special interest to me is the *bulssitong*, or fire pot, which was used for storing live embers of charcoal. (Typically made from earthenware, the *bulssitong* was shaped like a brazier with an inner pot and an outer pot. The inner pot, which actually held the live embers, was made from soft clay mixed with lots of sandy soil and could hold an ample amount of charcoal.) In

Inlaid celadon

the days before matches and lighters, how were people able to keep fires lit in their kitchens where food had to be cooked multiple times a day? These live embers were so important that allowing the fire to die out was one of the "seven misdeeds for a housewife." In addition, fire was equated with the kind of fortune that brings in wealth, so giving an ember to someone else was regarded as giving away one's luck with money. Embers properly handled could stay live for around a week in the *bulssitong*. In the winter, clay braziers were used inside to both keep a room warm and keep an eye on the fire.

Jeotgaldok, used to store fermented and pickled seafood, were mainly made in kilns in coastal areas where the seafood was caught. The *jeotgal* was packed into the jars on-site and transported to other areas. Other examples of pottery that found their way into every aspect of our daily lives include *tteoksiru* for steaming rice cake, *sojut gori* for distilling soju (a hard alcohol made from rice or other starches) and oil lamps.

Jagi (porcelain), unlike *dogi*, has a glossy finish. It is translucent and gives off a clear sound when tapped. Earthenware makes a dull *puck* sound when it breaks, but porcelain

makes a higher-pitched *clink*. The most well-known form of Korean porcelain is inlaid celadon. Unlike Chinese celadon, which was diverse in form, Korean celadon was diverse in pattern. Inlaid celadon was inspired by the *cheongdong eunnipsa* method, in which grooves were carved into brass bowls and inlaid with silver thread to create patterns.

Like Chinese celadon, Korean celadon is the color of jade, but it differs from Chinese celadon in many other respects. It is much closer to a pale jade. Pale jade, which is native to Korea, is known for its high quality and beautiful color. Also, the shape of Korean celadon is very simple and restrained. As a worldwide exporter of pottery, China began making celadon in many different shapes in order to meet demands. While a variety of shapes and figures can be found in Korean pottery, the celadon—wholly native to Korea—seems to have intentionally retained its simplicity of shape. The shape of Korean celadon reflects the natural lines found in Korea: resembling sometimes the curve of an earthenware jar and sometimes the mountains and streams, its line flows like water that runs without rest. The bohemian feel of *buncheong* stoneware and the simple yet elegant style of white porcelain developed from the unique beauty of this inlaid celadon. The fact that they are not more widely known and their value has not received proper recognition is not just an aesthetic loss for Koreans but for people all around the world.

In *Geschichte der Kunst des Alterthums* (*History of Ancient Art*), Johann Joachim Winckelmann wrote that "noble simplicity and quiet grandeur" were the defining feature of classic Greek art: "Like an ocean, which is always calm deep below even though the surface may be churning, the expressions of Greek figures reveal a soul that was always grand and calm, despite appearing to be excited with passion." For me, I first learned about "noble simplicity" not from Greek sculpture but from Korean porcelain. I suspect that the reason Korean pottery was able to achieve a universal human aesthetic of simple beauty without having to pass through different developmental peaks in terms of color and form was largely due to the influence of the natural environment. Perhaps Korea's natural landscape of mountains and streams, which embodies tranquility without sudden changes, filled Korean pottery with a beauty that quiets human obsession and ambition, a beauty that becomes deeper and richer over time.

In fifteenth century Japan, during the Muromachi period, the tea ceremony flourished as people sought piece and relief from the social insecurities brought about by the chaos of war. The reigning aesthetic of the time was one of stillness, melancholy and bleakness. For tea aficionados who sought out that aesthetic, the most fitting tea bowl was *buncheong* stoneware from Korea. *Buncheong* stoneware was not made in the official government kilns but by potters scattered all over the country. With its folksy, casual style, *buncheong* stoneware was a good match for the aesthetics of the Muromachi tea drinkers. The Japanese became very fond of the *buncheong* stoneware tea bowls brought over from Korea, and they called them Goryeo *dawan* or Joseon *dawan*. The *Kizaemon O Ido*, sixteenth century Korea's first tea bowl, has left behind many a story and is currently designated as a national treasure in Japan.

As for how the Joseon *dawan* was used in Korea, opinion is split four ways: everyday porcelain used with little ceremony, a bowl used by monks, a utensil used in ancestral rites or a bowl for drinking tea. Being a tea drinker, I cannot help but think that it must have been used as a tea bowl. Perhaps beauty is a universal language. Even nowadays, if I simply show, with no explanation, a tea bowl to someone who has no knowledge of Korean pottery, they say it is pretty and cradle it in both hands as they examine it this way and that.

The word "brand" as it is used in marketing originated from the practice of branding cattle. It was in turn an Old Norse or ancient German word, dating back approximately five thousand years, that meant "to burn." Cattle were branded so that they could be distinguished from one another in order to protect individual property rights.

As the face of a product, a brand combines a symbol and a name to differentiate a seller's products or services from that of competitors and to stand out in the marketplace. In a broader sense, it reflects a product's identity, from its physical attributes to its quality, packaging and image.

Chinese porcelain was reborn in Denmark as "Royal Copenhagen" brand porcelain. There are many such examples of people borrowing something that is not part of their own culture and turning it into an outstanding brand. If Korean pottery—inlaid celadon, *buncheong* stoneware, white porcelain—and its unique aesthetic were modernized, it could certainly take off as a global brand.

Pottery and Me

Recently I installed a potter's wheel in my house and have been practicing making pottery with the aid of a book. Pottery can be made easily without having to go through the entire process as it is done in Mungyeong. You can even buy pre-wedged clay. But there is a big difference between trying the basics first and skipping ahead a step. So I decided to wedge my own clay. I was dripping with sweat by the time I was done, but it was refreshing nonetheless.

I put the clay on the wheel and took a deep breath. I stepped on the pedal, and the wheel began to turn. In order to throw clay, you have to be in control of it. It takes focus to find the center. If you lose your focus, the center is lost. If the center is lost, the pottery will not be balanced. So you have to become one with the clay.

As I became more familiar with the clay, I began to relax. I was able to mimic what I had learned to some extent. But it was not easy to get the right shape and an even thickness. By the time I finished throwing the clay and cleaning up after myself, three or four hours had already gone by. I was still a long way from making a bowl and carving out the foot. The first time I tried to carve the foot, I carved out too much. In fact, there were enough scraps of clay leftover to make a whole other bowl. After that, I just kept practicing putting clay on the wheel and shaping it into a bowl.

"Put the clay on the wheel, smooth it out and shape the bowl all in one stroke." Cheon's words echoed in my ears as I tried to sculpt the clay. They say it takes a total of ten thousand hours to master anything. Even if I were to practice for three hours a day, it would take me at least ten years to become an expert. They say, back in the old days, potters had to make over three hundred bowls a day. Even though they had no choice in the matter at first, by practicing it over and over, day after day, they naturally became master artisans.

Making pottery is complicated, and there are many ways to fail. Getting through the entire process step by step without a single mistake is only possible if you have enough skill behind you. Even if you do complete the process flawlessly, it is rare that you have managed to create a "true piece of work." Having repeated over and over again the process of struggling to shape the clay only to ruin it, I don't think I could bring myself to throw out the "rejects" once they have been fired and glazed.

After a lot of practice, I finally managed to create a bowl to my liking. But I ruined it while -trying to carve the foot. Go figure. If I had at least practiced carving the foot before reusing the clay on my previous attempts, I might have been able to save it... As they say, "After death comes the doctor."

"Put the clay on the wheel,
smooth it out,
and shape the bowl
all in one stroke."

The timing of the wheel, the delicate
handiwork, the feel of the clay as it
turned beneath my hands.

捐

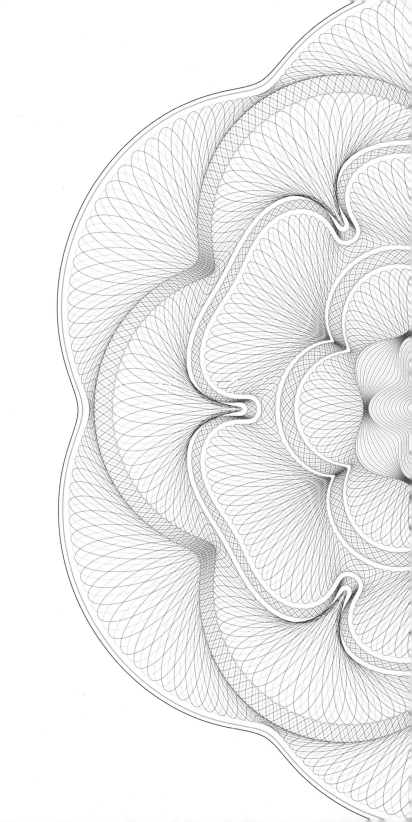

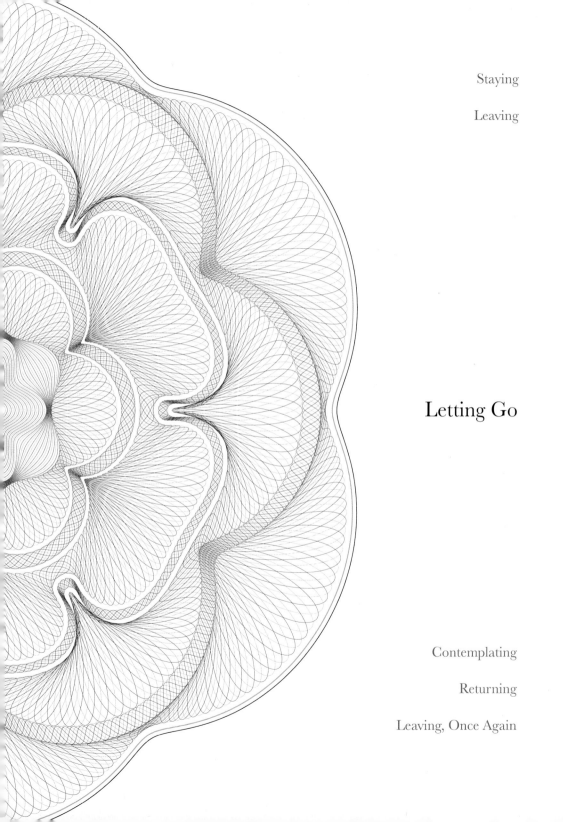

Staying

Leaving

Letting Go

Contemplating

Returning

Leaving, Once Again

Hwangnyongsa and Mireuksa Temple Sites 08

An Ancient Thousand-Year-Old Capital

Gyeongju

Gyeongju is one of Korea's ancient capitals, which ruled for over a thousand years and whose history may have extended even beyond that. It was the capital city of the Silla Kingdom, where it was called Seorabeol. It was also an international city in its day, doing brisk trade with merchants from advanced countries with developed civilizations, such as the Tang Dynasty, the Byzantine Empire, the Saracen Empire and the Magadha Kingdom. Just like Kyoto in Japan and Rome in Italy, Gyeongju bears many traces of a time long past and is still redolent with age-old stories.

Gyeongju was a planned city built at the heart of society, economics and politics on the Korean peninsula just fifteen hundred years ago. The city consisted of smaller districts called *bang* that were 6.5 acres (26,400 square meters) in size and made up of ordinary houses and wells surrounded by walls and alleyways. Gyeongju had three hundred and sixty of these *bang*, which were arranged in orderly rows. According to the *Samguk yusa*[1] (*Memorabilia of the Three Kingdoms*), at its height, Gyeongju had 178,936 homes, for a rough estimate of over 800,000 residents. Considering that Korea currently has no more than eight cities with populations of over a million (Seoul, Suwon, Incheon, Daejeon, Gwangju, Ulsan, Daegu and Busan), Gyeongju was truly grand in scale. Government offices, temples, markets and other facilities were established in the more heavily populated areas. Markets were typically held near Buddhist temples, as the surrounding area was usually crowded with people. Taxes were collected when items were bought and sold, and merchants were watched to make sure they did not cheat the scales. If an argument arose, thirty government officials were on hand in the marketplace to mediate. Chang'an, the capital of the Tang Dynasty at the time, had twenty-eight marketplace officials, which gives some sense of the scale of Gyeongju's marketplace. It was a bustling and prosperous ancient metropolis.

To see an ancient city is to be moved by its quiet beauty. There, one can escape the stress of the modern city with its sharp edges and enjoy the relaxed, peaceful pace of an older time. Cities are known for their enormous, splendid buildings that give free reign to ambition. But they can seem oppressive to those who live there. I think people become the center of attention only in a simple, restrained space. I have often observed architectural beauty of this nature in the works of the Japanese master architect Tadao Ando[2].

Winter was nearing its end but had not yet lost its chill. Just the day before, we were hit with a heavy snowfall on the freeway, but the sunlight in Gyeongju was so warm, I felt affectionate towards everyone for no reason. Was it the excitement I was feeling? In Gyeongju, where green pine forests greeted the eye everywhere we looked, even the sunlight seemed to come to life. Though the glories of the past had not been reproduced down to the last detail, the sublime beauty of the scenic sites and historical temples all over the city were untouched by the ravages of time.

I was lost in thought when one of my traveling companions,
who never says no to a snack, tugged at my sleeve, telling me we had
to try *Gyeongjuppang*, a famous local pastry. Their slogan—*You Won't
Find It Anywhere Else*—was enough to hurry our steps.
As we entered the bakery, the entire pastry-making process was laid
out before us, and the freshly baked *Gyeongjuppang* (also called
Hwangnamppang[3] after the district where they were first made)
looked tantalizing. The round pastries were stuffed with a sweetened
red bean paste that melted in our mouths and delighted all of us.
My snack-friendly companion, who is nuts about *Gyeongjuppang*,
said it was the first time he had tried one while it was still warm.
He piled a napkin high with the contents of the free sample tray and
stuffed it in his pocket. When I looked at his brightly smiling face,
I could not bring myself to scold him. So instead I bought another box
and apologized to the owner.

Hwangnyongsa Temple Site

Our goal in traveling to Gyeongju was to visit the site where Hwangnyongsa (Golden Dragon Temple) once stood. Hwangnyongsa was famous for its immense size. Over two hundred and fifty feet (eighty meters) high and over seven acres (29,090 square meters) in area, it had the largest wooden pagoda in East Asia at the time. It is said that when the nine-story wooden pagoda (an integrated structure built using advanced techniques that are difficult to recreate today) burned down due to war, the ash blocked out the sky for weeks. The temple was said to also include a large Buddhist temple bell (*beomjong*[4]) four times the size of the Emille Bell (also known as the Bell of King Seongdeok) made from eighty tons of melted copper, and a gigantic gilt bronze Buddha statue made from enormous amounts of gold. I could not help but wonder how they came by such huge amounts of copper and gold.

I was reminded of how modern cities around the world dove into the race to build skyscrapers. It seems that ancient cities were no more

immune from the reckless rivalry over building bigger and bigger structures. Once the Silla Kingdom built Hwangnyongsa, the Baekje Kingdom responded by building its own grandiose temple called Mireuksa. Was this, too, the result of the political aims of those in power, who sought to keep the people on their side and show off their strength? By harnessing the faith of the people and focusing on the realization of a single task, they could unify hearts and minds. This was the hidden meaning behind these "Buddhist works." People believed that great religious projects, such as building temples, would help to usher in a new world.

But even if that had been their intent, how different were the people who participated in those major civil engineering projects from people today? If they built those towering pagodas because they yearned to reach a more perfect world, then are not our skyscrapers also an expression of our desire to attract investment and the satisfaction of economic achievement?

Traces of a Cultural Giant

I stood in the desolate field where all that remained was Hwangnyongsa's foundation stones and was gripped by a sense of awe. The realization sunk in of the terrifying potential of human beings who cling all the more tenaciously the more barren things become. Perhaps technology in those days was better than we think, but I was still amazed by the willpower of those good men who fought to overcome so much adversity and uncertainty.

I went up to a single tree standing in an empty field.
In this place, once home to enormous spirits and relics,
the relics have vanished and only the spirits hover about,
leaning against one lonely tree.
I could be looking upon the same sight
that someone from Silla looked upon.
If the people of Silla dreamed of *Bulguk jeongto*[5]
(Pure Land Buddhism) and filled the land
with colossal structures,
what am I to fill this place with?

Drive and Longing: The Nine-story
Wooden Pagoda of Hwangnyongsa Temple

Gyeongju is currently in the midst of a project to develop itself as a city of history and culture. Part of the aim of this project is to rebuild Hwangnyongsa Temple, including the nine-story wooden pagoda. Expectations are as high as the colossal budget and manpower that is being invested, along with the long-pending aspirations of many. The pagoda must have been great solace to people in those days before television and Internet. Farmers returning home after a hard day in the fields must have looked at that distant pagoda and dreamt of future abundance. Women must have gathered in their courtyards as the sun was setting to look at the pagoda, the small details of their daily lives becoming secret stories passed from mouth to mouth. People must have come out in the dead of night, glimpsed the pagoda between the stars and found their heart's balance. I hope that rather than a simple reproduction, our nine-story wooden pagoda will inspire hope and a strength that will amaze us, just as the World Cup did for us in 2002.

> Each time an enormous stone was cut and wood was chopped
> and stacked in place, a dream was being built one step at a time.
> I build a nine-story wooden pagoda and climb the stairs to look out.
> The queen is very proud of the finished pagoda.
> A great temple, from which it seems a golden dragon
> will ascend to heaven at any point, dedicated to protecting
> the homeland, has been born.
> I can see the young monk Wonhyo[6] hard at work
> in the alleyways of Seorabeol.
> And Princess Yoseok[7] running away as she swallows her tears…
>
> I felt a slight tremor in my chest.
> All at once, the flow of time shifted back to the present
> and reached my heart.
> Where should I build that dream?
> What should I build?
> Why aren't these things possible nowadays?
> Such work is cultivated in the heart and cannot be accomplished
> through technology alone.
> I listened politely to the detailed explanation
> of the temple's style and meaning,
> but I could not seem to grasp a single word.

Mireuksa Temple Site

We left Gyeongju and headed for the city of Iksan in North Jeolla-do Province. Our destination was the temple grounds of Mireuksa, built during the Baekje Kingdom, which is naturally associated with Hwangnyongsa of Silla. The birthplace of Baekje's King Mu[8], Iksan was where he dreamed about moving the seat of government out of Sabi, the original capital. He lived there for many years before heading to Sabi.

As far as we know, three places served as the capital of Baekje—Buyeo, Gongju and Mongchon Toseong (Mongchon Earthen Fortress) in present-day Seoul—but none show evidence of any royal palaces. Instead, the only such site is found in Iksan. At the site of the old palace in Iksan's Wanggung-ri (Palace Village), a stone pagoda that bears the "Baekje silhouette"—with thin but broad stone roof tiles and eaves that stretch out flat then flare slightly at the ends—quietly stands its ground. At the moment, the pagoda's only companions are some cherry trees that were planted thirty years ago and a pine forest some meters off, but soon this site too will be restored, and one more place worth visiting will be brought back to life.

Mireuksa Temple once occupied the entire space that now holds a museum and parking lot. At the time of its foundation, it was an enormous temple spread over forty acres (165,000 square meters) that took thirty-six years to build. The stone pagoda of Mireuksa is in the process of being disassembled and repaired. Viewed from the center of the large temple, the pagoda being repaired is called Seotap (West Pagoda, National Treasure No. 11), and the one already restored is Dongtap (East Pagoda). During the Baekje era both stone and wooden pagodas were popular. The open-mindedness and flexibility of the people of Baekje is evident in the line of the eaves and the experimental way with which they made the first stone pagoda modeled on the form of a wooden pagoda. I cannot help but think that diverse and creative ways of thinking are rooted in being open to all possibilities.

I looked at the mountains, valleys and lake surrounding the Mireuksa. Temple site. I closed my eyes and pictured how majestic it must have been: an enormous wooden pagoda, the main hall, the long corridors and the two stone pagodas. The water came right up to the temple, close enough to bring a boat alongside it. Inside the temple where hundreds of monks once lived, there was even a kiln for firing the clay roof tiles. When the temple bell solemnly tolled for the evening service, the setting sun hung bright red above the three-foot-tall gargoyles sitting on the eaves.

I opened my eyes and placed my foot on one of the large stone steps that led up to the main hall. My foot is eleven inches long, yet there was still a good four inches leftover, both front and back. I was told there are no other steps this big to be found anywhere in the East. Just based on the stone's size, one can approximate that the temple was considerably large.

Mireuksa also had a majestic wooden pagoda like the one at Hwangnyongsa. It is estimated that it stood roughly 164-196 feet (50-60 meters) high, twice the height of the stone pagodas that stood on either side, so it must have been splendid. Suddenly, the music I heard in the car on the way to Iksan came to mind, and I hummed it to myself as I was leaving.

J.S. Bach: Goldberg Variations -1. Aria
Glenn Gould

I stood in the middle of the stone
that supported the pagoda's central pillar,
ran my finger over thousand-year-old dirt,
and met myself from a thousand years ago.

The Other Tale of Seodong

Mireuksa Temple was built by King Mu and his wife, the queen. In their youth, they were known as Seodong and Seonhwa, respectively. They are both described in the *Samguk yusa*: the young King Mu as *giryang nancheuk*, "being of unfathomable talent and generosity," and Queen Seonhwa, who was still a princess, as *miyeom mussang*, "unparalleled in loveliness and beauty." King Mu, the finest man of his generation, met Princess Seonwha, the most beautiful daughter of the Silla royal family—how is that not the stuff of legend? As if that is not dramatic enough, theirs was a marriage between the royal families of enemy kingdoms.

> Princess Seonhwa
> Fell in love on the sly,
> And embraces Prince Seodong
> Under cover of night.

This song, called Seodongyo, is one of the oldest *hyangga*[9] (poems written in native Korean) that have come down to us from the past. Seodong of Baekje made up the song on purpose to spread false rumors about the Silla princess so that he could make her his wife. This silly yet covert plan ensured that the story of their love would be remembered through the ages.

Cast out of the royal family because he was the child of a concubine, Seodong sought out the beautiful princess of an enemy state and managed to win her heart by using his sharp wits. Though he knew he was merely a puppet king, Seodong still decided to bring Princess Seonhwa to Baekje. And Seonhwa in turn became the heroine of a great love story in exchange for abandoning her family and country to follow her beloved husband. The finishing touch on their romance was the construction of Mireuksa, a Buddhist temple the likes of which had never been seen and would never be seen again.

Recently a discovery was made of new *sari jangeom*[10] (Buddhist relics) at Mireuksa Temple, much to the excitement of those working in cultural fields. It also ignited a heated debate, however. The relics included a Buddhist urn containing the remains of a cremated monk and a gold plate with an inscription that indicated that Mireuksa was not built by Princess Seonhwa but by the daughter of Sataek, a high-level Baekje official. For a while, there was debate over the veracity of the tale of Seodong, but when you consider the circumstances, not everything falls into place.

I once asked the head monk of a very old, traditional Buddhist temple about the story. He said that when the construction of a temple takes place over a long period of time, records of the founder who first begins the construction are enshrined inside the main Buddha statue in the main sanctum. Later, when pagodas, bells or other major features are added, records of the people who contributed to their construction or progress reports on the construction are enshrined directly inside the pagoda or bell itself, or inside Buddha statues or altar paintings that are kept in the new buildings. In other words, the monk explained, the records that come out of a pagoda only indicate the contributions

that were made to its construction, and they do not refer to the establishment of the temple as a whole. Not only does that explanation make logical sense, but I also personally hope that it is true. I cannot help wanting to bury away the all-too-practical sequel to a beautiful legend.

A romantic thought springs to mind: Was Mireuksa Temple King Mu's Taj Mahal? Being from an enemy country, his wife might not have received the treatment she was accorded as a queen by the aristocrats of Baekje. And even as king, he would have been able to do little about it. Though it would have been cruel for two people in love, King Mu might have had to take more wives in order to assuage the unhappy aristocrats. He would have been unbearably sorry. And he might have wanted, therefore, to build the biggest temple on earth as a gift to his queen. Wouldn't he want to express his love for her in the biggest and best way possible? Of course, these Buddhist works were primarily indicative of the strong competition for state power, but I cannot help but think his decision to push ahead with the temple was partly motivated by such feelings.

I went in secret to the place where their portraits were kept and burned a stick of incense to offer my sympathy for their troubled love.

Mireuksa's Stone Pagoda Shining in the Moonlight

The night is deep.
Alone on a dark hill in the moonlight,
a magnolia tree, three stories high,
stands in full blossom, more majestic than elegant.
I look down past my feet,
down at what is left of Mireuksa.
The silence is powerful enough to blast away
the suffering of midday, the harsh sunlight, and the stinging sandstorm.
The night is so dark,
the lights of a few houses that can be seen
seem to flicker and fade out.
I stand in the moonlight,
look from one end to the other
of where Mireuksa once stood.
Seotap's *simjuseok*[11] is being rebuilt;
workers labor long into the night beneath a new slate roof.
The wide steps that once led to the main hall,
now a playground for insects.
Beneath the pagoda's lotus lantern, the *badaeseok*[12] gathers dew.
I slowly walk over and stand before Dongtap.
Backlit by the moon, its silhouette appears starker.
The stone looks older in the dark than in the day.
I sit before the new pagoda
and lean my body against a thousand-year-old stone.
The stone is soft, but the night is without breeze.
I regret not having a fan to dry the sweat on my forehead.
One moon, one pagoda, one stone—
I lean both body and heart against them,
close my eyes, and go back a thousand years.
When I open my eyes, the silhouette of the pagoda
is no different than the one that came before.
This new stone, unmarked by time, is as yet unloved.
But in another thousand years,
when Dongtap holds the warmth of generations of people,
it may then prove to be the most loved.
After a while, I lift my head.
The insects and the owls are silent.
The magnolias in full bloom fall to the ground,
leaving bare spots on the branches.
I brush off my pants and rise, press my hand into the stone pagoda,
and pray that it will hold the warmth from my flesh
and from my dreams for a thousand years.

觀

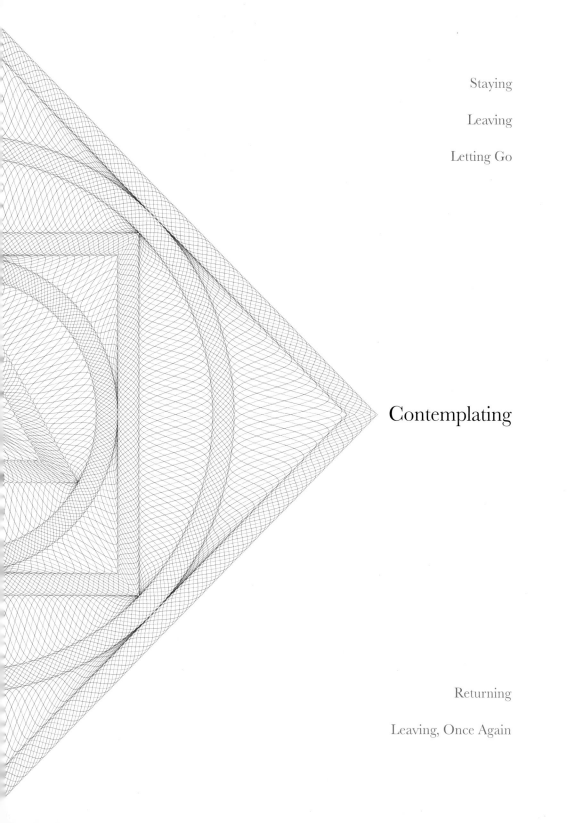

Staying

Leaving

Letting Go

Contemplating

Returning

Leaving, Once Again

A Dreaming King

Hangeul: The Korean Alphabet

Pearl S. Buck, the famous author of *The Good Earth*, once called Sejong, the fourth king of the Joseon Dynasty, "Korea's Leonardo da Vinci." What commonality could she have found between a genius of the Renaissance and the feudal lord of a tiny Asian country who died two years before da Vinci was born? In a word, it was the "depth and diversity of their innate talent." The scholarly King Sejong's greatest creation was hangeul, the Korean alphabet.

When hangeul was created, its official name was *Hunmin jeongeum*, or "Proper Sounds for the Instruction of the People." *Hanja* (characters borrowed from Chinese) had been used for writing up until that time and were all but the exclusive property of the *sadaebu* (scholar-officials), which made daily life difficult for the common people and for women and children of all classes, as they were typically excluded from learning *hanja*. The promulgation of a writing system that made it easier to read and write also enabled the Joseon era's Confucian ideology to penetrate more deeply into people's lives and opened up communication between the social classes. Social groups that had once been separated by a wide gulf, including farmers and the literati, women and the male scholar-officials, began to communicate more easily with one another.

The letters of the Korean alphabet were created based on East Asian philosophy. The three basic vowels represent heaven (·), earth (—), and human beings ( ]). According to the *Hunmin jeongeum haerye* (*Explanations and Examples of the Proper Sounds for the Instruction of the People*), otherwise known as the first hangeul handbook, "Heaven and earth originally sprang forth from one source, and all things in the universe were given shapes and sounds according to the *yin* and *yang* and the five elements. For that reason, hangeul was modeled after the shapes of heaven, earth and human beings." While the vowels are comprised of the three basic vowels—representing heaven, earth and human beings—and their various combinations, the consonants, from ㄱ to ㅍ, are also representations of the points, lines and planes that make up all the shapes found in the universe. Furthermore, the final consonant ㅎ is composed of all three basic vowels: · , —,] .

Because the composition principles behind hangeul are so simple, it is very easy to learn. Jeong In-ji, one of King Sejong's scholars, even wrote, "A wise man masters hangeul before the morning is over; a stupid man can learn it in ten days." In light of this fact, I cannot help but think that no other alphabet in the world comes so close to the aesthetics of simplicity as hangeul.

Korean is the only writing system that uses a homographic alphabet in which each character represents only one sound. That is how closely the sounds of the language were analyzed in creating hangeul. James McCawley, an eminent American linguist, said, "Of the existing writing systems, hangeul was the most inventive and occupies a special place among the world's writing systems. It is the only writing system that breaks sentences down into words, syllables and phonemes at the same time that it fundamentally maintains the basic syllabary characters. It is amazing that Koreans achieved this in 1440. Even by the linguistic standards of today, five hundred years after hangeul was created, their work was outstanding."

Korean has the most phonemes of all the world's languages; it is said that 12,768 phonemes can be created. As *Hunmin jeongeum haerye* boasts, indeed "even the sounds of the wind, a crane, a rooster crowing and a dog barking can be written down phonetically" using hangeul. After its invention in the fifteenth century, hangeul also incorporated phonetic symbols from other languages, including Japanese, Chinese, Manchu and Mongolian. Thanks to the ease and conciseness of hangeul, the illiteracy rate in Korea is almost zero. In 1989, UNESCO even created the King Sejong Literacy Prize to honor individuals, organizations and institutions that contribute to eradicating illiteracy around the world.

King Sejong the Great

In nearly five thousand years of history, only two Korean monarchs earned the title "the Great," and there is no dispute among Koreans about who they are. One was King Gwanggaeto the Great of the Goguryeo Kingdom, whom I portrayed in the television series *Taewang sasingi* (*Legend*), and the other is the man whose face appears on the ten-thousand-won bill: King Sejong the Great of the Joseon Dynasty. These two kings can be said to represent Korea's military and literary history. King Gwanggaeto is known as a "conqueror king," while King Sejong is remembered as a "scholar king."

Known as a bookworm in his childhood, King Sejong the Great was said to have read every book a hundred times. At that rate, it seems like you would not simply be memorizing the book but transforming the neurons in your brain. While studying history and researching King Sejong, I was continually surprised by the breadth of his studies and the interest he took in every field. He seemed to truly understand the "importance of information," as we would put it nowadays. That said, information alone is not what matters. What made him all the more great was the fact that he created a logical system for ongoing conversation, discourse and debate. This led to many creative inventions and the discovery of talented individuals. He was even accomplished at ceremonial music, creating a new type of court music known as *Jongmyo jeryeak*[1] (traditional court music for the royal shrine ritual), which surpassed Chinese court music. King Sejong was "Joseon's Renaissance Man" who established Jiphyeonjeon, or the Hall of Worthies, to pursue scholarly endeavors, and wrote music with the help of Bak Yeon[2] and Maeng Sa-seong[3].

It is truly moving that King Sejong continued to engage in rigorous debates, as well as constantly seeking counsel and trying new experimentation, even after creating the unprecedented new writing system of hangeul. He never renounced or suppressed those who opposed the adoption of hangeul. Rather, he welcomed the opportunity to question and test out his ideas. He engaged in extensive debates with Choe Man-ri, a court official who actively opposed the adoption of hangeul; he sent scholars as far as Liaodong, China to seek counsel; and he wrote *Yongbi eocheonga*[4] (*Songs of the Dragons Flying to Heaven*) with great care to test out the new writing system. His meticulous approach to problems was applied to all of his policies, from the outstanding agricultural manual *Nongsa jikseol* (*Straight Talk on Farming*) to the arrow-firing rocket launcher *singijeon* ("god machine arrow") and the *cheugugi*, a scientific device for measuring rainfall. All of these are

Jiphyeonjeon Hall

examples of King Sejong's successful motivation, process and results.

I have always thought of history as a treasure trove. But while studying up on Korean culture, I also realized that studying history unlocks the door to culture. During the Joseon Dynasty, a system called *gyeongyeon* was maintained, wherein the king and his officials, along with official speakers who recited the classics and recorders who kept careful notes, would hold discussions of a selected text. The recorder took down everything without showing any partiality to the king, who was not even allowed to peruse what was being written. It is said that King Sejong held one of these meetings every single day for thirty years. Following his coronation, his first words to his chief secretary Ha Yeon were said to be, "Let us talk." Engaging in dialogue even with others who do not necessarily agree with your opinions—or perhaps especially with those who disagree with you—is undoubtedly the shortcut to greater achievements. Those who give up on dialogue with themselves and with the world cannot avoid becoming stagnant and corrupt.

> "To govern well, you must look back upon the course of previous generations, during both peaceful and turbulent times. To do so, you need only refer to historical documents." (King Sejong, June 28, 1441)

Statue of King Sejong the Great to be installed at Gwanghwamun Pla
(Photo provided by Seoul City H

King Sejong even saw to it that the streets of Seoul were widened to make it easier to fight fires, and roof tiles were changed to make them more affordable. The example he set at the start of his reign, when a large fire broke out in Seoul and a famine had been ongoing for seven years, demonstrated the strength of his character. It is said that during the great famine, he turned his back on his royal bedchambers to live in a tiny thatched-roof cottage and ate simple, mostly vegetarian meals. According to records, his officials worried greatly about this, as the king was known for his various ailments as well as his fondness for meat, but he refused to bend. It was his style to lead others by example rather than by orders. There are not many leaders who respond to times of crisis first by humbling themselves.

There are countless stories about his humanism. He even created three different types of maternity leave for slaves. Government slaves were originally given seven days' leave to care for their children, but he increased it to a hundred. Expectant mothers were given a reprieve from service one month before delivery, and later their husbands were given paternity leave as well. King Sejong looked upon the lowly slaves who had no one to care for them with pity and did what he could to ensure that the common people led comfortable lives.

We talk a lot about compassion. No matter how capable, intelligent and rational people are, if they are lacking in compassion for others, we judge them as lacking in humanity. Some people have claimed that a culture of compassion will ruin Korean society, but I believe that is a misunderstanding caused by the misuse of compassion. We all have desires. We all have hopes and wishes. Our words for them may vary, but it is the same in every culture. If I want something and you want something, then isn't compassion acknowledging and giving each other what the other person desires—giving freely and without hesitation? Isn't the phrase "unconditional love" just another way of saying "compassion"? I think the idea that compassion runs through all of life's necessities is one of the characteristics of our culture. Perhaps culture is the expression of that desire. In the end, it is just the gathering and collecting of that which you desire for yourself. Nowadays people are saying that we should emulate King Sejong's outstanding leadership and excellent politics. It is said that he was not just a great king but also a good and wise king, which shows how truly loved he was by the people and that he was a true leader who won over their hearts.

A true leader—that is what we most need in every facet of our society today.

With each step I took through the Hall of Worthies, I sensed the passion of those long-ago scholars.

The Evolution of Hangeul

Each time I use a keyboard or cell phone, I think about how easy it is to type in hangeul. It must have played a big role in why Korea became an Internet powerhouse so quickly. No other writing system is so economical in terms of time and space when it comes to digital efficiency.

One time, a friend of mine who had just bought a new cell phone bragged about his lightning fast speed, saying that he had sent a hundred text messages that day. All I could do was marvel, as I lack such tremendous skill. Sometimes, during my silly musings, I imagine that if I had been born into an English or Chinese or even Arabic-speaking country and had to type out long texts in one of those languages, I would become exhausted and give up halfway through that dauntingly laborious task.

Lie Sang-bong is a fashion designer who fuses hangeul into his designs. He is an artist who discovered in the most Korean of letters a new visual language for communicating with the world. His work in the Paris prêt-à-porter fashion show was praised as a "representation of oriental yet modern aesthetics" and "balance between fashion and geometric beauty." Considering that hangeul included the concept of design right from its inception, this seems only natural.

Lie first used hangeul in high-end cell phones designed for CEOs, but to his surprise, consumers in their twenties responded strongly to the design. He decided to expand the line to include T-shirts and other clothing items. He did not become aware of hangeul's aesthetic value through a process of self-discovery but rather chanced upon it by accident. Later on, it became a quest for Korean identity. As our talk deepened, we turned to the subject of our interest in Korean culture in general. He said that using hangeul in his designs was what made him finally realize how much of our culture was disappearing, which really got me thinking. The hardships he experienced in his work actually instilled in him a sense of duty to improve things. He came up against a great deal of prejudice and frustration while also having to break through his own preconceived notions. Of all the difficulties he experienced, what I thought was most regrettable was the level of respect currently accorded to artisans. I decided then that I would do everything in my power to help them. For example, I heard that many people have trouble finding old *hanbok* that they are interested in buying. Also, I learned that the owner of a famous jewelry company is working hard to spread Korean culture in Kyoto. These stories have helped me to figure out what my role should be.

"Hangeul not only has artistic value but is effective at conveying emotion.
To foreigners, it looks like a beautiful, modern, abstract painting.
The response was so positive that foreign buyers requested that hangeul designs
be incorporated into the clothes."
Recalling Lie's words, I reflected on hangeul as an art form.

Jokduri, a traditional cap worn
by women on special occasions

How great would it be to save the beautiful *jokduri* from the traditional
Korean wedding dress and display it in your living room after the
wedding? You could tell your children about it and make it a symbol
of your family's love for each other.

It would be a piece of Korean culture with a story of its own.

Hangeul design:
teacup and saucer

Hangeul design:
memo cube

Can you imagine how difficult it would be to speak a different language than the one you write?
What if there were no letters you could use to express yourself the way you want to?
Maybe it would be like the early days of personal computers in Korea,
before we had Internet access?
If our words and our writing system were different,
then perhaps I would not be able to write this either.
It is thanks to the dreams of King Sejong the Great, who loved his subjects,
that we have received the magnificent gift of hangeul.

People with Dreams

If love's bondage is a dream,
then so is liberation from the world.
If laughter and tears are dreams,
then so is the illumination of no-mind.
If the laws of all creation are a dream,
then I'll attain immortality in the dream of love.

[Translated by Francisca Cho in *Everything Yearned For: Manhae's Poems of Love and Longing*, published by Wisdom Publications, 2005]

This poem, "If It's a Dream," was written by Manhae Han Yong-un. He said that if everything were a dream, he would dream of love, and he seemed to shun the idea of a life without dreams. Other people probably think I have it all—wealth, popularity and fame—but I always tell myself that the moment I start believing I have it all is the moment I stop living. I do not want to become jaded like that. I will always have my dreams, for they are what make me truly alive.

A long time ago, I saw a newspaper article about a survey that asked, "Which decade was the most memorable for Koreans?" To my surprise, most people said the 1960s through 1970s. The second most common response was the period of Korea's liberation from Japan in 1945. What surprised me even more was that even people who were born after those decades mostly had the same response. Why did most people choose such difficult decades, when we had not yet recovered from the wounds of war, rather than the 1980s and 1990s, when the country enjoyed economic success and played host to the Olympics? Perhaps it is because the periods most deeply engraved in our memories are those where we suffered as well as triumphed. I think the most memorable times for anyone are those times when we separate from someone we love or when we heal our wounds alone after undergoing a difficult experience. Maybe it is because, in the midst of deep despair and suffering, we yearn all the more after our hopes and dreams, and we remember those moments as ones of becoming more human, and our lives, that much richer.

Perhaps the times of our most wretched suffering, and every moment after in which we work to heal ourselves, can be called the times in which we are dreaming. When we train ourselves constantly and dream of the future we want, then that is the moment we most intensely recognize our own existence. A person without dreams is a person who is already dead. Anyone who says they do not need dreams or do not dream at all is merely in the grip of a nightmare. So I want to dream the best dreams possible. King Sejong's dream was for the people to be happy, and that dream became the cornerstone for the invention of hangeul.

After the Korean War, people must have dreamed of a quick escape from suffering. Then in the 1970s, people must have dreamed of becoming affluent through economic development. Did they succeed? Or do we still carry those dreams deep inside of us because they have not yet been made real? If the needs and sufferings of the past made us who we are today, then I wonder which of today's needs and sufferings will make us who we will be tomorrow. Isn't that what we are supposed to find out? Culture is a dream that we dream together. If you know a person's dream, you can know the person. When I consider what we have been hoping for historically, I think it must be a shortcut to knowing our culture. Like something King Sejong the Great once said, if those of us who are to become a page in history keep dreaming and working to achieve our dreams, then the work we do now will be embraced and treasured by future generations.

There is a dream I really wish would come true,
and I am working towards it little by little.
At this moment, in which
I dream my own dream,
I am happy to be able to dream.

Gyeongbokgung Palace and an Ancient Map of the Sky 10

Philosophy of the Night Sky

The Night Sky

I look up at the night sky. Whenever I gaze out into that empty space and let my mind go blank, not only do I confront myself head on, I feel reenergized. But lately the night sky over the heart of the city is troubled. It looks pale, as if choked with smog. The lights of the city have rapped on the ceiling of the sky, waking it, and left it groggy. Dazed, the sky is neither bright nor dark, much to my dismay. As a result, I find myself turning more often to the countryside where I take photo after photo of the dazzling night sky radiant with stars. Only then does this stifling feeling in my chest lift and let in some air.

When did I start to forget, to drive from memory that vast, unknown universe stretching on forever between the stars? Right above my head is a world of mystery unlike anything down here on earth. They say if you feel overwhelmed, look up at the stars; if you are overcome with ambition, look at the stones and flowers beneath your feet. We make our lives richer when we turn our gaze to that forgotten world and free our imaginations. That is how myths and legends are born.

The Industrial Revolution flooded society with the belief that science and technology would make us all-knowing and all-powerful. Yet our lives do not seem to have advanced that much. Sometimes the process itself is more enjoyable than the end result, like when we can see our lives improving, our relationships deepening, our children growing up, and things going according to plan. Likewise, we enjoy the process of learning new things. To know something also means to know that some things are unknown. Never forgetting that some things are unknown or unknowable seems to be good for us. It makes us humble and pure. And it makes us try harder. It fills us with the desire to learn. Too much and we are made fools, too little and we are made arrogant. But in the right amount, the unknown can be good for us.

A view from home:
Hangang River below, sky above

Ancient Planetarium

Since ancient times, the sky has been central to human culture. The sky was the spiritual pillar around which the laws of human nature were explained, norms and measures for daily life were established, and people's hearts and minds were cultivated. Astronomy, or the science of reading the sky, was also a practical necessity, as it helped people study the climate for farming and sailing and preparing for natural disasters. For ancient people, the night sky was more "real" than anything else.

I took a more significant look at Korean astronomy after becoming curious about hangeul and its creator, King Sejong the Great. King Sejong was interested in every branch of study, and he was a particularly excellent astronomer. During his reign, he invented the world's first rain gauge, sundial and water clock. That is why the front of the ten thousand-won bill in Korea shows King Sejong with the *Irwol obongdo* (*Painting of the Sun, Moon and the Five Peaks*) in the background. The five peaks symbolize Mercury, Venus, Mars, Saturn and Jupiter. For Koreans, who were mostly farmers, the sky governed all natural phenomena. It was revered as such, and King Sejong's efforts to gain access to the sky's secrets made him an even better and wiser king who cared for his subjects.

Astronomy is a study of the most fundamental observations of the location of celestial objects in relation to time and space. It can be called the oldest of the natural sciences, as it began in the Old Babylonian period with the development of astrology and the creation of a calendar. Kim Il-gwon, who studies the history of astronomy, wrote, "Examining people's anxieties about the sky is one of the biggest keys to understanding Eastern cultures. That means studying what the sky was like to them and what impact it had on them."

The *Cheonsang Yeolcha Bunya Jido* Astronomical Map

The back of the ten thousand-won bill gets more interesting. There we find a picture of the *Cheonsang yeolcha bunya jido* (*Chart of the Constellations and the Regions They Govern*, National Treasure No. 228), created in the Joseon Dynasty and features the Big Dipper and various constellations. The world's second oldest astronomical map, which was carved in stone, the *Cheonsang yeolcha bunya jido* shows the constellations divided into twelve sections and includes the Milky Way and 1,467 stars (or 282 constellations) visible in Korea. On the left side of the map is a round object called *honcheonui*, which was created by King Sejong the Great. It was an astronomical clock used to measure the positions and movements of celestial bodies. These images alone demonstrate how advanced Korean astronomy was back then, an achievement not found in many other parts of the world.

After the *Cheonsang yeolcha bunya jido* was created in 1395, it became the standard astronomical calendar used throughout the Joseon Dynasty. The text in the margins of the map is an account of how the map was made. It suggests that this map was based on another map from the Goguryeo era.

"Long ago, the original stone carving of this astronomical map was kept in Pyeongyangseong Fortress[1]. Then war broke out, and the stone was cast into the Daedonggang River for a long time, after which it could no longer be used to print maps. But soon after King Taejo founded the Joseon Dynasty, someone presented him with a single rubbing that had been made from it. King Taejo regarded it as extremely precious and ordered the Gwansanggam[2] (Office of Meteorology and Astronomy) to have the map carved again in stone."

Based on scientific analysis of the positions of the constellations on the map, it is presumed to have been created in the first century CE near Pyeongyang (approximately 39°N), the capital of Goguryeo, in an area located along latitude 40°N.

(Image provided by the National Folk Museum of Korea)

While the kingdoms of Goguryeo, Silla, Baekje and Goryeo drew many different worldviews and religious ideas from the night sky, the founding of the Joseon Dynasty resulted in the loss of that diversity due to the totalizing impact of Neo-Confucianism, which emphasized mental discipline. It could be called a retrogression of the imagination. Perhaps they thought that imagination alone was not enough to keep people in line. The royal celestial ceremonies that had been passed down since Goguryeo until the founding of Joseon were discarded one by one. Eventually, the Sogyeokseo (National Taoist Temple), which had overseen Taoist rites, was dismantled, and rituals related to the sky vanished without a trace.

But in the agricultural society of Joseon, celestial worship could not be eliminated entirely, even if they were denounced as superstition. Interestingly enough, those ritual duties shifted over first to palace women, then again to shamans outside of the palace, and to temples, eventually becoming the responsibility of ordinary commoners. Shamans and monks used to be summoned to the royal court in times of drought to stand in the scorching sun for days on end, in the hopes that the sky would take pity on them and send down rain. But with the advent of the Joseon Dynasty, Taoism and Shamanism were driven to the fringes of history and had no choice but to clasp hands and unite in order to eke out a survival alongside the common people, with the relatively long-lived and robust organization and structure of Buddhism at its center.

Some folk beliefs, such as the belief that the stars of the Big Dipper control the lives and fates of human beings, survived the changes that took place in the Joseon Dynasty. From ancient agricultural societies to the middle ages, kings strengthened their power by monopolizing information about the climate. But from that point on, the celestial realm was rejected by the royal palace and came to rest with the people. The folk beliefs that have remained to this day are the vestiges of this historical shift.

Chilseong is an abbreviation of *Chirwon seonggun* (Ursa Major), i.e. the Big Dipper. It was believed that the Big Dipper brought rain to increase the harvests, made people wealthy and granted them long lives. These religious beliefs were introduced to Korea during the Three Kingdoms period but did not develop beyond that. After the *Byeongja horan*[3], the second Manchu invasion of Korea in 1636, however, these beliefs spread widely among the people. They viewed the Big Dipper as a deity that controlled the life expectancy of their children. The fusion of Buddhism and the "Seven Star Deity" initially took place in China, but Korea was the only country that created a separate shrine (Hall of the Big Dipper) within Buddhist temples that was dedicated to the Seven Star Deity.

Each of the stars was entrusted with a different task. The first star (*Tamnang seonggun*) gave luck to one's descendants; the second (*Geomun seonggun*) eliminated obstacles and disasters; the third (*Nokjon seonggun*) eliminated bad karma; the fourth (*Mungok seonggun*) granted whatever a person was looking for; the fifth (*Yeomjeong seonggun*) removed one hundred types of obstacles; the sixth (*Mugok seonggun*) spread good luck and virtue far and wide; and the seventh (*Pagun seonggun*) granted long life.

(Photo provided by TSG Productions, LLC)

King Gwanggaeto the Great and the Four Gods

In many ways, the television show *Taewang sasingi* (*Legend*) left an indelible mark on me. It was my comeback performance after a long absence, and each episode was as demanding on everyone as shooting a feature-length film. The knee and shoulder injuries I sustained on set seem like they will take a long time to heal.

I believe deeply in fate, both in regards to people and work. Just like everyone else, I am not immune to the happiness or hurt that accompanies the events of our lives. But I consider it more important to look back and ask myself if I tried my best, regardless of what the outcome was. So even after I have completed a project, if I have a chance to study the topic in greater detail, I am likely to take that opportunity and study hard rather than be lazy.

When we were shooting *Legend*, my schedule was so packed that I did not have time to study up on the Four Gods that appeared in the show or learn about the constellation. So that may be why, when the opportunity to study East Asian astronomy for this project came up, I took a special interest and put a great deal of effort into it. Though it is an unfamiliar field for me, the stories and philosophy it contains reflect a surprising amount of Korean history and culture.

The night sky is imagined as an enormous sphere with a boundless radius. A celestial sphere, in other words. This sphere has its own celestial equator and twenty-eight constellations. The moon takes twenty-seven to twenty-eight days to orbit the sky, passing through a different constellation each day before returning to its original place. The number twenty-eight was chosen for the ease with which it could be divided into north, south, east and west.

The Four Gods are guardian spirits formed from the twenty-eight constellations; they each represent a direction and season of the year. During an excavation at Jeongbaek-ri in Pyeongyang, a copper mirror was found with the following inscription: "The Blue Dragon of the East and the White Tiger of the West repel inauspicious things, while the Red Bird of the South and the Black Tortoise of the North balance *yin* and *yang*."

In addition to *Bukdu* (Seven Stars of the Northern Dipper, i.e.

On the Lunar New Year holiday, Koreans traditionally get together to enjoy a game of *yunnori*. *Yunnori* is a very old game originating back to the ancient Gojoseon Kingdom (c. 2333 BCE). The courses marked out on the game board (*yutpan*) for the pieces (*yunmal*), or "horses," are said to represent the North Star surrounded by the four guardian constellations. The game ends when a player's game pieces have all passed through one of the various possible routes along the spaces marked on the board and reached the southernmost square. This square represents the Southern Dipper. The Northern Dipper controls heaven and the afterlife, while the Southern Dipper oversees the lives and longevities of people on earth. So it seems that winning at *yunnori* by being the first to pass through the Southern Dipper signifies receiving good health and a long life. Considering how some knowledge has traditionally been passed down through games in Korea, this interpretation does seem plausible.

Today's *yunnori* game boards are square but they used to be round, probably to represent the movements of heavenly bodies as they turned like a wheel in the sky. The game board has twenty-nine spaces. The central space represents the North Star, and the remaining twenty-eight spaces are the twenty-eight constellations that rotate around it. Perhaps in ancient times, people sought to project the celestial laws into people's

Goguryeo Map of the Five Gods
(Image provided by Sagyejeol Publishing)

Yunnori game board
(Image provided by The National Folk Museum of Korea)

lives by capturing them in a game.

On the *Cheonsang yeolcha bunya jido*, Canopus is depicted above the Big Dipper. Canopus is the second brightest star in the night sky after Sirius. It can be glimpsed on the horizon at dawn on the autumn equinox and in the evening of the spring equinox from the southern coast of Korea and Jejudo Island. The belief that sighting this star brings longevity first became popular during the Han Dynasty (206 BCE-220 CE) in China and lasted through the Joseon Dynasty in Korea. Come fall, I am considering taking a trip south to do a little stargazing.

the Big Dipper) and *Namdu* (Six Stars of the Southern Dipper, i.e. the Milk Dipper in Sagittarius), *Dongsimbang* consists of six stars in the constellation Scorpius in the east, and *Seosambeol* consists of six stars in the constellation Orion in the west. Because of their positions, when *Dongsimbang* is rising over the horizon, *Seosambeol* is just dipping below it. These distinct constellations are one of the most defining features of the murals found inside the walls of Goguryeo-era tombs.
[Source: *Goguryeo Constellations and Myths*, Kim Il-gwon, Sagyejeol Publishing]

In the mid-Joseon Dynasty, a scholar named Kim Mun-pyo wrote a history of the Goryeo Kingdom, called *Junggyeongji*[4]. In it, he explained *yunnori*.

"The circle on the outside of the game board represents the sky, and the square in the center represents the earth. Hence, the sky encircles the earth. The spaces on the board are modeled after the twenty-eight constellations in the middle of the stars. Hence, the North Star holds the center position and is surrounded by all the other stars. The routes around the board contain the utmost logic: The short route that starts from the north and heads east, then passes through the center to return to the north is the short path of the sun at winter solstice. The route that starts from the north and heads east then goes all the way west before returning to the north represents the spring equinox. The route that starts in the north and heads east then goes all the way south before returning to the north represents the autumn equinox. And the long route that starts from the north and heads east, then goes all the way south and all the way west before returning to the north is the long path of the sun at summer solstice."

Thus, ancient Koreans cast their agricultural forecasts by tossing *yunnori* sticks onto the game board and analyzing the spring, autumn, winter and summer solstices. Even a simple *yunnori* board contained all the heavens, the earth and the universe.
[Source: *Our History of the Sky and Stars*, Kim Il-gwon, God's Win Publishers, Inc.]

Gyeongbokgung Palace and the Constellations

Ancient people modeled their palaces after the constellations. This was the same for Gyeongbokgung Palace, the royal seat of the Joseon Dynasty. Inside the palace, the throne hall, called Geunjeongjeon, where the king and his officials discussed state administration, represented the North Star at the center of the sky. When you step inside the gate that leads to the throne hall, wide granite foundation stones spread out before you, on top of which sits the stately Geunjeongjeon. On the right and left sides of the courtyard in front of the hall, stone markers (*pumgyeseok*) indicate where the king's officials stood according to rank. Iron rings were embedded in the ground to tie off large tents that were pitched on hot, sunny days.

Geunjeongjeon Hall was named by Jeong Do-jeon, one of the king's most distinguished scholars, and dedicated to King Taejo, the founder of the Joseon Dynasty. The name indicated that the king was to tend to state affairs in the morning; keep the company of virtuous men in the afternoon; devote himself to the study of laws in the evening; and rest at night. But the name did not mean he had to be unconditionally diligent at all tasks, but rather that he had to have a diligent understanding of

his duties as king. Also, the name "Gyeongbok" was taken from a poem in which the speaker wishes for a virtuous king who would usher in a golden era that would last for ten thousand years. The palace was named Gyeongbok in the hopes that everyone—from the king to every commoner—would gaze upon it and appreciate it for generations to come in lasting peace.

The floor inside Geunjeongjeon Hall is covered in dark square tiles. The color black signifies the north. The other colors used to decorate the inside of the hall represent the king, such as crimson and plum. Outside, a cast iron basin called *deumu* was placed near the hall and kept filled with water to frighten away evil spirits that liked to cause fires. Though it was put there for symbolic purposes, it could probably used in a pinch for putting out an actual fire.

The carvings of the *sabangsin*[5] (four guardians) and twelve animal gods
on the stone balustrade looked as friendly as cartoon characters.
They sat with their heads turned towards Geunjeongjeon Hall,
as if keeping a watchful guard.
I mused to myself, 'Wouldn't it be fun to find the one statue
that is looking in the wrong direction and chastise it for neglecting its duties?'
Though Confucianism is pictured as solemn,
these small adornments seem filled with humor.
The fact that these were permitted when the palace was built
draws attention to their aesthetics and sense of optimism.

Every corner of Gyeongbokgung Palace is filled with such meaningful delights.
Gyeonghoeru Pavilion, where a bronze dragon sits beneath the water to ward off a fire,
seems to mimic the contours of Korea's mountains, sky and water in miniature.
Without the strange and ethereal backdrop of Mt. Inwangsan speckled with white rocks,
that feeling would likely be halved.
Gyeonghoeru looms like a clean, sharp gust of wind in the dead of winter
that seems to cut right through you.
Only when the rocky mountain, pine trees
and lotus pond become one is Gyeonghoeru complete.

Gyeonghoeru Pavilion

Standing here, I think about the sad fate of the vanished dynasty,
and I regret how easily the traces of that culture have been wiped away.
Koreans have lost the love and respect that other countries show
for the royal family and its descendants.
The monarchy could not have been entirely about shoring up authority
and sucking the blood and sweat of the people.
The democratic nature of the *gyeongyeon*,
where the king and his officials openly discussed politics, begs otherwise,
and there was the sophisticated culture and technology
that went into food, clothing and shelter, as well as the care
and respect they showed for the people.
I believe the royal family is yet another treasure trove of Korean culture
with its intersection of tragedy and sanctity.

Stars Full of Wishes

In Hwasun, South Jeolla-do Province, there is a Buddhist temple called Unjusa. The temple is famous for the thousand stone pagodas and Buddha statues that were once scattered around the grounds and the surrounding area. It is an eerie sight to behold. The statues are not uniform in shape or appearance, and they do not match the traditional structure of the temple. In this place, with its eclectic traces of Buddhism, Shamanism and Taoism, which were officially repressed during the Joseon Dynasty, the marginalized common people must have dreamed of a new world while creating these pagodas and statues. But in their hours of darkness, they turned not to the *Sakyamuni* Buddha but the *Chiseonggwangyeorae* Buddha, the one that reflected their faith in the seven stars of the Big Dipper, which contained the wishes of the alienated classes. In other words, they turned to the North Star.

The *Chilseong bawi* (Seven Star Stone) is a large stone sculpture that depicts the Northern Dipper. In the position of the North Pole is a large *wabul* (Reclining Buddha) statue. There were those who believed the legend that when the stone Buddhas rise, a new world will dawn. Their hopes and frustrations can be read in those unfinished, reclining Buddhas.

Buddha statues of Unjusa Temple

The positions of the other pagodas and statues match the positions of the stars in the sky, with the larger ones representing brighter stars. The temple is a map of the universe. It also represents the bold resistance of faith and a sensitive vision of the universe that was repressed by the rationality of Neo-Confucianism. It is logos[6] and pathos[7], the duality of the human spirit torn in two directions. The unending challenge of realizing an ideal world was passed down over the ages through the history of Korean folk religion. So while Unjusa Temple appears more chaotic than other temples, it is all the more inspiring for it. If the *Cheonsang yeolcha bunya jido* is the summation of ancient astronomy, then Unjusa Temple is a precious artifact inscribed with that map. I stood at the center of that chaotic universe and looked back on the longings inscribed in each of those faded stones.

Finally, a clear sky.
Tonight, the North Star would shine more brightly.
In the television series *Winter Sonata*, my character Jun-sang gives his beloved
Yu-jin a necklace with a pendant resembling the North Star.
It signifies the fact that his love for her will never change.
But when he decides to give up on their relationship, she casts the necklace into the sea.
Does throwing away the necklace mean she is throwing away his love?
Jun-sang's love for Yu-jin continues to shine like the North Star
from its constant perch in the night sky.
Even if we do not attach meanings to the stars,
they are always there, giving us light and courage.

So tonight, I look up to the stars.

National Museum of Korea 11

Finding the Roots of Culture

Janggyeonggak Pavilion

Haeinsa is a Buddhist temple located in Mt. Gayasan of South Gyeongsang-do Province. The temple is known as a treasure trove of Korean culture, as it is home to the *Tripitaka Koreana* (also known as the "Eighty Thousand Tripitaka"), the world's oldest collection of the entire Buddhist canon carved onto over eighty thousand wooden printing blocks and stored inside the temple's Janggyeonggak Pavilion. The blocks were created as a form of prayer for divine assistance in protecting the country from Mongol invasions. Fifty thousand people labored day and night to carve the Buddhist scriptures onto more than eighty thousand wooden printing blocks. To ensure that their prayers would be heard for ten thousand years, the boards were lacquered and stored in a well-ventilated building.

The *Tripita Koreana* was nearly destroyed several times. Once, the Venerable Seongcheol[1], a famous monk who was nicknamed the "Tiger of Mt. Gayasan," severely scolded a disciple who had set fire to his finger in front of Janggyeonggak Pavilion as a form of ritual immolation. He was not so much worried about the disciple as he was astonished that anyone would put the pavilion at risk of fire, however briefly. During the Korean War, an American pilot received orders to bomb Haeinsa Temple. Thanks to the courage and fortitude of the officer, who disobeyed those orders, Janggyeonggak Pavilion was spared. But the main reason this legacy has survived for over eight hundred years is the remarkable architectural technology that went into building the pavilion. It is also the reason Janggyeonggak Pavilion (National Treasure No. 52) was designated as a UNESCO World Heritage Site in 1995. As I thought about how the pavilion has protected the *Tripitaka Koreana* all these years, I tried to remember where Korea's other cultural heritages are housed. Just as important as creating new cultural assets—if not more important—is collecting, preserving and caring for existing ones.

The *Tripitaka Koreana* was carved over a period of approximately twelve years, from 1237 to 1248. Contrary to popular belief, which holds that the blocks were made from white birch, the blocks were actually made from the wood of wild cherry and wild pear trees, as revealed by a recent examination under an electron microscope.

The technique of woodblock printing was first developed in the late Silla Dynasty and continued through the Goryeo Dynasty. *The Tripitaka Koreana* is the only case in the entire world, however, where the original wooden blocks have survived intact, rather than just the printings produced from them. According to data released by Haeinsa Temple, there are a staggering 81,258 boards in total.

National Museum of Korea

Museums are vessels of culture. London has the British Museum; Paris, the Louvre; Vatican City, the Vatican Museum; Washington D.C., the Smithsonian; and New York, the Metropolitan. Falling in line right behind these cosmopolitan museums is our very own National Museum of Korea in Seoul. In his autobiography, *My Life with the Museum*, Dr. Kim Jae-won, the first director, includes many entertaining behind-the-scenes stories about the National Museum. I heard the stories from the current director, Choe Kwang-shik, and wanted to pass them along to others.

According to Choe, when World War II ended in 1945, Dr. Kim, who has since passed away, was living in Germany. He was summoned back to Korea and hastily appointed director of the National Museum. With the peninsula divided and war clouds on the horizon, Dr. Kim realized that the Gaeseong Museum (built in 1931 and located in what is now North Korea) was in imminent danger of being bombed, and he had the museum's collection of artifacts quickly moved to Seoul. On June 25, 1950, the Korean War broke out. Within three days, North Korean troops had captured Seoul. The city remained in northern hands until September of 1950, when UN forces landed at Incheon on September 15. When Seoul was recaptured by UN forces, the North Korean troops ordered Dr. Kim to pack up the museum's artifacts and move them back to Gaeseong. But he used his wits to outsmart them. He stalled for time by having the artifacts packed up during the day then secretly unpacked at night, thus preventing them from being taken back to North Korea. As packing cultural artifacts requires professional expertise, the North Korean troops' hands were tied. Then, on January 4, 1951, the UN forces that had recaptured Seoul were forced to retreat from the capital. Dr. Kim risked his own life to ensure that all of the artifacts were evacuated south to Busan before leaving the city himself. Thanks to the efforts of a few brave souls like Dr. Kim, these historical artifacts have survived to this day, weary from the ordeal but thankful nonetheless.

The first overseas exhibit of Korean cultural assets did not take place until 1957, after the flames of war had subsided. At that time, there were no specialists within Korea who could translate the materials for the exhibit into English, so with the help of a foreigner, Dr. Kim had to create an English catalog himself. He also had to handle every aspect of the tour on his own, from planning to negotiations to exhibition. Nevertheless, the National Museum was able to leap forward and establish itself as the sixth largest museum in the world in just fifty years. Though I have not been to every museum in the world, I have been to several of the most well-known ones and can say with certainty that the National Museum of Korea is on par with them in terms of size, collections and facilities.

It had been a while since I last visited the National Museum of Korea. Some of my staff who took a taxi to the museum told me that the driver did not know where it was and let them off a fifteen-minute walk away, right in front of the War Memorial of Korea² near the Yongsan army base. Had people been losing interest in the museum since it was relocated from Gyeongbokgung Palace to Yongsan? The museum is easily accessible using the Seoul subway system (Subway line No. 4, Ichon Station), but when I thought about the taxi driver, I wondered if the problem was that not enough people had gone to see the new location yet.

The new National Museum wiped away all of my preconceived notions of museums as dark, stuffy places. Built on a site totaling over three million square feet (over three hundred thousand square meters), the museum rises up like an enormous wall. My favorite part was the open-air plaza, where I first saw the Magnum photo exhibition. Mt. Namsan was visible in the distance, looking like a large framed painting. In fact, everything there seemed to turn into a work of art.

The enormous doors were a bit oppressive, but inside, the vaulted ceilings brought the sunlight in and seemed to brighten every corner of the building. The effect was like sunlight through a lattice door. In an instant, all my tension vanished. Standing between the rooms at the far end of the long corridor, *they* were waiting for me.

Choe Kwang-shik gave me a personal tour of the exhibits.
At first, it felt as if there was an unbridgeable gulf of time between me and
the glass-encased artifacts. Perhaps they had been waiting an eternity for someone
to come along who would properly appreciate them. I felt an irrational burst of
remorse at the thought that I lacked that kind of discerning eye.

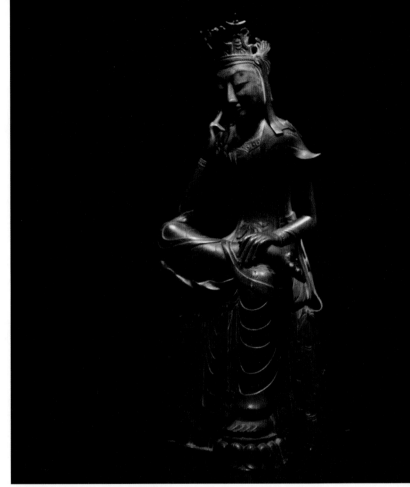

Gilt-bronze Semi-seated Pensive Bodhisattva Maitreya (National Treasure No. 78)

When you see the Pensive Bodhisattva in person for the first time,
you realize that it is more than just a simple religious symbol
but a work of art that represents Korea as a whole,
from the Korean face to the Korean sense of beauty.
When they were first made,
the statues became very popular and were produced in large numbers.
Of those, two have survived to the present day (National Treasures
No. 78 and 83). There is one more to keep them company, however—
the wooden Miroku Bosatsu statue, Japan's National Treasure No. 1.

Guy Sorman, a French culture critic, once said, "France has the Eiffel Tower, Japan has Mt. Fuji, and Korea has the Pensive Bodhisattva." The famous French writer André Malraux even asked to be left alone for an hour to take it in. I understood completely. The Pensive Bodhisattva is exhibited alone in a darkened room to encourage contemplation. I was guided through the somber entrance where I was greeted by a beautiful "living" being. The Pensive Bodhisattva is neither too big nor too small, but just the right size for holding in your arms. If I could only touch it, I imagine, my fingers would find skin and fabric rather than cold metal. Its exact age is unknown, and no one even knows if it came from Silla or Baekje, but the face is clearly Korean. The face is all too familiar, recognizable on some deep, genetic level.

The Pensive Bodhisattva I saw was National Treasure No. 78. It has a minimalist, feminine appearance. In contrast, National Treasure No. 83, which I viewed in a photograph, has more exquisite, beautiful detailing in the clothes. Also, the angle of the wrist is very realistic, and the emotional expression conveys warmth. The statue is so lifelike that it seems it will reach enlightenment at any moment and arise. Japan's Pensive Bodhisattva is quite similar in appearance to this one. The beauty, elegance and exquisite detail of these figures are unparalleled. When Dr. Choe told me that the museum rotates these two Pensive Bodhisattva statues so that only one is on exhibit at a time, I decided I would have to come back to the museum so I could be moved again.

Korean and Japanese scholars have been arguing for a long time about whether the Pensive Bodhisattva was originally Korean or Japanese. I think that rather than arguing over the question of ownership, it is more important that people know Korea and Japan had a long, close relationship of cultural exchange, which has left them with just three such statues today. I picture them together, these three statues that could have been brothers. How proud an accomplishment would that be, to inform more people around the world of their beauty?

If someone were to ask me to show them
what Korea looks like,
I would show them the Pensive Bodhisattva.
I doubt anyone would be disappointed.
I could describe it as Korea's version of
The Thinker[3].

백제금동대향로

百濟金銅大香爐

BAEKJE INCENSE BURNE

National Treasure No. 287

My Favorite Korean Cultural Assets

Splendid Baekje: Gilt-bronze Incense Burner

The Baekje Gilt-bronze Incense Burner (National Treasure No. 287) was excavated from a temple site in the village of Neungsan-ri, Buyeo in 1991. Incense burners were mainly used in Buddhism, but the depictions of mountains and fields, musicians playing instruments, tigers, deer, trees and stones suggest a Taoist influence. The people of Baekje used their unique sense of aesthetics and artistry to blend and fuse these two religions.

I enjoy burning candles and incense at home,
but I have yet to find an incense holder that I like.
Though I am not necessarily looking for something
this enormous and fancy, I do wish that small,
diverse styles of incense burners would come back
into fashion. I would also very much like to try
my hand at designing incense burners myself.

Dynamic Goguryeo: Ancient Tomb Murals

Because the Goguryeo Kingdom was mostly located in present-day North Korea and points further north, very few cultural artifacts from that kingdom have been found in South Korea. In fact, though there have been some museum exchanges with the Korean Central History Museum in North Korea, most of the artifacts and scholarship on the Goguryeo Kingdom have been collected from China or Russia.

'Korea's cultural artifacts are still wandering around out there,' I thought.

Goguryeo's ancient tomb murals, which are on exhibit in Ji'an of Jilin Province in China, are full of energy and movement. In 2009, the world-famous *hanbok* designer Lee Young-hee collaborated with the museum to put on a successful fashion show with clothing inspired by the fashions depicted in the Goguryeo-era murals. Perhaps with the help of the museum, which conducts close historical research of ancient cultures, the costumes seen in television series and movies could become much more detailed and historically accurate.

A Fondness for the Unfamiliar: The Gaya Confederacy

Little is known about the culture of the Gaya Confederacy. Most of the artifacts from that period consist of ironware, as the area was rich in iron deposits. In terms of national resources, they were comparable to today's oil-producing countries. For that reason, they did not necessarily have to pool their strength. Though they were small groups, about five or six in number, there was never a unified Gaya. Eventually, they were conquered by Silla, which was able to grow bigger on the strength of those iron deposits. Gaya's ironware culture became the foundation on which Silla was able to unify the Three Kingdoms. Silla absorbed Gaya's culture intact, perhaps because of Gaya's high level of cultural achievement. One could even say that the glory of Unified Silla was built on the glory of Gaya.

"Why am I so drawn to Gaya? Perhaps I was from Gaya in a past life."
One of my staff members overheard me and said, in full seriousness,
"No, you were from Goguryeo. After invading Gaya,
you fell for the beauty of Gaya women."

Could be...

Exquisite Metalwork: Bronze Kundika

Korea's National Treasure No. 92, a Goryeo Dynasty bronze kundika (ewer) inlaid with silver, is astonishing in its detail. Even with modern technology, this kind of work would take a long time to produce. Though the original color has been lost somewhat, the years have given it a much deeper, more exquisite patina. Kundikas were ritual water vessels used by monks. The designs etched into the sides of the vessels are strange and beautiful in a way that is rarely found today. It looks so unusual that, without proper explanation, it would be hard to tell that it is Korean. I cannot imagine how much focus it took to complete just one of these exquisite works of art. Nor can I imagine what could possibly compare to the pride of having created one of these.

Handwriting with Personality: The Signatures of Great Men

One of the exhibits had an especially fun concept. It was a collection of the signatures of kings and literary figures from the Joseon Dynasty, as well as literary figures from China, that were found in ancient documents. In my line of work, I am constantly signing autographs, so I pay a lot of attention to handwriting. I even recently began practicing traditional calligraphy, a litter at a time. Handwriting says a lot about a person. It is intriguing to see whether the handwriting of well-known historical figures matches up with our images of them. I think it would be nice to find a single Chinese character that sums me up so I could use it as my autograph.

태종
(太宗, 1367–1422)

이황
(李滉, 1501–1570)

이이
(李珥, 1536–1584)

Behind the Scenes at the National Museum

In the museum archives were many more artifacts not on display. If people do not show interest in a museum, the budgets are reduced, which in turn makes research and restoration difficult. As it turns out, culture is easy to preserve. The trick is interest and care. When people take interest in a museum, they grow to like it, and the more they like it, the more often they go. Over time, this adds up to cultural development.

If traditional Korean culture were difficult and boring, it would not be made the subject of so many television shows and movies. I think I could happily chat for hours with anyone who takes a great interest in Gaya, which stood out amongst the Three Kingdoms for its ironware, or the countless secret stories of the Silk Road, which connected Europe and Asia.

On the day I visited the museum, early modern works from Japan were on exhibit. The purpose of a national museum is not merely to exhibit the artifacts of that country alone. Cultural exchange with other countries is also important, as is introducing other cultures to the people of that country. But what I thought at first were paintings on loan from Japan turned out to all be part of the museum's permanent collection. Furthermore, the early works of those painters were rare pieces that are hard to come by, even in Japan. How did these paintings come to be housed in Korea? It turns out Japan had requested that Korea purchase them back in the days of Korea's first museum, the Imperial Household Museum established by Emperor Gojong of the Greater Korean Empire (1897-1910). It seems that the wheels of history are always turning, driving exchanges between different cultures. Each artifact as well seems to have its own destiny.

The men and women who have worked and will work to protect Korean heritage

Whenever a problem arises,
the wisest thing to do is to try to go back to the beginning.
When a relationship goes awry,
think back to the first time you met.
When something you are doing goes wrong,
think about why you started doing that thing in the first place.
I believe the answer to our uncertain futures can be found
back at the starting point, i.e. in history.
The past is the key to the future, and that key is kept safe inside museums.
I think the ideas that are the source of creation are all found in museums.
When we have to design something or come up with practical ideas
for daily life, we should start by visiting a museum.
Perhaps there we can discover new images, designs and ideas
that would not have occurred to us otherwise.
A museum is a teacher that stands in the same spot for a long time.
When we gaze upon objects that show us the plain truth of the past,
as if transporting us there by time machine,
we can learn about the forgotten roots of culture.
To know your roots, to return to the starting point,
does not mean staying in the past but rather searching for a new future.

Museums are alive.
Though they have often been dismissed
as boring places filled with dusty notions and relics of a bygone era,
my earnest hope is that the true value of museums
and the cultural assets they contain will be rediscovered.

逞

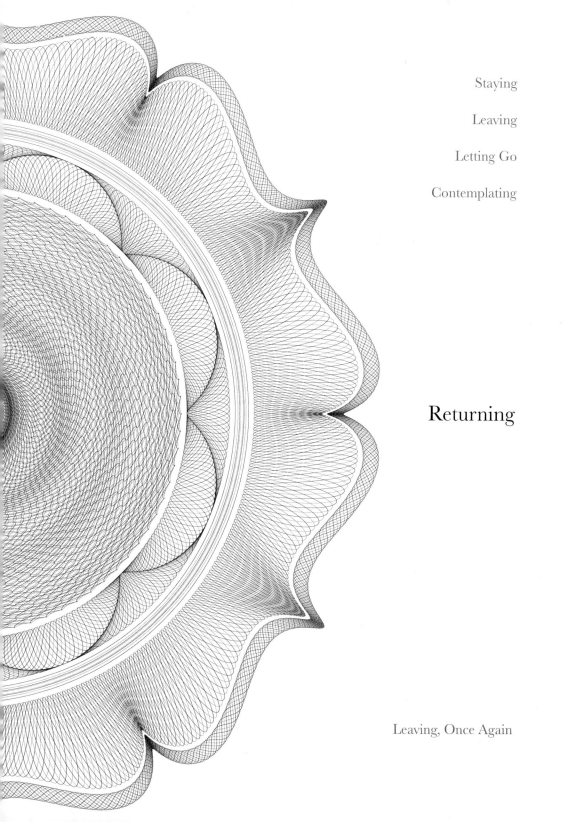

Staying

Leaving

Letting Go

Contemplating

Returning

Leaving, Once Again

Wine and Song 12

Rediscovering Forgotten Flavors
and Aromas in Nature

First Taste of Home-Brewed Alcohol

Ten years ago, a close friend and I traveled to the west coast together, where we chanced upon a restaurant that served Hansan *sogokju*[1], a traditional alcohol that dates back to the Baekje Kingdom. Entranced by the deep flavor and rich aroma, we drank nearly half a gallon (two liters) between the two of us that night. We should have been plastered, but I was clear-headed and in a great mood the whole night. Several years went by after that, but I never forgot the taste of that alcohol. I looked all over the country but I couldn't find a *sogokju* that tasted like that batch from my memory, probably home-brewed by someone's grandmother in her tiny kitchen.

I wanted to discover the unknown flavors of those home-brewed alcohols that I had learned about, the sense of style and indulgence that goes hand in hand with alcohol, and the uncovered potential of Korean alcohols that are reviving once-lost traditions. As luck would have it, the last leg of our field research took us to Gurye in South Jeolla-do Province, right at the foot of Mt. Jirisan. At that point, I was feeling a little unsettled and dissatisfied. We had been hard at work on the road whenever we had time, but it seemed like we were still overlooking something. I was also startled to see how quickly time was passing. I wanted the last leg of our journey to be a meaningful one and an opportunity to show my appreciation for those who had joined me on my travels. So after much deliberation, I decided on alcohol. And I thought having some music would add to the fun. For this journey into wine and song, we were accompanied by Park Rok-dam, poet and president of the Korea Traditional Liquor Institute, and Ubong Yun Jin-cheol, a master of the Boseong *pansori* performance.

Gurye is a small, rural township located at the southern end of Korea. Most of the residents are farmers, including a lot of elderly Koreans who have enjoyed long lives thanks to the clean air and water. In fact, so many of the residents are elderly that six out of eight villages in Gurye have been dubbed a "longevity village." Mt. Jirisan is a high mountain with many deep ravines; an analysis of the spring water has shown it to be very beneficial. This spring water may be the secret to the long lives of Gurye's residents. In fact, it could even be called a fountain of eternal youth.

Korea has a long tradition of making alcohol. During the Three Kingdoms era, alcohol was exported to China, and in the Goryeo Dynasty, a distillery was established in China to make *goryeoju* ("Goryeo liquor"). In the Joseon Dynasty, more diverse methods of brewing and distilling alcohol were developed, and many people enjoyed home brewing grain wine, which is second only in aroma to fruit wines.

Home-brewed alcohol was made from water, rice and a fermenting agent called *nuruk*[2]. Over two hundred varieties of alcohol could be made depending on how long the alcohol was fermented, which flavors were added (including flowers, medicinal herbs and pine) and which rice-based starter was used (including a rice porridge called *juk*, a steamed white rice cake called *baekseolgi*, and arieties of rice dough, such as *godubap*[3], *gumeongtteok*[4], *songpyeon*[5], *injeolmi*[6], *gaetteok*[7], and *beombeok*[8]). Different fermentation methods could produce *balhyoju*[9] (brewed alcohol), *jeungnyuju*[10] (distilled alcohol), *honseongju*[11] (aged alcohol) and *iyangju*[12] (twice-brewed alcohol). The end product could be *takju* (raw, unrefined alcohol) or *cheongju* (clear, refined alcohol) depending on the filtering method.

Home brewing began in the homes of aristocratic *yangban* families, who regularly entertained guests. The alcohol served in those homes reflected that family's level of class. The importance of alcohol is made apparent in Korea's first cookbook, *Eumsik dimibang*. Of the one hundred and forty-six recipes in the book, fifty-three were for alcoholic beverages, twenty-four of which were refined alcohols.

We spread out a straw mat in the small courtyard and sat down. There were six different alcohols for us to try: *songiju*, which is made from pine mushrooms and becomes mellower the longer it is fermented; *songnyeongju*, which is made from pine cones; *sogokju*, which was made in the winter from rice and a small amount of *nuruk* and brewed for sixty days, and which first taught me the allure of home-brewed alcohol; *gwahaju*, a summer wine that holds up well in the hot weather; *makgeolli*, which had been flavored with *sansuyu* (Japanese cornelian cherry) for which Gurye is famous; and *gamhongno*, a strong 40- to 45-proof liquor.

Roughly four hundred years ago, when home brewing was in its prime, the three best alcohols produced by the Joseon Dynasty were hard liquors: *igangju* (made from pear and ginger) from Jeonju, *jungnyeokgo* (made with bamboo sap) from Jeolla-do Province and *gamhongno* (made with herbs and honey) from Pyeongyang. Liquors like *gamhongno* that have the suffix 로 (*ro/no*, "dew") in their names are distilled twice, making them very strong.

The aroma of *gamhongno* is similar to wine. Despite the high alcohol content, the flavor is smooth, unlike the bitterness usually associated with hard liquors. But the flavor does start off strong then mellows out. There is something of the strength of a woman in this alcohol: a potency that coils inward and subsides. It is like a strong wine that inspires a slower, more delicate approach, rather than a greedy rush to drink as much as possible. While *soju* is a good drink for reconciliation as it numbs you, opens up your heart and inspires unity, *gamhongno* is a drink fit for celebration, well-suited to times when you want to stand out and make an impression on your drinking companion.

Drinking alcohol in moderation is good for your metabolism. The home-brewed alcohol that our mothers made was not for themselves but for the family. It was made to be served at ancestral memorial services, to one's parents and to guests. But as with anything, excessive consumption is a bad thing. The universal principle of "everything in moderation" applies to alcohol as well. I think two or three glasses a day is appropriate. Though everyone's intake will vary based on their body type, most people can break down around twenty-five grams of alcohol the day after drinking. That is roughly the amount that is found in two or three shots of *soju*. So Korean mothers never served more than two or three shots of alcohol a day. Also, that was the only way they could ensure that they did not run out before the next batch was ready.

But of course drinking in moderation is not always easy. The tipsier you get, the faster the glass is refilled. When the alcohol is on your tongue and the aroma is in your nose, there is no such thing as moderation. The alcohol at our celebration flowed freely. My face turned the same shade as the sweet, red *gamhongno*.

At one point, there were as many different flavors of traditional alcohol as there were varieties. But sadly that diverse tradition ended ninety years ago. In 1907 the Japanese Governor-General of colonized Korea issued a liquor tax, after which hundreds of varieties of Korean alcohol disappeared. Then, due to a crackdown on bootlegging in 1916, every type of alcohol was standardized into one of three categories: *yakju* (refined alcohols such as *cheongju*), *takju* (unrefined alcohols such as *makgeolli*), and soju. After 1917, home brewing was brought to a complete stop, and alcohol manufacturers were newly allocated to each district. Even after the establishment of the Republic of Korea in 1945, bootlegging was prohibited for nearly forty-eight years in accordance with the national liquor law. Furthermore, the disappearance of traditional alcohols that are mainly made from rice accelerated with the food shortages following the Korean War and the Grain Management Act of 1965. Home brewing recipes that had been passed down orally and acquired through trial and error were not recorded for preservation.

In 1123, during the reign of King Injong of the Goryeo Dynasty, an ambassador sent by Emperor Huizong from the Song Dynasty in China wrote a book called *Seonhwa bongsa goryeo dogyeong*, which was a detailed account of what he observed in Goryeo. In it, he described the customs of its people: "When they drink, the people of Goryeo do not do so in moderation but instead drink to their hearts' content until they are inebriated."

This is very old proof of Koreans' tendencies to drink to excess. Of course, every culture on the planet must be similar in its enjoyment of alcohol. But I cannot help but laugh at the fact that Koreans' love for alcohol would leave such a deep impression that it would even merit being recorded in a book.

Jeokbyeokga: Battle of the Red Cliffs

Pansori master Yun Jin-cheol took out a drum and fan and began to sing. The traditional Korean music known as *pansori* can be performed anywhere, even without a formal setting, as long as there is a singer and a folding screen and mat for a stage. This is what is called *sarangbang sori*, a kind of impromptu performance for personal guests.

Pansori is an interactive performance between the singer and the audience. The singer must have rapport with the audience in order to convey the emotions in the story. Listeners who do not understand the language tend to mistake *pansori* for just sad songs. The appeal of *pansori* lies in the fact that all of the roles are played by a single performer who injects the music with wit and satire. Therefore, audience participation is a big part of a *pansori* performance. The audience calls out "*Eolssigu!*" and "*Jo-ta!*" in positive response to the performance, which spurs the singer on further. The audience can also call out when it will not disrupt the performance, such as when the singer is catching his or her breath or there is a pause in the rhythm. Only when the singer has established the proper rapport with the audience can the relaxed pace and liveliness of *pansori* be understood. You feel happy together, then sad together. Unfortunately our own group did not quite get the timing, and we just sat there blankly. So the drummer, called *gosu*, set the rhythm and alerted us to when we should call out.

Pansori is divided into *dongpyeonje* and *seopyeonje*, or the eastern and western schools of *pansori*, respectively. *Dongpyeongje* is more broad and masculine, with less emphasis on technique, rather like the striking of a large iron hammer. In contrast, *seopyeonje* is delicate, savory and soft with a small, relaxed sound. Masters of *seopyeonje* are skilled at the melancholic *gyemyeonjo*, a sorrowful mood similar to a minor key in Western music.

Up until the eighteenth century, there were twelve *pansori* songs in existence, but the number dropped in accordance with audience preferences. Currently, five *pansori* songs are still performed, all of which are based on the Confucian concept of filial piety: *Chunhyangga*, *Simcheongga*, *Heungboga*, *Jeokbyeokga* and *Sugungga*. In the late Joseon Dynasty, Shin Jae-hyo documented six *pansori* pieces, including one called *Garujigi taryeong*. All six survived down to the modern period. But after the passing of Park Dong-jin, no one was left who remembered how to perform *Garujigi taryeong*, so the number dropped to five.

Drinking Games

Drinking in Korea often leads to games with some devilish rules. Though no one knows exactly when it began, Koreans have made a tradition of shouting "One shot!" before downing alcohol. I used to think that the origins of this custom were simply unknown. But I recently came across a book that explained that these types of drinking games, with rules and penalties, have been in existence since the Silla Kingdom. Perhaps even Kim Cheon-taek, the famous singer-poet of the late Joseon, coaxed others to "one shot" while saying, "Don't even think about not finishing the glass I've poured for you!"

Of the more than thirty thousand artifacts unearthed from Anapji, a pond built during the Silla era, one item was of particular interest: a fourteen-sided die made from oak with Chinese characters engraved on each side. This die, called *juryeonggu*, was used in drinking games. The engraved characters mostly indicated penalties.

Samjan ilgeo: Drink three shots at once.
Gokbi jeukjin: Share shots with arms entwined.
Yangjan jeukbang: Drink two shots at once.
Geumseong jakmu: Dance alone with no accompaniment.
Nongmyeon onggwa: Do not move while your face is being tickled.
Jachang jaeum: Sing and take a shot alone.

I marveled at how similar our twenty-first century drinking games are to those that were played by people a thousand years in the past. It is funny, too, to think that a simple drinking game can contain a thousand years of history. I also mused about the possibility of using the die to teach people about both traditional Korean alcohol and our drinking culture through this simple game.

Juryeonggu
(Image provided by the Gyeongju National Museum)

Brewing Alcohol

Are there any Korean alcohols that have the same vitality as wine? Is there a traditional alcohol that grows wiser and more mature with age, like people? One that ripens and becomes richer with the passing of time, like bottled wine? Can rice, water and *nuruk* alone produce that kind of fullness of flavor and aroma? As the night wore on and we continued to tip our glasses back, my mind filled with curiosity about the secrets behind traditional Korean alcohol.

The first time I learned to appreciate wine was during a trip to Paris. After stopping off in England for a shoot, the staff went back to Seoul, while I put on a backpack and jumped on a train by myself. At the time, I was not all that interested in wine, but I wanted to experience the charm of travel and thought of something I saw in a movie once. So everyday I bought a bottle of wine and carried it back to my hotel room in a paper bag. That was how I started drinking wine. I drank five or six bottles during my stay in Paris. One day, I left a bottle of wine uncorked in the room. I had not cared for the flavor, so there was wine leftover in the bottle. When I returned, the room was filled with the scent of flowers. The bouquet was distinctly different from the way it smelled the night before. It occurred to me that this might be what was called "breathing." With my new-found interest, I returned to Korea. Since then, I began with a bottle or two and am now a full-fledged wine drinker.

One of my close friends is Yi Jun-hyeok, a professional sommelier. Jun-hyeok is so skilled at what he does that you can ask him anything about wine and he will be ready with an answer. What sets him apart from others is that he is far more interested in drinking wine than in collecting it. But this is significant. He believes that sommeliers should always taste wines for themselves before recommending them, rather than blindly trusting wine critics. There is a lot I can learn from my friend, who prefers experience to possession, and we frequently meet to share a drink of wine. "Why not learn about traditional Korean alcohol first," I suggested to Jun-hyeok, whose dream is to own his own winery, "then apply those skills to making an even more amazing wine?" He took me up on my suggestion and went with me to meet Park Rok-dam, an expert on traditional Korean alcohol.

Park greeted us with an easy smile. A poet, his way of talking and even his every movement exuded poetry. In Park's presence, even Jun-hyeok carried himself in a more mature, dignified way than usual. As they say, "Seeing is believing." We saved the discussion for last and began with some hands-on training.

Dongjeongchun

The alcohol Park taught us to make is called *dongjeongchun*. It is one of the hardest traditional alcohols to make. But we thought that by starting with the most difficult, we could more easily understand the principles behind the other alcohols. Also, Park hinted that, of the four hundred and thirty traditional alcohols he had tasted, this one had the best flavor and aroma. He said he found it the most satisfying to make. In fact, he usually enjoys drinking with other people, but this was one alcohol he said he might prefer to drink alone. Even though I knew I would not get to drink the alcohol the same day we bottled it, I started feeling impatient for a taste.

Dongjeongchun is known for having the best flavor, aroma and color: a heavy sweetness that sticks to your mouth like honey, a fragrant bouquet of fruit and a clear color with a subtle sparkle. It takes discipline, devotion and effort to produce all three of these. Not only that, but it takes two months and over seventeen pounds (eight kilograms) of rice to make just half a gallon (two liters) of *dongjeongchun*. The brewing process is difficult and low in yield, because the starter is made from a type of rice dough called *gaetteok*, to which no water is added. Furthermore, the rigorous fermentation process means that the recipe for *dongjeongchun* has a high rate of failure. It must have been an overwhelming task for commoners to try to make this kind of alcohol, as it uses so much rice, a staple food.

Making *Dongjeongchun*:
The Drink that Captured the Heart of Su Dongpo[13], the Chinese Master Poet

① Wash four pounds (1.8 kilos) of short-grain white rice in water one hundred times, or until the water runs clear. Leave the rice to soak then wash it again, rinse it well and grind it into a fine powder.

② Mix the rice powder with boiling water to form a dough. Shape the dough into three flat patties. Poke holes through the centers to make *gumeongtteok*.

③ Add a bowl of water to a large pot, and place the *gumeongtteok* in an earthenware steamer. Place the steamer inside the pot, and steam the *gumeongtteok* until they are soft. Before they can cool, mash the *gumeongtteok* up and shape them into small ball-shaped pieces. Leave the dough to cool completely.

④ Mix the cooled dough with 15-18 ounces (450-500 g) of powdered *nuruk* and knead thoroughly. Place the kneaded dough in a large earthenware jar, and seal the jar tightly. The dough will ferment and form the starter for the alcohol.

⑤ After the starter has fermented for a day or two, move the jar to a cool place and allow it to ferment for another day or two.

⑥ Late at night on the third day, wash seventeen pounds (eight kilograms) of glutinous rice a hundred times, or until the water runs clear, and leave the rice to soak overnight in fresh water.

⑦ Early the next day, rinse the soaked rice and sieve it to remove the water. Put the rice in an earthenware steamer and place it inside a pot. Hard-steam the glutinous rice to make *godubap*. Spread the *godubap* out thinly on a straw mat and cool it completely.

⑧ Mix the *godubap* evenly with the alcohol starter and place it back inside the liquor jar. Seal the jar tightly and cover it with a cloth wrapper. Store the jar at room temperature for two to three days to allow the mixture to ferment. Then move the jar to a cool spot for the after-fermentation stage, when the alcohol will age for sixty days.

⑨ To check if the alcohol is ready, light a match and hold it just inside the jar. If the flame wavers or does not go out, insert a long cylindrical strainer into the jar and leave it there for three to four days. Afterward, the strainer can be used to scoop out the alcohol. Bottle the alcohol and age it another two months to further improve the flavor and bouquet.

* The alcohol starter for *dongjeongchun* must be fermented for four days, but Park had prepared some in advance. The one that we made was used four days later.

Discipline

When it comes to making traditional Korean alcohol, the raw rice must be processed properly, whether it is being hard-boiled for *godubap* or made into *tteok*. Rice is a staple food of Korea. By making alcohol from something that is eaten every day, food allergies or intolerances can be reduced, and people may feel a stronger affinity towards it. Since *godubap* and *tteok* play a decisive role in the taste of the alcohol, the rice must be handled carefully to keep it from being under or overcooked. Generally, Korean alcohols are brewed from *juk* (rice porridge), *baekseolgi* (steamed white rice cake), *beombeok* (mixed grain porridge) or *godubap* (hard-boiled rice).

Devotion

Dongjeongchun is made from an alcohol starter called *gaetteok*. (The alcohol base, or *sulmit*, is a crude liquor made from rice or other grain that has been steamed, boiled into a porridge, or ground into a powder and used to make dough.) To make *gaetteok*, hot water is slowly added to rice powder, which cooks the rice, and is stirred with a wooden paddle. The mixture is kneaded to ensure that the moisture is evenly absorbed into the rice powder. The dough is then formed into flat patties, and holes are poked through the center. (This type of *gaetteok* is called *gumeongtteok*.) This process was so strenuous that I broke into a sweat. It seems fitting that the same verb in Korean, *bitda*, is used to refer to both making alcohol and making pottery. I thought about how not a single piece of clay is wasted when making pottery. Now that I have tried making alcohol as well, every grain of rice seems precious to me.

Effort

Nuruk is added to the *gumeongtteok* and kneaded by hand for an hour and a half, or until the dough is ready to begin fermentation. The dough starts off very stiff but eventually softens to the consistency of porridge. It takes such a considerable amount of strength that it is hard to imagine how women were able to do this work. Suddenly I understood what Park meant when he said that women, who had to do this work several times a year back in the old days, must have felt liberated when prohibition laws were introduced.

After the entire process was complete, *deotsul* (a mixture of steamed rice and crude alcohol) was added and the jar was sealed. The jar was wrapped in cloth and stored in a warm room. Once the alcohol had aged for two months, the *dongjeongchun* would be ready to drink. According to Park, the longer the alcohol ferments, the richer the bouquet and the mellower the taste. Jun-hyeok enthusiastically agreed, saying it was the same for wine. I looked at the two of them. It seemed my sommelier friend had learned through drinking alcohol what Park had learned through making alcohol.

Showdown: The Brewer vs. The Sommelier

After our exhausting attempt at home brewing, we each busied ourselves preparing dinner. Park Rok-dam bustled about, setting out white porcelain cups and Korean alcohol. Never one to lose, Jun-hyeok took out a large bag that he had brought with him. He opened it to reveal twelve wine glasses. He had brought his Riedel wine glasses, which I normally only use when I have company. I set out some kimchi, vegetable fritters and meat.

While we were setting the table, Park served *gambyangju*, which is made by kneading *songpyeon* made from short-grain white rice for the starter, and adding a *deotsul* made from hard-boiled glutinous rice. The aroma of the *gambyangju* pulled me in, and I found myself holding out my cup. Stirred by professional curiosity, Jun-hyeok used one of his own wine glasses for the Korean alcohol, instead of the porcelain cup, and dipped his nose into the glass. At the sight of Jun-hyeok sniffing away with his face and nose stuck inside that tiny opening, as if determined to suck up and identify every smell, everyone burst into laughter. But Jun-hyeok did not even flinch, staying focused completely on the glass.

#1. At the Traditional Liquor Research Institute

Yi Jun-hyeok (YJH below)

How did you get so much aroma from just rice, water and nuruk*?* (Jun-hyeok lifts his head to reveal a bright-red ring around his nose and mouth.) *It has floral notes... but it's not made from flowers, right?*

Park Rok-dam (PRD below)

(With a sharp gleam in his eye.) *Doesn't wine have a floral scent even though it is only made from grapes? We call that* banghyang, *a scent resembling a flower. So you call those "notes" in wine? different alcohols are made using different* nuruk *and different methods for processing the rice, then the scent changes, too. Secondary ingredients make a difference as well.*

Jun-hyeok raises the glass to his lips, as if the alcohol has passed his aroma and viscosity test. Park's eyes follow the arc of his hand. Everyone holds their breath. Jun-hyeok rinses the *gamhyangju* around inside his mouth as if gargling. His eyes widen.

YJH

(His voice suddenly grows louder.) *This is great! If I were to compare it to wine, I would have to say it has the aroma and body of the best dessert wines! You see, when a wine is made well, the flavor develops as you drink it. The flavor of this* gamhyangju *rises slowly, very slowly, like a fog billowing up gradually. Wow!*

PRD

(The crease in his forehead finally smoothes out, and he relaxes, crossing one leg over the other.) *Many Korean alcohols are made using only hard-boiled rice, but you can't get that kind of flavor that way. You have to use the softer rice dough to get that flavor.*

YJH

(Unable to peel his eyes off of the *gamhyangju*, with its strong viscosity and cloudy color, so unlike that of wine.) *Now I understand why you said you were never all that drawn to wine. With an aroma like this, it's understandable. To be honest, I had no idea Korean alcohol could taste this good.*

PRD

(As if gazing into the distance and reminiscing.) *I was nervous at first. I didn't know if people would like this kind of alcohol. I was not confident I could change people's preconceived notions that Korean alcohol smells musty or that I would be able to create something that tasted good. But now I am confident. Even those picky Europeans have tasted my alcohol and thanked me afterward. So I feel obliged to host as many tastings as possible.*

As if something has only now occurred to him, Jun-hyeok puts down his glass of *gamhyangju,* takes out several bottles of wine and sets them on the table one by one.

YJH

Today I brought a 2003 Colgin from the US that costs one to two million won, a 1995 Chateau Le Pin and a 1990 Chateau Petrus from France that cost three to four million, and a 2001 Gunderloch Rothenberg Riesling T.B.A from Germany that costs one to two million. Those prices are from when I bought them five years ago, so they have probably gone up a little since then. Of course I don't mean that the price says anything about the quality. But I wanted you to have the chance to taste a lot of different wines, so I chose these based on what I think is good.

As if his turn has come at last, Jun-hyeok fills everyone's empty wine glasses with the 2003 Colgin. He gives off an air of confidence somehow. It is apparent that Jun-hyeok is eager to hear his opinion, but Park takes his time breathing in the scent of the wine. Then he sets the glass down without tasting it. Jun-hyeok's eyes never leave the glass.

PRD

The reason there are so few people who make traditional Korean alcohol for a living is because it is difficult to expect the price and reception it deserves from customers. If you could get a million won per bottle, like this wine, more people would probably give it a try. Mr. Yi, if Korean alcohol were a million won per bottle, do you think people would order it in restaurants?

YJH

If it tastes this good, then definitely! You need to let more people know how good this is and how amazing the flavor is. With this kind of quality, your alcohol can definitely be competitively priced.

PRD

Why, thank you, young man... You know, after just three glasses, I start to have an allergic reaction to the alcohol. I'm not much of a drinker. But I have no choice but to drink a lot if I am to taste test the alcohol that I make. What would you guess happens? Even after drinking an entire bottle and falling down drunk, I have never once had a hangover the next day. So it goes without saying that the quality of my alcohol is very high.

Jun-hyeok leaps up and places on the table a Pétrus that he has decanted the day before. Other wines can be allowed to breathe directly in the glass. But Jun-hyeok has used a teakettle instead of a decanter. Everyone stares at him in amazement. Park finally takes a careful sip of the Colgin. Jun-hyeok appears tense.

PRD

(Relaxing) *Mm... Good length. Smooth. Very nice.*

YJH

(His whole face lights up.) *Just as I thought, since you're a Korean alcohol expert, wine is no problem for you. Colgin is a "cult wine" from California. Only three thousand bottles are produced a year. Robert Parker, a famous wine critic, gave it 95 out of 100 points. It's aged for as much as three years in oak barrels.*

(He continues filling everyone's glasses.) *I first tried wine seven or eight years ago. At the time I thought it was wrong to sell wine that I had not tasted myself. Of course I still think that way. Anyway, for three months I drank only wine, after which I began to understand it. That's my excuse anyway for why I drank so much wine.*

PRD

(As if carefully calculating something.) *If I think back... on how much I spent on rice... just to brew alcohol... it would come to around 230 million won. That's about thirteen 15-ton trucks worth of rice. My wife wanted to kill me.* (Laughs.)

I poke Jun-hyeok in the side and quietly ask him how much he has spent on wine so far.

YJH

(Whispers.) *Enough to buy a nice apartment south of the river. Don't you dare tell my wife!*

Sorry, Jun-hyeok... for not keeping my promise.

PRD

In the old days, brewers could tell from the aroma and flavor the pre-fermentation treatment and alcohol strength as well as the fermentation method and period. Jun-hyeok, when you drink wine, can you tell how long it was aged?

YJH

I can tell the grape variety, the vintage, and the region about seventy to eighty percent of the time, but I can't tell how long it's been oak-aged.

PRD

Actually it is unfortunate that sommeliers don't make their own wine. But it's even more unfortunate that there is no classification system or systematic fermentation standards for Korean alcohol. Probably no more than one percent of the Korean population has even tasted traditional alcohol. Everyone who has tried it says they love it, though.

I finally butt in on the two experts' conversation.

Me / BYJ

Lately people's taste in wine is becoming more and more uniform because of the point system used to critique wine. It's like they're losing their own sense of taste. But it's also clear that the point system has helped to globalize wine.

YJH

(Nodding enthusiastically.) *You're right. More brewers like Park should do research and create standards of performance for traditional Korean alcohol. It seems like someone needs to make that effort now.*

PRD

Yes, there are so many alcohols that need to be researched and restored. There's another type of alcohol called songgyechun. *It smells like pine and cinnamon, even though it's not made from either of those things. But no one can figure out what the source of that aroma is.*

Me/BYJ

Don't we have to distinguish between traditions that have to be restored and things that can move forward in a modern, scientific way, and develop them separately?

PRD

You're young, so of course you have a lot of interest in modernization. I want the same thing.

Just then, the *songsunju* made from rice, *nuruk* and pine needles is brought out. Jun-hyeok pours the *songsunju* into a wine glass with a look of interest. Then he sticks his nose in the glass again and takes a sniff.

YJH

Ah, this one smells just like a dessert wine.

PRD

That's a good word for it. Songsunju *was the best dessert wine made by families of the aristocracy.*

YJH

Really? Then you should try this dessert wine from Germany. It's the best there is. Gunderloch Rothenberg makes two hundred and forty bottles a year from Riesling grapes. Wine Spectator *magazine gave it a perfect score!*

Park tastes the Gunderloch Rothenberg and cocks his head then takes another sip.

Surprising. I don't know if you two will believe me, but it's very similar to the dongjeongchun *you bottled today.*

Jun-hyeok and I turn and look at each other, as if on cue.

YJH

You mean you can get this flavor and aroma from rice? (Suddenly drops to his knees and kneels in a manner exuding the deepest respect.) *Sir, I will be back in two months to taste that* dongjeongchun!

Everyone laughs at Jun-hyeok's determination.
Park smiles a very satisfied smile.

PRD

Young man, I'm just as surprised to hear you can get this flavor from a grape. I guess I learned a thing or two about wine today as well!

Park's young apprentice serves us a snack of cold steamed chicken and dried roast shrimp. The food is presented beautifully, and everything is in neat, bite-size pieces.

PRD

(Around a mouthful of shrimp) *Hm... the smell is overpowering the alcohol...*

His apprentice flushes with embarrassment. But the fact that someone as young as the apperntice would pursue a traditional art of his own accord is impressive in itself.

PRD

Chicken... ah, it's wrapped in tofu. That's excellent. Did you know? With traditional alcohol, the flavor and aroma are improved by making it in large batches rather than small ones.

YJH

(Stops eating in surprise.) Then what is the ideal batch? Likewise with wine, the bigger the bottle, the better the flavor is. The best is what's called a magnum, which is the size of two regular bottles.

PRD

Traditional alcohol tastes best when it's made from 176 pounds (80 kilograms) of rice. That makes about 53 gallons (200 liters) of alcohol.

YJH

The best barrel size for aging wine is also around 59 gallons (225 liters). That's an oak barrel called a barrique. Wow, what a coincidence!

Furiously trying to keep up as I jot down everything they are saying, I butt in with one comment.

Me / BYJ

I can't believe how similar Eastern and Western alcohols are! Maybe that's why Korean alcohol tastes and smells just as good as wine. It's been on its way out for a long time, and it will take just as long to restore it to its former glory. But the fact that the two have so many similarities means that we have a lot to learn from each other.

Jun-hyeok appears deep in thought.

YJH

I think Korean alcohol is just getting started. You only have to taste it once to agree that the flavor and aroma are superior. It has a lot of potential. Sir, since I can't buy this alcohol, I'm going to come back later if I get a craving. I'll bring more wine. We can swap.

Everyone has a friendly laugh at Jun-hyeok. Park raises his glass. Everyone follows suit. Wine glasses and porcelain cups are mingled together and filled with alcohol.

PRD

Thank you everyone for your hard work today, and for sticking it through to the end. I appreciate all your praise of this traditional Korean alcohol. I feel inspired by the rich flavors and aromas of the wine I enjoyed today. I want to learn more about the design, the science behind how it is distilled, and the secret to winning so many admirers the world over and keeping them for such a long time. Thank you again.

And of course, Jun-hyeok makes a few final words of his own.

YJH

Sir, I will be back in two months. I'll be waiting for that finished dongjeongchun.

#2. On the Ride Home

During today's drunken conversation, I learned anew about how delicious, stylish and scientific traditional Korean alcohol can be, and I was amazed at its potential. The steps we can take to help preserve and develop traditional home brewing are quite simple: we can stop the extinction of traditional home-brewed alcohol by sharing and appreciating this precious cultural heritage with more people. I look forward to the day when hundreds of long-lost home-brewed alcohols will have been recovered and restored to their rightful place, filling everyone's porcelain wine cups and intoxicating them with their aroma. When that happens, I hope the rhythm and melody of tradition will be heard together, and that smiles will spread across the faces of many good people.

Hanok 13

My Dream House

Landscape of a House

When the Romanian writer Constantin Virgil Gheorghiu,
author of *The 25th Hour*, first saw the Korean countryside,
he remarked, "It's like looking at a scroll of calligraphy."

– Lee O-Young, *Encyclopedia of Korean Culture*, Design House

Usually when people see the East Asian countryside, landscape paintings
come to mind. But Gheorghiu's gaze stopped not on the mountains
but on the winding paths between rice paddies. Why did he say they
reminded him of calligraphy scrolls?

I, too, have spent a long time staring at a photo of those winding
paths. Back then, everything I was going through, both big and small,
felt like they were happening in the last night's dream. When I looked
at the photo, I would imagine there was a house at the end of the path,
and it felt more real to me than anything else at the time. Perhaps I thought
that path would lead me to another world, away from the fierce, dizzying
competitiveness of the here and now, into one that would embrace me
warmly. My desire to live in another world conjured up the image of a house.

The image of escape offered by the peaceful countryside came to
Gheorghiu in the form of a calligraphy scroll, and to me as a house.
Perhaps all of us who began our lives somewhere ordinary dream of
spending our later years somewhere cozy.

Hanok, traditional Korean houses, are eco-friendly structures that
embrace the four seasons. One of the most striking features of *hanok*
is the complementary structure of *ondol* (also known as *gudeul¹*) and

*maru*²: the former refers to the underfloor heating system that draws heat from the stove to directly beneath the floors to warm them in winter, while the latter refers to the raised central floor that enables air to circulate and cool the house in summer. *Ondol* and *maru* are unique features of traditional Korean houses that make it possible to overcome both the heat waves and cold spells brought about by the distinct seasonal changes experienced on the Korean peninsula.

Hanok have even earned the nickname "summer house" for their outstanding ability to keep the heat out. The secret is their remarkable ventilation and temperature control. In a traditional Korean house, rooms are arranged to the right and left of a large wooden-floored hall, called *daecheong*, which can open on the remaining two sides to allow air to circulate. On hot, sticky summer days, you can sit on the *daecheong* and look out at the landscape of sky and mountains unfolding beneath the eaves, crack open a watermelon, and feel the sweat that has been running down your spine turn cold before you know it. But it does not end there. On frosty winter nights that freeze the tip of your nose, you can tiptoe quickly across the *daecheong* and scurry beneath your nice soft blankets waiting for you in a warm room. The colder the days grow, and the icier that raised wooden floor becomes, the more you treasure the warmth of that spot on the floor closest to the stove.

Considering the warm floors, *hanok* could also be called a "winter house." The unusual image of people crowding into a sizzling hot room in the dead of winter to thaw themselves out is a familiar sight for Koreans. In fact, there is no better treatment for people who are tired, sick, pregnant or just getting on in years than to bask on a hot floor. Korea must be the only place in the whole world where people enjoy warming their bones not on sand or in water but on an ordinary floor, and not singly but huddled together with others. In fact, *ondol* has even been made into an entry in the Oxford English Dictionary, underscoring the uniqueness of this Korean invention.

The finest example of an *ondol* room in Korea can be found in Chilburam (Seven Buddhas Hermitage) near Mt. Jirisan; the room was named *ajabang*, or *aja* room, because the shape of the flues beneath the floor resembles the Chinese character for *a*: 亞. According to temple documents, it takes one week and at least three cords of firewood to fully heat the room. Once heated, though, the flues stay warm for forty days. The nonpolluting and energy-efficient invention of *ondol*, which is estimated to have been in use on the Korean peninsula since before the Goguryeo era (37 BCE - 668 CE), was nothing short of revolutionary. Not even parts of the world like Eastern Europe or the northernmost parts of North America, which endure bitterly cold winters, have anything that can compare to *ondol*'s ability to beat the cold.

I prefer winding roads to straight ones.
If a straight road represents ambition,
then a curving one brings to mind contemplation.
Just as the sight of a beautiful view or location makes us think,
"I'd like to build a house there,"
so falling in love makes us think,
"I'd like to build a house in their heart."
There, you would learn anew everyday
the feeling of being alive and supporting each other.
By giving my life to another, I find true love.
Love is not achieved within yourself but is conceived in another.
It is an inevitable path that none can avoid, and I believe that it is God's love.

Another attractive feature of *hanok* is the harmony of logic and romance. The windows are built at just the right height so that when you are lying down, you cannot be seen from outside, but if you are sitting up, you can rest one arm on the sill and gaze out at the scenery. When the windows are open, the world outside seems as if it will come spilling into the room at any moment.

There are few walls inside a *hanok*, and doors often fill the roles of walls. *Bunhammun* are a special type of folding door that serves as room dividers when closed, but can be lifted and latched to the ceiling to open up the space. By turning small divided spaces into one large open space, the house can be made more spacious and airy, and it can accommodate many people at once. *Bunhammun* can be installed between rooms and along the *toenmaru*, the narrow wooden porch that runs along the outside of the room, to make cozy spaces when closed or to invite the scenery in when opened. It also gives people the emotional satisfaction of being able to see and feel the seasons changing.

Hanok are built from all-natural materials—clay, stone, wood and paper—that can later return to nature. The posts, rafters, doors, windows and floor are made from wood; the walls are made from a mixture of straw and clay; and the doors and windows are covered in *hanji*, traditional Korean paper. The floors as well are papered with *hanji* and polished with soybean oil.

Ironically, *hanok* is both eco-friendly and human-centered. The dimensions of the entire house are based on the size of the *kan* (the space between two pillars), and the *kan* in turn is determined by the size of the people living in the house. If the resident of the house is short, then the ceilings are built lower, or the overall size of the building is made smaller. Conversely, the house is built a little bigger for a tall person. Even if you searched the entire architectural history of every time and place on earth, you would never find a more human-centered design.

According to *De Architectura*, written by the ancient Roman architect Marcus Vitruvius Pollio around the first century BCE, "Proportion is a due adjustment of the size of the different parts to each other and to the whole; on this proper adjustment symmetry depends. Hence no building can be said to be well designed which wants symmetry and proportion. In truth they are as necessary to the beauty of a building as to that of a well formed human figure." But this assertion was related to the golden ratio of architecture and the physical body, not to the standard of *hanok*, which was based on the relationship between living people and architecture.

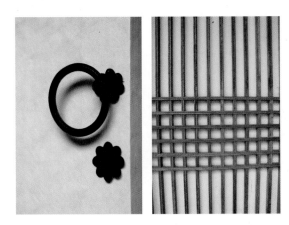

Bunhammun

The beauty of eco-friendly *hanok* is maximized by several architectural features. The *toenmaru* is a half-open space where a person can sit and enjoy the scenery, but it can also be lengthened and a banister added to make this narrow porch into a passageway. The *toenmaru* helps to soften the boundary between house and nature. The graceful eaves of the roof that curve up at the ends like traditional Korean socks seem to invite the moonlight in. Though the eaves can be seen as one part of an architectural style concerned with beauty, they are also a product of the science of architecture: taking the axis of the earth's rotation into account, the eaves protrude at just the right height to block sunlight in summer and let in sunlight in winter. Also, the uppermost ridge of the roof known as the *yongmaru*[3] ("dragon's spine"), has a characteristic line called the *hyeonsuseon*[4] (known in English as "catenary"). Traditionally, Korean houses were built in the shelter of mountains or hills; the ridgeline of the roofs were said to mirror these *dwitsan*, or "rear mountains." In other words, houses were built to harmonize with the natural surroundings. It is said that the *domoksu*[5], or master carpenter, would build the roof, which rose up at both ends and dipped ever so slightly through the middle, by tying a straw rope between the pillars on each side of the house and slackening or tightening the rope until the curve harmonized with the surrounding mountains.

Recently, people have gone beyond talking about "well-being" and are embracing "ecology." *Hanok* have long been ignored due to the preference for artificial beauty, but perhaps now *hanok* will earn proper recognition as an ecological living space.

Once, I stayed overnight in an old house in Andong. Though I normally toss and turn in my sleep, I slept very soundly that night. It was as if the house rocked me to sleep. There was a sense of perfect unity, as if the house and I shared the same breath and the same pulse, an emotion the likes of which I had never felt before. *Hanok* is alive. It breathes and moves.

This is how a *hanok* breathes: when the house becomes damp, the wood and clay inhale; when it is dry, they exhale. Slender drafts slip in through the paper used to seal the doors and wander about the room. The breeze circulates the air, regulates the humidity, and ushers in the outside world before heading back out. Lying with your back against the hot floor as a cool breeze touches your face—it is difficult to imagine this feeling without having experienced it for yourself. I love that breeze. When I wake before dawn and reach one hand out to open the door or window, still snuggled up in my blankets, the frozen night sky and the stars pour into the room.

This is how a *hanok* moves: when something is wrong with the house, the wood twists and squeaks, but the house would never suddenly collapse. It would warn you long before that. With a few bangs of the hammer, the house's health is restored. When the aches and pains of old age get to it again, it whines to let you know. The house is like an organism that slumbers and grows old alongside you. There is no need to knock, as even the floor squeaks to let you know when someone is approaching. That, too, is part of its subtle beauty. As the years go by, the house does not grow old but rather warm and filled with stories.

A store made from a renovated *hanok* in Samcheong-dong

Hanok Transformed

Hanok are expensive. Construction costs are much higher on average than other buildings. Ambitious plans for a new *hanok* village were even rescinded due to the high costs involved. *Hanok* require a lot of materials and manpower to build. In the late Joseon Dynasty, the *Silhak* (Practical Learning) philosopher Dasan Jeong Yak-yong wrote in *Mokmin simseo* (*Admonitions on Governing the People: Manual for All Administrators*), "Draw the designs for your own house and ask around quietly about the cost for building it. Then choose the most suitable offer among those and build your house." In other words, get an estimate and choose the most affordable option.

Hanok cannot compete in price, but they last a long time. A house must be built to last. It is said in Korea that even the mountains and rivers change every ten years; nevertheless, life inside the *hanok* has to go on for generations. Korean pine does not change or warp even after thousands of years. *Hanok* made from Korean pine have stood the test of time and continue to stand strong before our eyes. These strong *hanok* were possible because there were people to plant pine trees. Mireuksa, the Buddhist temple site I visited previously, was marked for restoration several years ago. But after Sungnyemun (more commonly known as Namdaemun) Gate was burned down, all of the lumber that was earmarked for Mireuksa went to Namdaemun instead. As a result, not only Mireuksa but many other historic sites that were set to be restored will have to wait until the supply of pine timber is back on track again. They say that concrete buildings barely last a hundred years. Is it far-fetched to argue that building something properly the first time is better than rebuilding it over and over?

I also think it is a good idea to change the way *hanok* are built. Recently in South Jeolla-do Province, *hanok* have become popular again. Architects have input the process of building a *hanok* into a computer so that the different parts can be modularized and assembled on-site. If this process is perfected, then we may see more *hanok* in our midst, and for less money and effort. Lately in places like the neighborhood of Samcheong-dong in Seoul, formerly residential *hanok* are being turned into charming cultural and commercial spaces, which exude a classiness that is quite distinct from large, fancy modern galleries. While modern buildings seem cold and commercial, where people have to make an effort to get to know the space, traditional buildings seem warm and friendly, as if to win people over.

This is not only the case in one or two neighborhoods. Recently, the fashion and design worlds have been emphasizing the idea of "storied" and "historied." Luxury is not something that can be bought only with money. When the Hôtel Le Meurice in Paris was going to be taken over by an American investor with enormous capital, city officials refused, saying, "Nobility cannot be bought with money." Likewise, there is something a little different about the type of luxury that wins people over. That difference is history. If *hanok* are understood as more than their exteriors but as "spaces with history," then perhaps they will be able to receive more love from people.

I would like to build a *hanok* on top of a New York skyscraper. Someone asked me if that would even be possible, but I say nothing is impossible. How amazing would that be to see a Korean house, a *hanok*, living and breathing in a city crowded with skyscrapers, that soars upwards in defiance of providence? Lately, more high-rise buildings have been adding public gardens to their roofs. If a single *hanok* were built on top of one of those buildings, it would add an accent to the dreary urban skyline. Many New Yorkers follow different trends in interior decoration, which have included Japanese, Chinese, Tibetan, Vietnamese and other Asian influences. I think the day is not far off when the Korean Wave will be felt in Hollywood, in the homes of movie stars, in famous restaurants, and in galleries, bringing the composed beauty of Korea to America.

Empty spaces fill with people's thoughts. Homes fulfill the important role of providing basic shelter, but they do many other things besides. Workshops, offices, restaurants and galleries are all homes as well. Among those is one that has shocked me the most: the *mumungwan* (gateless passage). I found out about this for the first time when I visited a Buddhist temple. This is a room at a temple where the occupant stays inside and does not come out for a set period of time or until he or she achieves enlightenment. One monk told me that the *mumungwan* is like a living tomb, a place where you decide that you would rather die than be reborn. While I am sleeping peacefully in my bed, someone somewhere is wide awake, fasting and struggling towards enlightenment. Our homes are similar and yet as different as night and day. Actually, I have had similar thoughts to the *mumungwan*. I thought that a home would fill up at first then at some point become empty again. We always start by cramming in as much as we can then slowly letting things go as we mature. Right now, I seem to be in the process of filling my home. It is strewn with books and filled with tools. Even the furniture is big. But with time, I will start to simplify my belongings, and eventually my home will be decluttered. Perhaps the fuller we feel on the inside, the fewer things we need.

If I build a *hanok* some day, I will take only books and lock myself inside, like a *mumungwan*. But what is truly shocking is that a true *mumungwan* would have to mean entering without any books or personal belongings. I find that very disappointing. Without books or anything else, how would you pass the time? I guess I still have a long way to go. The realization that I am not yet ready to let go of anything leaves me feeling dejected.

Evening skyline of New York

In the future, I will build a *hanok* and fill the rooms
with my dreams and entertain my friends there.
I would like the bedroom to be small and simple.
My parents will live in the main room, where I will build
a cabinet in the back wall on the warm side of the room
so they can store snacks for their grandchildren.
Instead of a separate library,
I will make a space where everyone can sit together and look at books.
I also want to include a tearoom and a workroom.
I want it to be a space not just for me alone but a space where everyone
who is like family to me can come together.
The tearoom would be small enough for five or six people to sit
with their knees touching, close enough to feel each other's breath.
Because if the space is too big, someone might feel left out.
I want to fill my house with stories that make everyone,
without exception, feel loved.

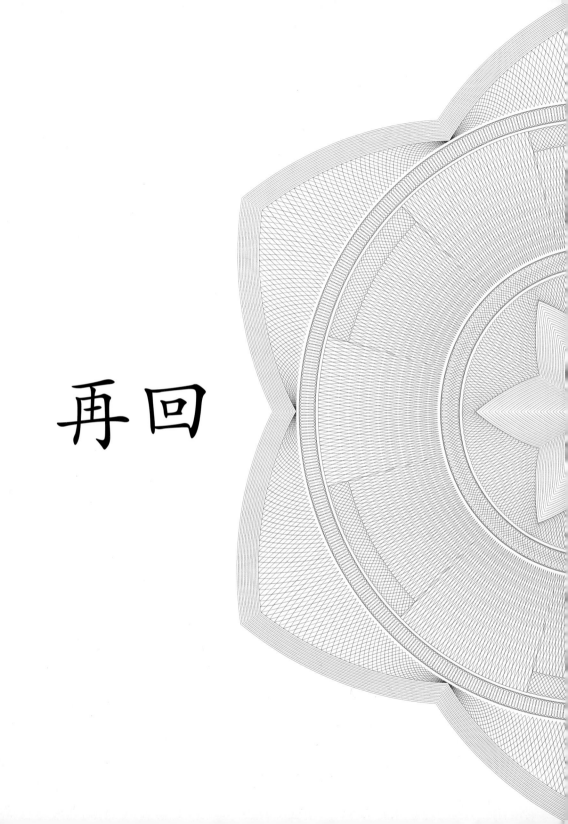

再回

Staying

Leaving

Letting Go

Contemplating

Returning

Leaving,
Once Again

Landscape [14]

Capturing Korea

The stride of a classical
Confucian scholar who
has devoted his life to
moral cultivation emanates
restraint and righteousness.

The sound of
the Dharma drum
echoing through
Mt. Cheongnyangsan,
flush with
pink lanterns
to celebrate
the birth of Buddha,
puts me at peace.

The woman's bent back and the man's sunburned arms
overlap with the vast salt flats.
My heart aches to see
the marks of long years of hard work.

A row of bamboo visible between the lattices of a sliding door
in a *hanok* reminds me of midsummer.

Just as I focus the camera on the beautiful sight of a line of women
in sun visors working in an onion patch,
a tractor sweeps by on the way to another field.
This is the busy life of a farming village.

An old boat, a mountain,
and a glimpse of the sea.

The view during a solitary
walk at dawn.
The moment is silent
but full of promise.
No other place—
not even the Maldives—
can compare to greeting
the morning on Wido Island
in the South Sea.

Another view of night seen from my house.
Seoul is truly a city that never sleeps.

The joy of Buddha's Birthday shows in the bright smiles
on children's faces.

I wish I could fly.
But I do not wish to wander aimlessly.
Sometimes I long to rest.
Now travel is both a beating of wings and a rest.
Because I have experienced a true journey,
and the beauty will live in my memory forever.

Letters from the Road

Experiencing one's own traditional arts and culture and writing a book about them is not an easy task for anyone. Nevertheless, you took the time to travel to every corner of the country and even came all the way to Japan to visit my museum. So it is with a glad heart that I congratulate you on the publication of *A Journey in Search of Korea's Beauty*, for which you experienced and endured so much. Studying your own culture, writing about the priceless cultural heritage that has been left to us by our ancestors, and introducing it to foreign and domestic readers alike is not only an act of love for one's own culture but a show of deep respect for other cultures as well.

I believe that the past is the foundation upon which the future is created. Therefore, I believe that the splendid achievement of your book will leave a lasting and meaningful impression. In addition, I hope that it will serve as a bridge between Korea and Japan, which share so much culture in common.

I will never forget the look of determination in your eyes, despite the subzero temperatures that turned your face red. It just makes me happy to know someone as fully committed as you are to serving the international community.

Jeon Yong-bok
Iwayama Lacquer Art Museum

You are never alone.
You say you will be together and want to be together.
Because you are pure. So you did not know you were already doing so.
You seem like a wise person who truly understands how to live for oneself.
Because loving culture is a good choice that means
cultivating and refining yourself.
In that spirit, you will brighten yourself and everything around you.
I am sure of this.
The people who love and care for you must be good people.
I want to praise them and tell them they made a fine choice.

Venerable Jeongnim
Gilsangsa Temple

There are so many different roads in the world. El Camino de Santiago, Jeju Olle, the Silk Road, the Noodle Road... the Tea Road!

The journey which began with making kimchi and scattering food to the spirits beside a pine tree on the bluff behind my house in Hongje-dong has led you to Unbuam, Baekheungam, the site of Hwangnyongsa Temple, the fog-shrouded tea fields of Seonamsa Temple... From Gurye to Seoul to Iksan, then Suncheon, Andong, Mungyeong... You have been on the road a long time. Your journey in search of Korea's beauty in the spirit of a young man's love for his country will come to be known as "The Yonsama Road."

I am happy to have undertaken that journey with you.
Many thanks!

Lee Hyo-jae
Hanbok designer

The Journey Ends

My journey in search of Korea's beauty is the most meaningful journey I have taken since becoming an actor. Everyone I met and all the experiences I had were unlike anyone and anything I had ever encountered before. I felt truly alive and filled with a passion and a drive I had never known before. It was the kind of journey that will remain with me forever. Every new experience moved me deeply and left me with something that went beyond just emotional impact, something that lingered and made me eager for the next leg of the journey. Before nature, before the deep spirit of art, before our enormous cultural heritage, I was but one equal soul. Now I think I understand why people take journeys. I returned home from my own journey with the joy of new connections and new experiences.

The start was rocky. There were times when the plan did not go as smoothly as I thought it would. Writing was far more difficult than I could ever have imagined, as was capturing good photographs. I feared I would not be able to complete the project well, and at times I even regretted undertaking it. But thanks to the meticulous care of the teachers I met on this journey, I was able to overcome those difficulties. Without their advice and encouragement, this book could never have been written. My teachers freely shared their knowledge and experience gained over many years, and I did my best to humbly accept what they had to offer and threw myself into experiencing all of it. The more I look at the material and the more I write, the more I begin to understand that which was so foggy to me before. My goal was to maintain a balance between writing down correct information, my teachers' stories, and my own impressions, but it was not so easy. As with any long journey, there was so much that happened, but in the end not all of those stories could be included.

During this journey, there were many people who stayed by my side from start to finish. If not for them, I cannot imagine that I would have taken even the first step. Because I took that first journey with them, now I believe I could do it any time on my own. I have the confidence that I could take off anywhere with only camera in hand and easily enjoy myself. Looking back, I realize that this journey gave new energy to my life, which had been lethargic and empty for some time, and in the future will help me to think deeply about the direction my life is going in. I feel like I have learned everything there is to know about life through this journey.

I look forward to setting off in silence along my path, not as an actor, but as a person.

I would like to once again convey my deepest gratitude and affection to everyone who helped me with this book: Lee Ja-eun, who made sure that the entire itinerary went according to plan; Venerable Jeongnim, who offered his perspective on culture and recommended many fine people; Lee Hyo-jae, who was the life of the party and made the journey a happy one; Hosan, the project manager, and Hwang Yong, the team leader, who both took on all the dirty work; Ho-il and Yeong-ho, the photographers who took great photos of me, and Nona, the editor who suffered on our behalf starting from the on-site work all the way up through post-production; and Pyo Jong-rok, who provided steadfast backing for this project.

Finally, to my family and the many people who have waited a long time for this book, I send you this postcard, filled with memories, straight from my heart.

Bae Yong Joon

Routes & Maps

route 1.

Seoul

Hyojae
Seongnagwon
Bugak Skyway
Gahoe-dong Hanok Village
Gyeongbokgung Palace
Sejong Center for the Performing Arts
Hangang River
National Museum of Korea

route 3.

Gyeonggi-do &
Gangwon-do Provinces

Jangjibang Paper Mill
Woljeongsa Temple
Manhae Village
Baekdamsa Temple
Mt. Seoraksan
Seoji Chogatteul Restaurant

route 2.

North Gyeongsang-do Province

Mungyeongyo Kilns
Mungyeong Saejae Mountain Pass
Cheongnyangsa Temple
Manhyujeong Pavilion
Mukgye Seowon Confucian Academy
Andong Hahoe Village

route 4.

South Jeolla-do Province

Sansuyu Village
Lee Jae-jong's Tea Farm
Ahn Hwa-ja's Studio
Seonamsa Temple
Shin Gwang-su's Tea Farm
Cheongmaesil Plum Farm

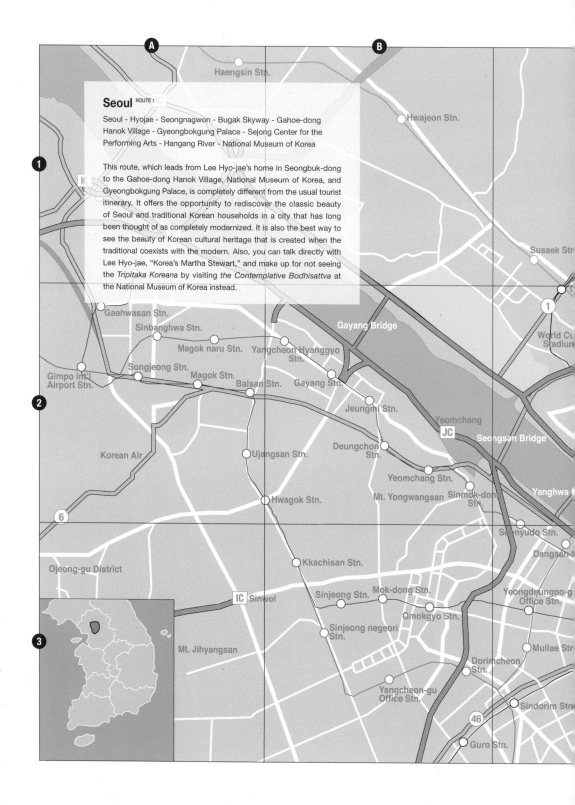

Seoul ROUTE 1 IC

Seoul - Hyojae - Seongnagwon - Bugak Skyway - Gahoe-dong
Hanok Village - Gyeongbokgung Palace - Sejong Center for the
Performing Arts - Hangang River - National Museum of Korea

This route, which leads from Lee Hyo-jae's home in Seongbuk-dong
to the Gahoe-dong Hanok Village, National Museum of Korea, and
Gyeongbokgung Palace, is completely different from the usual tourist
itinerary. It offers the opportunity to rediscover the classic beauty
of Seoul and traditional Korean households in a city that has long
been thought of as completely modernized. It is also the best way to
see the beauty of Korean cultural heritage that is created when the
traditional coexists with the modern. Also, you can talk directly with
Lee Hyo-jae, "Korea's Martha Stewart," and make up for not seeing
the *Tripitaka Koreana* by visiting *the Contemplative Bodhisattva* at
the National Museum of Korea instead.

Haengsin Stn.

Hwajeon Stn.

Susaek Str

Gaehwasan Stn.

Sinbanghwa Stn.

Gayang Bridge

World Cu
Stadiun

Magok naru Stn.   Yangcheon Hyanggyo
Stn.

Songjeong Stn.   Magok Stn.

Gimpo int'l
Airport Stn.   Balsan Stn.   Gayang Stn.

Jeungmi Stn.

Yeomchang
JC   Seongsan Bridge

Korean Air   Ujangsan Stn.   Deungchon
Stn.

Yanghwa

Yeomchang Stn.

Mt. Yongwangsan   Sinmok-don
Stn.

Hwagok Stn.   S anyudo Stn.

6   Dangsan

Ojeong-gu District   Kkachisan Stn.   Yeongdeungpo-g
Office Stn.

IC Sinwol   Sinjeong Stn.   Mok-dong Stn.

Omokgyo Stn.

Sinjeong negeori
Stn.   Mullae Str

Mt. Jihyangsan   Dorimcheon
Stn.

Yangcheon-gu
Office Stn.   Sindorim Stn

46

Guro Stn.

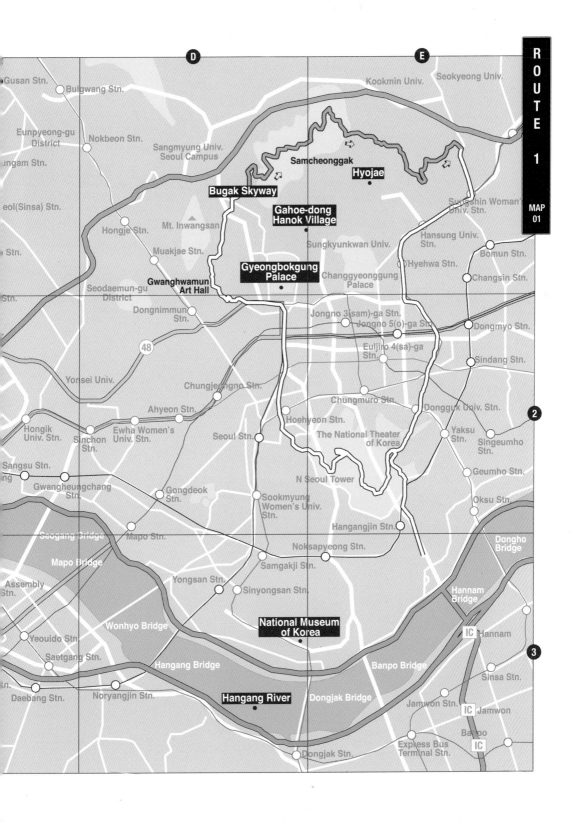

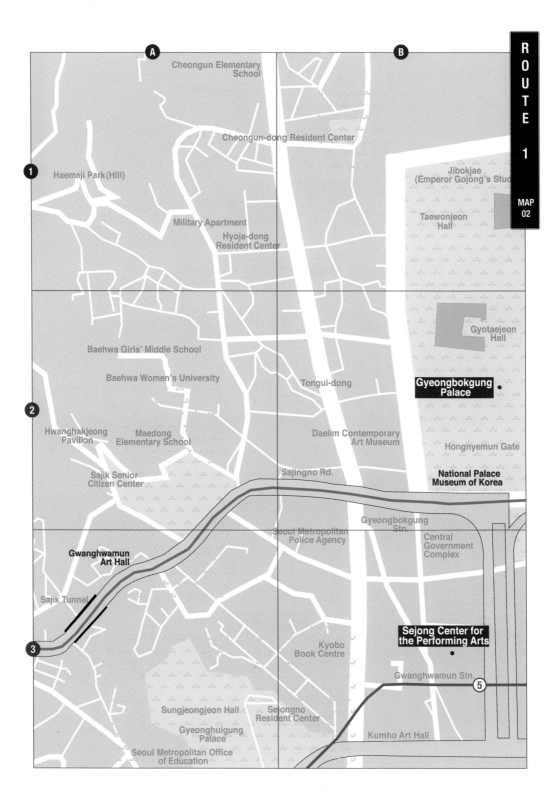

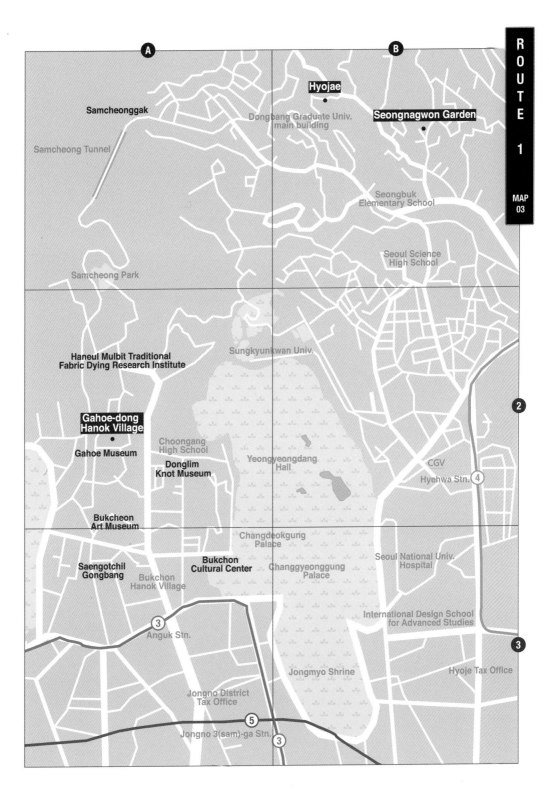

A

B

Hyojae

Samcheonggak

Dongbang Graduate Univ.
main building

Seongnagwon Garden

Samcheong Tunnel

Seongbuk
Elementary School

Seoul Science
High School

Samcheong Park

Haneul Mulbit Traditional
Fabric Dying Research Institute

Sungkyunkwan Univ.

2

Gahoe-dong
Hanok Village

Gahoe Museum

Choongang
High School

Yeongyeongdang
Hall

CGV

Donglim
Knot Museum

Hyehwa Stn. 4

Bukcheon
Art Museum

Changdeokgung
Palace

Saengotchil
Gongbang

Bukcheon
Hanok Village

Bukchon
Cultural Center

Changgyeonggung
Palace

Seoul National Univ.
Hospital

3

3
Anguk Stn.

International Design School
for Advanced Studies

3

Jongmyo Shrine

Hyoje Tax Office

Jongno District
Tax Office

5
Jongno 3(sam)-ga Stn.

3

Hyojae

Address

314-9 Seongbuk-dong, Seongbuk-gu

Telephone

02-720-5393

This is the workshop of Lee Hyo-jae, *hanbok* designer and *bojagi* artist, who also creates wedding *hanbok*.

Seongnagwon

Address

2-22 Seongbuk-dong, Seongbuk-gu

One of the last surviving Joseon Dynasty-era villas in Seoul, this was the home of Prince Imperial Ui, the son of King Gojong (the 26th king of the Joseon Dynasty and the first emperor of the Korean Empire).

Bugak Skyway

A scenic ten-kilometer drive that follows the ridgeline of Mt. Bugaksan from Jahamun Gate and over the Arirang Pass, it was opened in 1968 and takes approximately thirty minutes to complete.

Gahoe-dong Hanok Village

Address

31 Gahoe-dong, Jongno-gu

One of the streets in Seoul with the most well-preserved *hanok*, it is regarded as an ideal spot for taking photos. This street is the fifth of eight in Bukchon designated by the city of Seoul.

Gyeongbokgung Palace

Address

Sejongno1-ga, Jongno-gu

Telephone

02-3700-3900

Web site

http://www.royalpalace.go.kr/

Royal palace of the Joseon Dynasty and historical landmark #117.

Sejong Center for the Performing Arts

Address

81-3 Sejong-ro, Jongno-gu

Telephone

02-399-1111

Web site

http://www.sejongpac.or.kr

The largest arts and cultural complex in Seoul, the Sejong Center regularly hosts various concerts and exhibitions. The facilities within the complex include a large and small theater, three exhibition halls, a convention center, a conference hall, meeting rooms, a fountain, a deck and Samcheonggak, a traditional pavilion.

Hangang River

Flowing through the center of the Korean peninsula, the Hangang River originates in the Taebaek Mountains and ends at the Yellow Sea. The two major branches of the river, Bukhangang River and Namhangang River, converge in the city of Namyangju. This river valley has been regarded as a key location on the peninsula since the Three Kingdoms era.

National Museum of Korea

Address

135 Seobinggo-dong, Yongsan-gu

Telephone

02-2077-9000

Web site

http://www.museum.go.kr

The flagship museum of Korean art and history, the National Museum collects and preserves Korea's cultural heritage and exhibits it to the general public, in addition to researching and investigating relics and ancient ruins.

Samcheonggak

Address

330-115 Seongbuk-dong, Seongbuk-gu

Telephone

02-765-3700

A traditional cultural performance space in Seoul.

Bukchon Art Museum

Address
170-4 Gahoe-dong, Jongno-gu

Telephone
02-741-2296

Web site
http://www.bukchonartmuseum.com

An exhibition space that brings together the traditional and the modern, the Bukchon Art Museum is engaged in active cultural exchange in East Asia with its collection of over 2,850 pieces that includes both modern and ancient art from Korea and China.

Bukchon Cultural Center

Address
105 Gye-dong, Jongno-gu

This restored *hanok*—once the home of Min Hyeong-gi, who was Minister of Finance in 1921 during the Japanese occupation of Korea—is the typical style of *yangban* home built in Bukchon before the 1900s. In 2002, the building was restored to an urban dwelling as part of the redevelopment of Bukchon by the city of Seoul, and was used as the Bukchon Cultural Center. Currently, it serves as an information center for the history and cultural properties of Bukchon.

Haneul Mulbit Traditional Fabric Dyeing Research Institute

Address
35-167 Samcheong-dong, Jongno-gu

Telephone
011-729-9970

Web site
http://www.macart.co.kr

Visitors can learn about natural fabric dyeing, traditional Korean knots and other women's crafts.

Gahoe Museum

Address
11-103 Gahoe-dong, Jongno-gu

Telephone
02-741-0466

Web site
http://www.gahoemuseum.org

Housed in a traditional *hanok*, this private museum contains 250 folk paintings, 750 amulets, 150 classical books and 250 relics of folk culture, for a total collection of 1,500 pieces.

Gwanghwamun Art Hall

Address
284-1 Sajik-dong, Jongno-gu

Telephone
02-722-3416

Korea's first permanent traditional performing arts theater, located in Gwanghwamun.

Donglim Knot Museum

Address
11-7 Gahoe-dong, Jongno-gu

Telephone
02-3673-2778

Web site
http://www.shimyoungmi.com/

Visitors can view and experience traditional arts and crafts using decorative knots. The collection includes traditional accessories that incorporated decorative knots, such as *norigae* ornaments, belts and pouches, as well as the materials used to make the knots, from thread to cords and other accessories.

National Palace Museum of Korea

Address
1-57 Sejong-ro, Jongno-gu

Telephone
02-3701-7500

Web site
http://www.gogung.go.kr

The National Palace Museum houses artifacts and cultural properties from the palaces of the Joseon Dynasty. The museum also engages in publicity and education and collects and publishes research and scholarly writings on the royal artifacts.

Saengotchil Gongbang

Address
17-11 Anguk-dong, Jongno-gu

Telephone
02-735-5757

Lacquerware studio where lacquerware is displayed and visitors can try lacquerware painting.

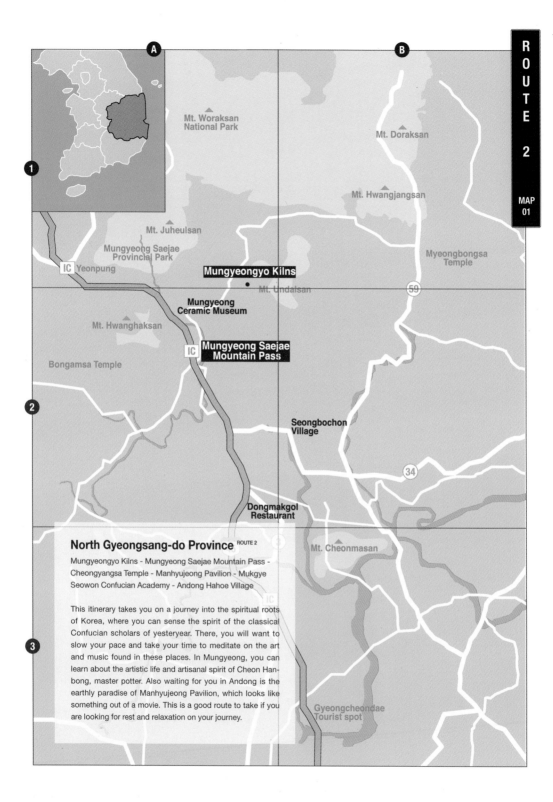

A

B

1

2

3

Mt. Woraksan
National Park

Mt. Doraksan

Mt. Hwangjangsan

Mt. Juheulsan

Mungyeong Saejae
Provincial Park

Myeongbongsa
Temple

IC Yeonpung

Mungyeongyo Kilns

• Mt. Undalsan

59

**Mungyeong
Ceramic Museum**

Mt. Hwanghaksan

IC **Mungyeong Saejae
Mountain Pass**

Bongamsa Temple

Seongbochon
Village

34

**Dongmakgol
Restaurant**

North Gyeongsang-do Province ROUTE 2

Mungyeongyo Kilns - Mungyeong Saejae Mountain Pass -
Cheongyangsa Temple - Manhyujeong Pavilion - Mukgye
Seowon Confucian Academy - Andong Hahoe Village

This itinerary takes you on a journey into the spiritual roots
of Korea, where you can sense the spirit of the classical
Confucian scholars of yesteryear. There, you will want to
slow your pace and take your time to meditate on the art
and music found in these places. In Mungyeong, you can
learn about the artistic life and artisanal spirit of Cheon Han-
bong, master potter. Also waiting for you in Andong is the
earthly paradise of Manhyujeong Pavilion, which looks like
something out of a movie. This is a good route to take if you
are looking for rest and relaxation on your journey.

Mt. Cheonmasan

IC

Gyeongcheondae
Tourist spot

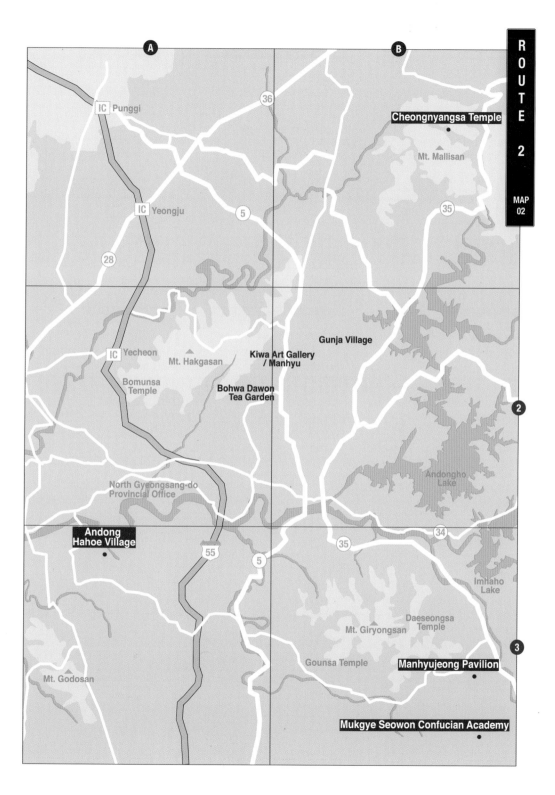

ROUTE 2

MAP 02

A

B

36

IC Punggi

IC Yeongju

5

28

Cheongnyangsa Temple

Mt. Mallisan

35

IC Yecheon

Mt. Hakgasan

Gunja Village

Kiwa Art Gallery
/ Manhyu

Bomunsa
Temple

Bohwa Dawon
Tea Garden

2

Andongho
Lake

North Gyeongsang-do
Provincial Office

Andong
Hahoe Village

34

55

5

35

Imhaho
Lake

Mt. Giryongsan

Daeseongsa
Temple

3

Gounsa Temple

Manhyujeong Pavilion

Mt. Godosan

Mukgye Seowon Confucian Academy

Mungyeongyo Kilns

Address
156-1 Dangpo-ri, Mungyeong-eup,
Mungyeong-si
Telephone
054-572-3090
Web site
www.문경도자기.com

Selected as one of Asia's leading cultural figures, artist Docheon Cheon Han-bong established this traditional pottery village to purse the artistic spirit of the common people.

Mungyeong Saejae Mountain Pass

Address
288-1 Sangcho-ri, Mungyeong-eup,
Mungyeong-si
Telephone
054-571-0709, 054-550-6421
Web site
http://saejae.mg21.go.kr

This place has been designated as National Scenic Spot #32.

Cheongnyangsa Temple

Address
Bugok-ri, Myeongho-myeon, Bonghwa-gun
Telephone
054-672-1446
Web site
www.cheongryangsa.org/

Nestled at the foot of Yeonhwabong Peak, Cheongnyangsa Temple was built by the Great Buddhist Master Wonhyo in the third year of the reign of Munmu of Silla (663 CE). At the time, it was the cradle of Silla Buddhism. The Yuribojeon Hall (Dharma Hall) has been designated as Tangible Cultural Asset No. 47 of North Gyeongsang-do Province.

Manhyujeong Pavilion

Address
1081 Mukgye-ri, Giran-myeon, Andong-si

This pavilion was built by Kim Gye-haeng, a prominent civil servant of the Joseon Dynasty, to spend his latter years. It has been designated as No. 173 on the list of cultural assets of North Gyeongsang-do Province.

Mukgye Seowon Confucian Academy

Address
735-1 Mukgye-ri, Giran-myeon, Andong-si
Telephone
054-851-6392

Mukgye Seowon is where memorial services are held for Bobaekdang Kim Gye-haeng and Eunggye Kim Ok-go. Located in the middle of a village not very far from the academy is the Kim family home, which includes Bobaekdang, a pavilion once used by Kim and nowadays used for ancestral memorial services.

Andong Hahoe Village

Address
749-1 Hahoe-ri, Pungcheon-myeon, Andong-si
Telephone
054-853-0109
Web site
www.hahoe.or.kr/

This important folk village was designated as Important Folklore Material No. 122.

Gunja Village

Address
25-1 Ocheon-ri, Waryong-myeon, Andong-si
Telephone
054-852-5414
Web site
www.gunjari.net

Gunja Village was settled five to six hundred years ago by Kim Hyo-ro of the Kim Clan of Gwangsan. The Geum clan of Bongwha, the descendants of a woman from the Kim clan, also settled there around the same time and continues to reside there today. Fronted by the blue waters of the Nakdonggang River, the village houses many cultural properties and has produced many famous people, on par with its long history.

Seongbochon Village

Address
23 Hogye-ri, Hogye-myeon, Mungyeong-si
Telephone
054-555-0001
Web site
www.sungbo.net/

This is a village where visitors can experience traditional culture firsthand. There are also many exhibits on display.

Dongmakgol Restaurant

Address
923-9 Mojeon-dong, Mungyeong-si
Telephone
054-556-8283

This restaurant serves local Korean dishes, including *mukbap* (acorn jelly on rice) and *yeongyang dolsotbap* (rice with medicinal foods in a stone bowl).

Bohwa Dawon Tea Garden

Address
Geumgye-ri, Seohu-myeon, Andong-si

Telephone
054-821-3572

This organic chrysanthemum farm is famous for its *hwanggukcha* tea. Visitors can sample and purchase chrysanthemum tea here.

Kiwa Art Gallery

Address
910 Taejang-ri, Seohu-myeon, Andong-si

Telephone
054-855-2267

Web site
http://kiwart.com/

Giwa art, or roof tile art, dating as far back as the Three Kingdoms period, can be viewed and purchased here.

Manhyu

Address
910 Taejang-ri, Seohu-myeon, Andong-si

Telephone
054-855-2268

Web site
http://manhue.com/

This is a traditional tea house located on the way to Bongjeongsa Temple. The name Manhyu means "a place to rest from ten thousand worldly desires." It is located inside an octagonal building made from pine.

Mungyeong Ceramic Museum

Address
360-10 Jiran-ri, Mungyeong-eup, Mungyeong-si

Telephone
054-550-6416

Web site
http://dojagi.mungyeong.net/

Mungyeong, which is famous for its ceramics, has been designated Intangible Cultural Property No. 10 of North Chungcheong-do Province in recognition of the many pottery craftsmen it as produced, and because of the many kiln sites that have been found where *buncheong ware* was produced since the early Joseon Dynasty.

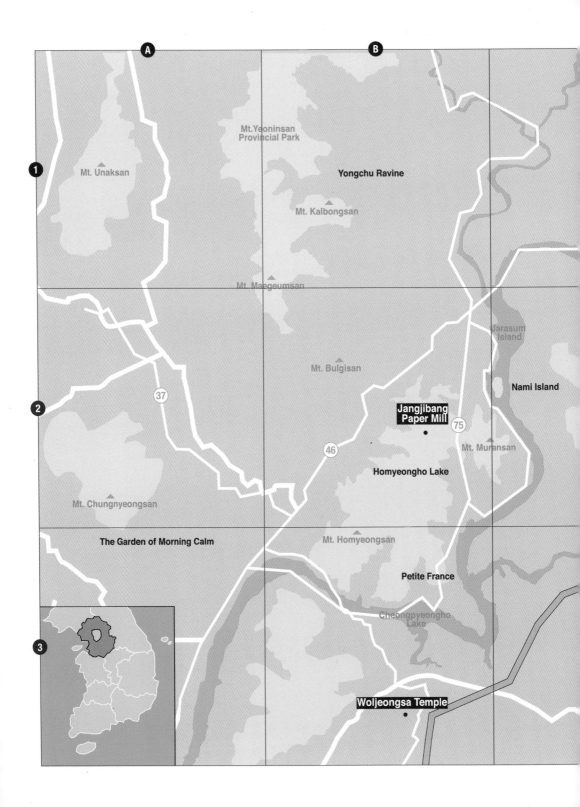

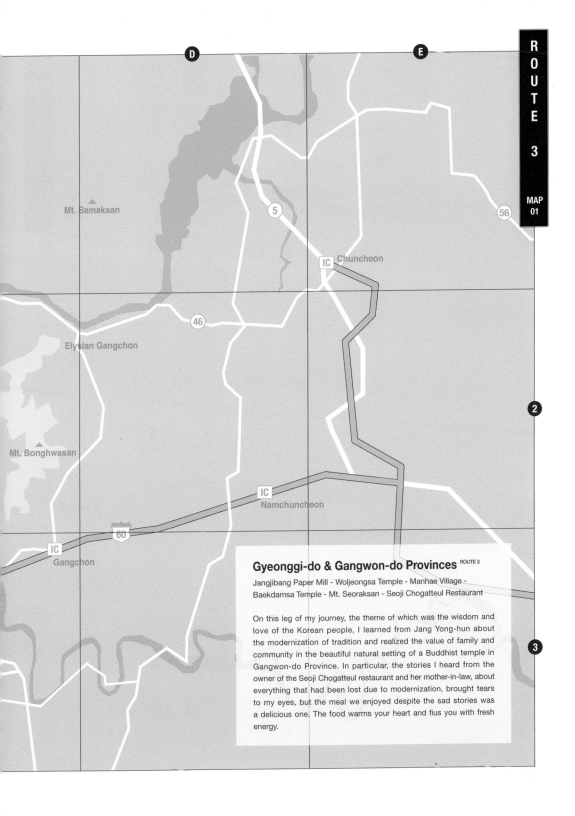

Mt. Samaksan

5

56

IC Chuncheon

46

Elysian Gangchon

Mt. Bonghwasan

2

IC
Namchuncheon

60

IC
Gangchon

3

Gyeonggi-do & Gangwon-do Provinces ROUTE 3

Jangjibang Paper Mill - Woljeongsa Temple - Manhae Village -
Baekdamsa Temple - Mt. Seoraksan - Seoji Chogatteul Restaurant

On this leg of my journey, the theme of which was the wisdom and
love of the Korean people, I learned from Jang Yong-hun about
the modernization of tradition and realized the value of family and
community in the beautiful natural setting of a Buddhist temple in
Gangwon-do Province. In particular, the stories I heard from the
owner of the Seoji Chogatteul restaurant and her mother-in-law, about
everything that had been lost due to modernization, brought tears
to my eyes, but the meal we enjoyed despite the sad stories was
a delicious one. The food warms your heart and fius you with fresh
energy.

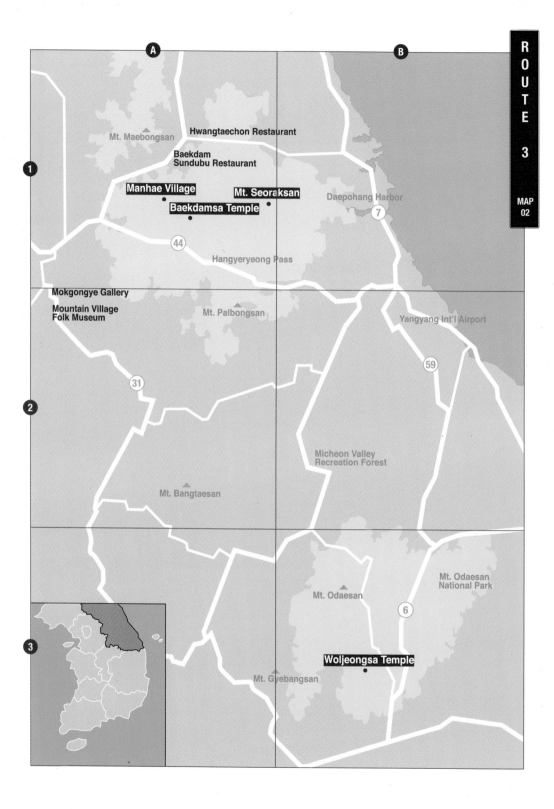

A

B

Mt. Maebongsan

Hwangtaechon Restaurant

Baekdam
Sundubu Restaurant

Manhae Village

Mt. Seoraksan

Daepohang Harbor

Baekdamsa Temple

7

1

44

Hangyeryeong Pass

Mokgongye Gallery

Mountain Village
Folk Museum

Mt. Palbongsan

Yangyang Int'l Airport

59

31

2

Micheon Valley
Recreation Forest

Mt. Bangtaesan

Mt. Odaesan
National Park

Mt. Odaesan

6

3

Woljeongsa Temple

Mt. Gyebangsan

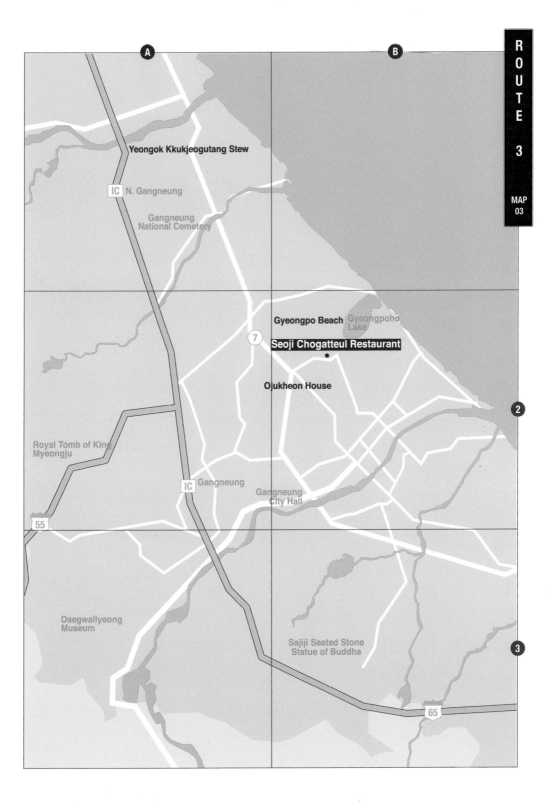

A

B

Yeongok Kkukjeogutang Stew

IC N. Gangneung

Gangneung
National Cemetery

Gyeongpo Beach Gyeongpoho
Lake

7 Seoji Chogatteul Restaurant

Ojukheon House

2

Royal Tomb of King
Myeongju

IC Gangneung

Gangneung
City Hall

55

Daegwallyeong
Museum

Sajiji Seated Stone
Statue of Buddha

3

65

Jangjibang Paper Mill

Address

1671-1 Sangcheon-ri, Cheongpyeong-myeon, Gapyeong-gun, Gyeonggi-do Province

Telephone

031-581-0457

Jangjibang means, "Where the Jang family makes paper." They grow their own mulberry trees for making traditional Korean paper.

Weoljeongsa Temple

Address

63 Dongsan-ri, Jinbu-myeon, Pyeongchang-gun, Gangwon-do Province

Telephone

033-339-6800

Founded in 643 by the Silla monk Jajang, this temple is located on Mt. Odaesan. The temple's cultural assets include an octagonal nine-story stone pagoda that was built to enshrine relics of the Buddha, and an epistle commemorating the renovation of Sangwonsa Temple at Mt. Odaesan.

Manhae Village

Address

1136-5 Yongdae-ri, Buk-myeon, Inje-gun, Gangwon-do Province

Telephone

033-462-2303

Web site

www.manhae.net

Manhae Village was built to honor the poet Manhae Han Yong-un and his thoughts on literature, freedom, progress and the Korean spirit.

Baekdamsa Temple

Address

690 Yongdae-ri, Buk-myeon, Inje-gun, Gangwon-do Province

Telephone

033-462-6969 / 033-462-5565

Web site

www.baekdamsa.org

According to legend, Baekdamsa (One Hundred Walls) Temple, was named for the one hundred small stone walls that stretch from the temple to Daecheongbong Peak of Mt. Seoraksan. Founded by the monk Jajang during the reign of Queen Jin-deok, 28th ruler of the Silla Dynasty, in 647 CE, the temple was first called Hangyesa, and is home to National Treasure No. 1182, the Wooden Amityus Buddha Statue.

Mt. Seoraksan

Address

713 Seorak-dong, Sokcho-si, Gangweon Province

Telephone

033-636-7700

Web site

http://seorak.knps.or.kr

Mt. Seoraksan is the third highest mountain in South Korea, after Mt. Hallasan and Mt. Jirisan. Located in the middle of the Baekdu Mountain Range, it has been called by different names, including Mts. Seolsan, Seolbongsan, and Seolhwasan, which all mean "sacred and noble mountain."

Seoji Chogatteul Restaurant

Address

259 Nangok-dong, Gangneung-si, Gangwon-do Province

Telephone

033-646-4430

This restaurant serves traditional Korean food prepared according to the recipes of the scholarly Jo family of Seoji Village, which have been designated as an important cultural property.

Nami Island

Address

198 Bingha-ri, Namsan-myeon, Chuncheon-si, Gangwon-do Province

Telephone

031-580-8114

Web site

www.namisum.com

This half-moon shaped island in the Northern Hangang River was not originally an island. It was created after the area was flooded with the building of Cheongpyeong Dam. Because of its lyrical appearance, the island is a popular location for film and photography, and it is most famous for the filming of *Winter Sonata*.

Gapyeong Yongchu Ravine

Address

Seungan-ri, Gapyeong-eup, Gapyeong-gun, Gyeonggi-do Province

Telephone

031-580-2066 (Information Center)

This ravine begins in Mt. Kalbongsan and flows around Ongnyeobong Peak. The ravine is twenty-four kilometers long and includes nine scenic outlooks.

Homyeongho Lake

Address

Cheongpyeong-myeon, Gapyeong-gun, Gyeonggi-do Province

Telephone

031-580-2514

This manmade lake was built at an elevation of 1755 feet (535 meters) on Mt. Homyeongsan. The scenic landscape with its beautiful mountain and the wide lake make it the second of Gapyeong's eight scenic sites.

Petite France

Address
616 Goseong-ri, Cheongpyeong-myeon,
Gapyeong-gun, Gyeonggi-do Province

Telephone
031-584-8200

Web site
www.pfcamp.com

This French village was built around the theme of
The Little Prince.

Baekdam Sundubu Restaurant

Address
568 Yongdae-ri, Buk-myeon, Inje-gun,
Gangwon-do Province

Telephone
033-462-9395

This restaurant specializes in *sundubu*, soft
tofu. The restaurant is famous for the tofu made
fresh on-site, fermented soybean paste made
from beans grown locally and dishes made with
hwangtae, half-dried Alaskan pollack.

Hwangtaechon Restaurant

Address
82 Yongdae-ri, Buk-myeon, Inje-gun,
Gangwon-do Province

Telephone
033-462-3109

This restaurant specializes in *hwangtae*, half-dried
Alaskan pollack, which is prepared on-site on fish
drying racks located right next to the restaurant.

Mokgongye Gallery

Address
430 Sangdong-ri, Inje-eup, Inje-gun,
Gangwon-do Province

Telephone
033-463-2233

This gallery collects woodcrafts produced all
around Inje County so they can be viewed in one
place.

Mountain Village Folk Museum

Address
415 Sangdong-ri, Inje-eup, Inje-gun,
Gangwon-do Province

Telephone
033-460-2085

Web site
www.inje.gangwon.kr/home/museum

This museum has a collection of around three
hundred items related to the folk life of people
living in mountain villages in Gangwon-do
Province.

Ojukheon House

Address
201 Jukheon-dong, Gangneung-si,
Gangwon-do Province

This wooden structure was built in the mid-
Joseon Dynasty. It is currently one of the oldest
residential buildings still standing in Korea, and it
was the birthplace of Yulgok, a famous scholar
and politician of the Joseon Dynasty.

Gyeongpo Beach

Address
Gangneung-si, Gangwon-do Province

Telephone
033-640-5129

Four miles (six kilometers) of sand surrounded by
pine trees, this beach is bounded by Gyeongpo
Lake on one side and the sea on the other.

Yeongok Kkukjeogutang

Address
69-7 Bangnae-ri, Yeonggok-myeon,
Gangneung-si, Gangwon-do Province

Telephone
033-661-1494

This restaurant specializes in a spicy stew made
from red chili pepper, fermented soybean paste,
mushrooms, vegetables and a freshwater fish
called *kkukjeogu* (floating goby) that is caught in
the rivers of Gangwon-do Province.

The Garden of Morning Calm

Address
255 Haenghyeon-ri, Sang-myeon,
Gapyeong-gun, Gyeonggi-do Province

Telephone
1544-6703

Web site
www.morningcalm.co.kr

This arboretum does not simply collect flora but
arranges it with the highest attention to Korean
aesthetics. Twenty gardens are organized
according to different themes.

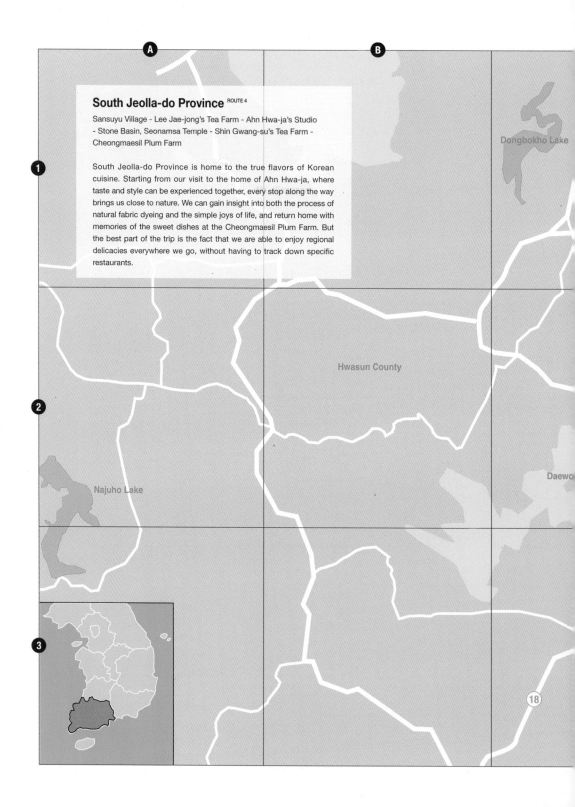

South Jeolla-do Province ROUTE 4

Sansuyu Village - Lee Jae-jong's Tea Farm - Ahn Hwa-ja's Studio
- Stone Basin, Seonamsa Temple - Shin Gwang-su's Tea Farm -
Cheongmaesil Plum Farm

South Jeolla-do Province is home to the true flavors of Korean cuisine. Starting from our visit to the home of Ahn Hwa-ja, where taste and style can be experienced together, every stop along the way brings us close to nature. We can gain insight into both the process of natural fabric dyeing and the simple joys of life, and return home with memories of the sweet dishes at the Cheongmaesil Plum Farm. But the best part of the trip is the fact that we are able to enjoy regional delicacies everywhere we go, without having to track down specific restaurants.

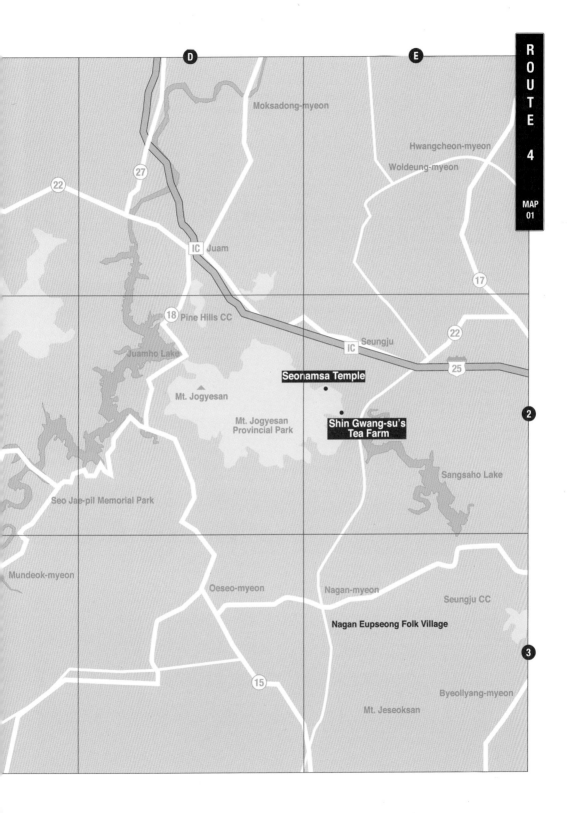

D

E

Moksadong-myeon

Hwangcheon-myeon

Woldeung-myeon

22

27

IC Juam

17

18 Pine Hills CC

Seungju

22

IC

25

Juamho Lake

Seonamsa Temple

Mt. Jogyesan

2

Mt. Jogyesan
Provincial Park

Shin Gwang-su's
Tea Farm

Sangsaho Lake

Seo Jae-pil Memorial Park

Mundeok-myeon

Oeseo-myeon

Nagan-myeon

Seungju CC

3

Nagan Eupseong Folk Village

15

Byeollyang-myeon

Mt. Jeseoksan

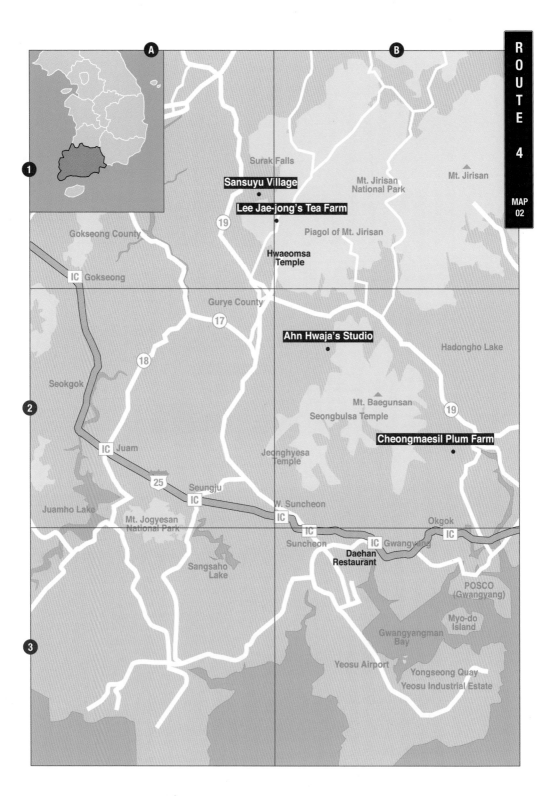

A
B
1

Surak Falls

Sansuyu Village

Lee Jae-jong's Tea Farm

Mt. Jirisan
National Park

Mt. Jirisan

Piagol of Mt. Jirisan

Gokseong County

(19)

Hwaeomsa
Temple

IC Gokseong

Gurye County

(17)

Ahn Hwaja's Studio

Hadongho Lake

(18)

Seokgok

Mt. Baegunsan

(19)

2

Seongbulsa Temple

Cheongmaesil Plum Farm

IC Juam

Jeonghyesa
Temple

25

Seungju

IC

Juamho Lake

Mt. Jogyesan
National Park

W. Suncheon

IC

Okgok

IC

IC

Suncheon

IC Gwangyang

IC

Sangsaho
Lake

Daehan
Restaurant

POSCO
(Gwangyang)

Myo-do
Island

Gwangyangman
Bay

3

Yeosu Airport

Yongseong Quay

Yeosu Industrial Estate

Sansuyu Village

Address

Sugi-ri, Sandong-myeon, Gurye-gun

Telephone

061-783-1039

The village is named after the *sansuyu* (dogwood) trees that surround the entire village. Tourists flock there in mid-March to see the dogwood trees in full bloom.

Lee Jae-jong's Tea Farm

Address

528 Sanbaragi, Tapjeong-ri, Sandong-myeon, Gurye-gun

Telephone

061-781-6685

This tea farm doubles as a research association for traditional tea culture. It is famous for its wild tea fields. Located in Sansuyu Village, visitors can stop by the Sanbaragi Cafe.

Ahn Hwa-ja's Studio

Address

429 Supyeong-ri, Ganjeon-myeon, Gurye-gun

Telephone

061-781-3031

This is the home of Ahn Hwa-ja, a master of natural fabric dyeing.

Seonamsa Temple

Address

802 Jukhak-ri, Seungju-eup, Suncheon-si

Telephone

061-754-5247

Web site

www.seonamsa.co.kr

A thickly forested temple of the Taego Order, many monks come to meditate in its buildings, which are open to many different practices.

Shin Gwang-su's Tea Farm

Address

660-1 Jukhak-ri, Seungju-eup, Suncheon-si

Telephone

061-754-5235

Web site

www.jagsul.com

Located at the foot of Mt. Jogyesan, this tea farm is an excellent location for viewing the surrounding sites while tasting tea.

Cheongmaesil Plum Farm

Address

414 Dosa-ri, Dap-myeon, Gwangyang-si

Telephone

061-772-4066

This farm specializes in developing and manufacturing food products made from *maesil*.

Daehan Restaurant

Address

Eumnae-ri, Gwangyang-eup, Gwangyang-si

Telephone

061-763-0095

This family-owned restaurant has been serving charcoal-grilled bulgogi, according to a traditional local recipe, for over forty years. The meat is barbecued using charcoal, brass braziers and copper grates.

Nagan Eupseong Folk Village

Address

Dongnae-ri, Nagan-myeon, Suncheon-si

Nagan Eupseong is a walled castle town located near the city of Suncheon. Built in the traditional style of Korean castle towns, Nagan Eupseong is surrounded by a fortress wall and intersected by the main village road that runs east-west, from one end of the wall to the other. Another road runs perpendicular to the main road, connecting the center of the village with the southern fortress gate. This type of building and road design was created to make the town fully functional as a self-contained city.

Hwaeomsa Temple

Address

Hwangjeon-ri, Masan-myeon, Gurye-gun

Hwaeomsa is a Baekje-era temple located in Mt. Jirisan National Park. The temple buildings were expanded greatly during the Silla Dynasty, and the contents of the temple have been designated as National Treasures.

TIP
INDEX

| 1. Elizabeth Keith | A British artist born in Scotland in 1887, Keith taught herself how to paint, having received a traditional girls' schooling that did not encourage the development of her artistic talents. In 1915, she traveled to Japan with her sister, Elspet, and her sister's husband, Robertson Scott. While she was living abroad, her artwork began to be deeply influenced by the cultures and lifestyles of East Asia. In 1919, she and her sister went to Korea, where they stayed for three months. Afterward, Keith's paintings and her sister's writings were published in a book entitled *Old Korea*: The *Land of Morning Calm*. | 21 |

| 2. *eomnamu* (Kalopanax tree) | The Kalopanax tree (*Kalopanax septemlobus*) is known by various names in Korean: *eumnamu*, *eommok*, and *gaedureup namu* in a regional dialect. The tree can grow up to eighty-two feet (twenty-five meters) high, and has large, thick branches. Yellowish-green flowers bloom in July and August, and the fruit of the tree, which is round and black, ripens in October. The tree is native to northeast Asia and is found in Korea, Japan, China, and other parts of the region. According to a traditional custom, farmers in the countryside stick the branches of the Kalopanax tree on their front gates to prevent malicious spirits from entering. | 26 |

| 3. *songjuk dugyeonju* | This traditional liquor has been passed down for over three hundred years by the head family of the Jo clan of Changnyeong. A medicinal liquor brewed from a mixture of bamboo leaf, pine needles and five different grains, the flavor is a refined balance of astringency and the delicate scent of pine. | 26 |

| 4. *motbap* | Rice seedlings are called *mo* in Korean, therefore, *motbap* refers to the rice eaten in the field during the busy planting season. | 26 |

| 5. *nudeok namul* | Also called *goreume namul*, these fresh sea greens are harvested from the beaches of Simgok-ri Village in the township of Gangdong-myeon near the city of Gangneung in Gangwon-do Province, on the east coast of Korea. Originally named *gorimae*, this edible seaweed can be eaten raw. As with other types of laver, the *gorimae* is rinsed clean, hung on bamboo frames and dried for several hours in direct sunlight. The dried *gorimae* is then brushed with perilla oil and lightly toasted over a fire, then eaten with rice. Fresh *gorimae* can also be used as an ingredient in *doenjang jjigae* (soybean paste stew). | 31 |

| 6. *dolnamul* | *Dolnamul* is a wild stonecrop (*Sedum sarmentosum*), a perennial variety of dicots (flowering plants with two embryonic leaves), found in the Korean mountains. | 31 |

| 7. *nongmak* | *Nongmak* (farm huts) are simple structures built near fields and rice paddies where farmers can seek shelter from the sun or take breaks while farming. | 31 |

| 8. *jeonggwa* | *Jeonggwa* is a generic term for a traditional confection that is made by preserving various fruits, ginger, lotus root, carrots or ginseng in honey or sugar. | 37 |

| 9. *jeongbuin* | *Jeongbuin*, which translates roughly as "noblewoman," was a title bestowed upon the wives of third- and fourth-rank civil and military officials. | 37 |

02. Kimchi

1. *jwajong* Also called *notgeureut* and *yugi* in Korean, these bowls are made by heating an alloy of tin and copper over a flame and hammering the metal into shape with a mallet. The city of Anseong in Gyeonggi-do Province is renown for its high-quality traditional metalwork. 53

2. *bangjja* *Jwajong* (seated bell) is used to signal the start of a service in Buddhist temples. A monk strikes the bell while seated, hence the name. 53

03. *Hanbok* and Housekeeping

1. *doryeon* The hem of a jacket or coat, *doryeon* also refers to the curve in the fabric at the bottom of a garment. 71

2. *dongjeong* The long white strip of fabric or paper trim inserted into the top of a jacket or coat collar. 71

3. *git* The collar of a jacket, or neckband. 71

4. *honghwa* Safflower (*Carthamus tinctorius*), also known in Korean as *itkkot*, is an herbaceous, thistle-like biennial plant. The petals are plucked early in the morning, while they are still wet with dew and dried. The dried petals are called *honghwa* and can be used in the treatment of gynecological disorders, menstrual cramps and stomach problems. The fruit of the plant can be pressed for oil. 72

5. *buncheong* A traditional gray to charcoal gray stoneware that is decorated with a white slip and glazed before firing, *buncheong* ware can be traced back to the origin of inlaid celadon. It is known for its practical forms characterized by an energetic, bohemian style, as well as the variety of ways in which it can be decorated. 84

6. *bapjubal* These lidded brass rice bowls are rectilineal in form, narrowing slightly at the base and wider at the top than at the bottom. 92

04. Black Lacquer

1. *Mugu jeonggwang daedarani gyeong* (Pure Light Dharani Sutra) The Pure Light Dharani Sutra is the world's oldest woodblock print, dating back to the Unified Silla kingdom. Three inches (8 centimeters) in width and 244 inches (620 centimeters) in length, the woodblock print was found inside the three-story stone pagoda, called *seokgatap*, at Bulguksa Temple in Gyeongju. It is believed that the sutra was printed from a woodblock at some point between 700-751 CE. The condition of the paper and the features of the reliquary confirm that the typeset is from the Silla era, which makes this a valuable relic that demonstrates how advanced Korean printing technology was at the time. This sutra is designated as National Treasure No. 126 and is currently housed at the National Museum of Korea. 126

| 2. *saengchil* | *Saengchil* is the fresh sap of the lacquer tree, extracted by cutting lines into the bark and collecting the grayish milky white sap that oozes out. The sap contains the compound urushiol, as well as moisture and trace amounts of latex and laccase. As the fresh sap of the lacquer tree lacks the gloss of processed lacquer and dries too quickly to be used for varnish, the sap is first processed according to its intended use. As oxidization causes the lacquer sap to turn its characteristic shade of black, the sap is stirred and beaten until it turns black, after which it is stored at 100-113°F (38-45°C). | 131 |

05. Temple Stay

1. *sumidan Altar*	*Sumidan* Altar is a special pedestal built to enshrine statues and images of Buddha.	137
2. *gasa* (saffron robe)	Derived from the Sanskrit word "Kāṣāya," referring to the brown or saffron dye traditionally used to dye Buddhist robes, *gasa* is the name of the square "saffron" robes worn by Buddhist monks and nuns in Korea. In Buddhism, there are five primary colors, known as *jeongsaek*: blue, yellow, red, black and white. Because monks and nuns are traditionally prohibited from dyeing their clothes one of these primary colors, their clothing came to be known as *bujeongsaek* (non-primary colored). The dyed fabric is cut and sewn into a rectangular shape, such that a bean placed inside would roll about in all directions without stopping. In warmer countries, like India, only the "saffron" robes are worn, but in the temperate region of northeast Asia, the robe is worn over a set of garments that completely cover the body.	138
3. *jangsam* (monastic garments)	The *jangsam* is the garment worn by Korean Buddhist monks and nuns, characterized by its long length and voluminous sleeves. The garment originated in China and was brought to Korea during the Three Kingdoms period along with the introduction of Buddhism. The term *jangsam* is also used to refer to the formal dress worn by women in the Joseon Dynasty.	138
4. *unsu napja* (cloud and water monks)	*Unsu napja* is a figurative term used to refer to itinerant monks and nuns who travel from temple to temple in search of different masters in order to reach enlightenment.	138
5. *Jaba hamgyeong* (*Samyukta Agama*)	The *Jaba hamgyeong* (*Samyukta Agama*, "Connected Discourses") is the most fundamental of the four extant collections of Buddhist scriptures. The others include the *Jangaham* (*Dirgha Agama*, "Long Discourses"), the *Jungaham* (*Madhyama Agama*, "Middle-length Discourses"), and the *Jeungil aham* (*Ekottara Agama*, "Increased by One Discourses").	146
6. *baru gongyang*	*Baru gongyang* refers to the meal eaten by Buddhist monks and nuns. *Baru* is the name of the bowl, and *gongyang* is the name of the meal. The meal setting consists of four bowls: the largest holds rice; the second largest, soup; the third, clear water, and the smallest, a side dish. The soup and rice are both served in exact amounts, neither too much nor too little. Proper etiquette requires rinsing the rice, soup and side dish bowls with the water in the third bowl, drinking the rinse water, and rewrapping the dishes.	160

1. Seon (Zen) Buddhism	Zen is a sect of Buddhism that is said to have been inspired by the Flower Sermon, in which Buddha gathered his disciples together for a Dharma talk, only to remain completely silent while twirling a flower. The only one of his disciples to correctly interpret what this meant was Mahakasyapa. Unlike non-Zen sects that emphasize study of Buddhist scriptures, Zen Buddhism emphasizes the transmission of thought through intuition and experience. Zen Buddhism was transmitted to Korea in 784 by a monk named Doui who brought it over from Tang Dynasty in China.	175
2. *Sungyu eokbul*	For five hundred years, the official policy of the Joseon Dynasty was *Sungyu eokbul*, "Promote Confucianism, Suppress Buddhism." An early-Joseon Dynasty scholar named Jeong Dojeon wrote a critique of Buddhism called *Bulssi japbyeon* (*Buddha's Nonsense*), which refuted Buddhism altogether. When the Joseon Dynasty was founded, the hereditary nobility of the former Goryeo Dynasty were in collusion with Buddhism. Because these former Goryeo nobles sought to prevent the founding of the new dynasty by wielding their vested rights, Taejo, the founder of the Joseon Dynasty, adopted a strict policy of anti-Buddhism. The privileges that had been continuously extended to Buddhist monks and temples since the Goryeo Dynasty were abolished, and the temples that were once located within the walled cities were packed up and moved deep into the mountains.	187
3. *dolhwak*	*Dolhwak* are small stone mortars, or stones carved to resemble mortars.	193
4. *Dongdasong*	*Dongdasong* was written in the late Joseon Dynasty by the Venerable Choui, who contributed greatly to the revival of tea culture in Korea by incorporating tea into Zen meditation. The title of the book means "Ode to the Tea of the East," i.e. Korea (from the perspective of China). Ven. Choui wrote this poetic exposition of the Korean tea ceremony in 1837 at the request of Haegeodoin Hong Hyeon-ju, the son-in-law of King Jeongjo. The thirty-one stanzas of the poem cover the history of tea, the many varieties of tea plants, the health benefits of tea, the way tea is made, the areas where tea is produced and the different qualities of those teas.	197
5. *yeomsaeng singmul* (salt / halophyte plants)	*Yeomsaeng*, or salt plants, grow in the salty soil near the ocean, salt lakes and other salt-producing areas. These plants include seaweeds and sea grasses. The cells of the plants have a high saline content, which enables them to exert osmotic pressure on the soil to draw in more water.	198

07. Pottery

1. *dawan*	*Dawan* started out as a roughly made bowl found in the homes of the lower or working classes in Korea, but it later came to be used for drinking tea. The finest example of this *dawan* was found during the excavation of Anapji, a pond located in the palace complex of ancient Silla. Called *Eonjeong yeongmyeong baekto bunjang togi dawan*, the bowl was made from white earthenware clay decorated with slip. Many different types of *dawan* were passed down over the years, including the black glazed *heugyu dawan* from the Goryeo Dynasty and the white porcelain *baekja dawan* of the Joseon Dynasty.	203

2. *duduok dawan*	The lightly multicolored *duduok dawan* has a flared rim and a slightly concave curve in the middle. The foot is left unglazed, revealing the color of the local clay. Also, the glaze is allowed to drip down and thicken around the foot, which is another one of the trademarks of this style.	205
3. *bunin dawan*	The rim of the *bunin dawan* juts out slightly, while the sides are convex. The bowl is heavily coated inside and out with a white slip, and designs can be carved into the unglazed parts to reveal the red clay beneath.	205
4. Gimhae *dawan*	Known for its bold appearance, the Gimhae *dawan* is characterized by the four small feet that flare out at the base and the scratch marks that cover the entire body of the bowl, as if raked with fingernails.	205
5. *bongtong*	The large furnace at the very front of a traditional Korean kiln, the *bongtong* plays the most important role in building up the temperature of a wood-fired kiln.	215
6. *Iphak dawan* (Standing Crane Tea Bowl)	Tea bowl decorated with an image of a crane.	222
7. *jato*	Highly pure kaolin clay.	224
8. *doto*	A collective term for the clay used as the raw material for making pottery, *doto* has a reddish cast to it.	224

08. Hwangnyongsa and Mireuksa Temple Sites

1. *Samguk yusa* (*Memorabilia of the Three Kingdoms*)	*Samguk yusa* is a history of the Three Kingdoms period in Korea that was compiled by the Buddhist monk Iryeon at Ingaksa Temple in 1281, during the seventh year of the reign of King Chungnyeol of the Goryeo Dynasty. The book contains the rise and fall of Gojoseon (2333 BCE-108 BCE) and other ancient kingdoms, myths, legends, religious texts, historical accounts, the royal lineage and chronology of the Three Kingdoms and the Gaya Confederacy, records related to Buddhism, tales of high Buddhist priests and the deeds of Buddhist monks. Though it was written from a Buddhist perspective centered on Silla, it is still important source material for ancient historical research, along with *Samguk sagi*. The book is also an important resource for studies of Korean language and literature due to the fourteen *hyangga* poems written in the *idu* style, in which Chinese characters are incorporated into Korean sentence structure (rather than following Chinese grammar). In 2003, a copy of the book, which contains volumes 3-5 of the original, printed in the early Joseon Dynasty was designated as National Treasure No. 306; a later copy, which contains volumes 1-5, was designated as National Treasure No. 306-2.	234
2. Tadao Ando	Born in Osaka, Japan on September 13, 1941, Tadao Ando (安藤忠雄) is a world-famous Japanese architect. After graduating from high school, he traveled all around the world, during which he was inspired by the works of Le Corbusier, a French architect from Switzerland, and began to study architecture. In 1969, Ando established the firm Tadao Ando Architects & Associates and won the Annual Prize from the Architectural Institute of Japan for his "Row House in Sumiyoshi." His body of work is characterized by a sense of peace and reverence in balance with nature. His best known works include the Suntory Museum in Osaka, the Nariwa Museum in Okayama Prefecture and the Church of the Light in Ibaraki, Osaka Prefecture.	234

3. *Hwangnamppang* — A local pastry invented in the neighborhood of Hwangnam-dong in the city of Gyeongju in 1939, this was the first instance of a sweetened red bean paste being used as a filling for a flour-based dough. — 237

4. *beomjong* (temple bell) — The *beomjong*, or Buddhist temple bell, is struck to summon people to the temple or to announce the time. The bell is also called *gyeongjong*, *dangjong* and *jojong* in Korean. It is believed that the moment one hears the bell, all worldly cares can be shed. Korean temple bells are so unique among Buddhist bells around the world that they have even been given the scientific name *Hangukjong* ("Korean bell"). Bells from the Silla period have been recognized as particularly outstanding. — 238

5. *Bulguk jeongto* (Pure Land Buddhism) — *Jeongto* (Pure Land) is where the Buddha resides. It is also known as the sacred Land of Bliss that can only be reached through enlightenment. In Mahayana Buddhism, the Buddha transmitted many different teachings in order to save all sentient beings, resulting in the creation of the paradise known as *Bulguk jeongto*, or Pure Land Buddhism. — 242

6. monk Wonhyo — A Buddhist monk from the Silla Dynasty, Wonhyo was on his way to study Buddhism in China when a sudden rainstorm forced him to take shelter in a cave. Overcome with thirst, Wonhyo reached out in the dark for what he thought was a gourd filled with fresh water. In the morning, he discovered that the cave was a tomb, and that he had drunk from a human skull filled with brackish water. The experience made him realize that purity and impurity are an illusion, and that the human mind can transform reality. Thus enlightened, he abandoned his journey to China and returned home. He spent the rest of his life working to popularize Buddhist thought. — 245

7. Princess Yoseok — Yoseok was the second daughter of King Muyeol, the 29th king of the Silla Dynasty. Yoseok had a relationship with Wonhyo and gave birth to a son named Seol Chong. — 245

8. King Mu — King Mu (? - 641) was the 30th king of Baekje. His name was Jang, and his nickname was Seodong. He maintained a policy of friendship with the Sui and Tang Dynasties of China in order to hold back the southward advancement of Goguryeo, and he also launched frequent attacks on Silla. In 627, he sent the Buddhist monk Gwalleuk to Japan with books on Buddhism, astronomy, geography and history. In the later years of his reign, he was given to self-indulgence and extravagance, including frequent civil engineering projects, which contributed to the fall of Baekje. — 246

9. *hyangga* — *Hyangga* are Silla-era poems written using the system known as *hyangchal* or *idu*, in which Chinese characters are incorporated into Korean sentence structure. They first appeared during the Three Kingdoms period and were prevalent throughout the Unified Silla period (668 CE – 935 CE). Towards the end of Unified Silla, *hyangga* began to fall out of use, and they were written down according to the fixed form of poetry native to Korea during the early Goryeo period. Extant works include the fourteen *hyangga* found in *Samguk yusa* and eleven *hyangga* recorded in *Gyunyeojeon*. — 253

10. *sari jangeom* (Buddhist relics) — Before *sari* (sacred relics recovered from the cremated remains of Buddhist monks) were enshrined within pagodas, they were placed inside containers called *sarigu*, along with other accessories. *Sari jangeom* refers collectively to the relics, the reliquary in which they are stored, and device used to enshrine the *sari* within the pagoda. — 254

11. *simjuseok* (central pillar)	The stone that forms the central supporting pillar of a pagoda.	257
12. *hadaeseok*	Stone slab at the base of a stone lantern ("lamp of enlightenment"). Also known as *mit batchimdol*, or foundation stone.	257

09. Hangeul and King Sejong the Great

1. *Jongmyo jeryeak*	The Jongmyo Shrine, or Royal Ancestral Shrine, is where the ancestral tablets of the successive kings of the Joseon Dynasty are enshrined. The *Jongmyo jeryeak* is the ceremonial music for the ancestral memorial rituals performed in the Yeongnyeongjeon (Hall of Eternal Comfort). This traditional court music has been designated as Important Intangible Cultural Property of South Korea No. 1, and was also inducted into the UNESCO list of "Masterpieces of the Oral and Intangible Heritage of Humanity."	264
2. Bak Yeon	A civil official and composer, Bak Yeon stressed the need for tuning instruments and compiling scores. Bak Yeon is one of the three greatest masters in Korean music history, along with Wang San-ak, who invented the *geomungo* (seven-string zither), and Ureuk, who invented the *gayageum* (twelve-string zither). Bak reformed court music by replacing the ceremonial music with native Korean music and pursuing perfect pitch based on the 12-note *yulgwan* (a woodwind instrument used for tuning) that he created.	264
3. Maeng Sa-seong	Maeng Sa-seong, along with Hwang Hui, contributed to cultural advancement in the early days of the Joseon Dynasty. With a gifted musical ear, he arranged Korean music and even made musical instruments.	264
4. *Yongbi eocheonga* (Songs of the Dragons Flying to Heaven)	First work written in hangeul, the songs praise the foundation of the Joseon Dynasty.	264

10. Gyeongbokgung Palace and an Ancient Map of the Sky

1. *Pyeongyangseong* Fortress	Pyeongyangseong Fortress was the capital city of the late Goguryeo Dynasty, located in current-day Jung-guyeok (Central District) and Pyeongcheon-guyeok (Pyeongcheon District) in Pyeongyang, the capital of North Korea. The fortress is North Korea's National Treasure No. 1.	284
2. Gwansanggam	During the Joseon Dynasty, the government officials of the Gwansanggam were in charge of astronomy, geography, meteorology, calendars and water clocks.	284

3. *Byeongja horan*
   (Second Manchu
   Invasion of Korea,
   1636)

After *Jeongmyo horan*, the First Manchu Invasion of Korea, which took place in 1627 during the Later Jin Dynasty, Joseon and Later Jin formed a close alliance with each other. But Later Jin continued to attack Ming China, and changed the terms of their relationship with Joseon from equality to suzerainty, demanding various tributes in accordance with the revised relationship. King Injo of Joseon took a strong stance in defiance of these orders. Later Jin then changed its name to Qing and was outraged when Korean delegates from Joseon refused to kowtow to Huang Taiji, who had declared himself emperor of the Qing Dynasty. Thus provoked, the Qing assembled an army of 100,000 troops and attacked Joseon. This was known as the *Byeongja horan*, or Second Manchu Invasion of Korea. King Injo and his men, who had taken refuge in Namhansanseong Fortress, were cut off without access to food or ammunition during the siege. After two months, the king surrendered and signed a peace treaty with the Qing, in which he accepted the terms of suzerainty.

285

4. *Junggyeongji*

A history of the Goryeo Dynasty.

287

5. *sabangsin*
   (four guardians)

Sabangsin refers to the four animal guardians who represent the four points of the compass: blue dragon, black tortoise, white tiger and red phoenix. The exact term is *sasin* (four gods). They watch over the four cardinal points (north, south, east and west), and the four seasons (spring, summer, autumn and winter). They also symbolize the Five Elements (metal, wood, water, fire and earth), as well as the four primary colors of blue, white, black and red. A yellow dragon is also often depicted in the center, between these four guardians. Paintings of the four guardians, along with the constellations, have been found in the tomb murals in Ji'an, China and Pyeongyang, North Korea.

291

6. *logos*

In philosophy, *logos* ("word," "reason") is the universal law or rule that governs the existence of matter. It also signifies reason and discernment in accordance with universal law.

298

7. *pathos*

In contrast to *logos*, *pathos* ("suffering," "experience") translates as emotion, impulse and passion.

298

11. National Museum of Korea

1. Venerable
   Seongcheol

Born in 1912 in Sancheong, South Gyeongsang-do Province, Seongcheol became a monk after finishing middle school and achieved enlightenment while studying under the Great Master Ha Dong-san. Seongcheol was famous for cutting all ties with the secular world and devoting himself completely to the search for Buddhistic truth. He was critical of Jinul's theory of *dono jeomsu* ("sudden enlightenment, gradual training") and promoted instead *dono donsu* ("sudden enlightenment, sudden training").

302

2. War Memorial of
   Korea

Located near US Army Garrison Yongsan in Seoul, the War Memorial of Korea is South Korea's only museum devoted to the history of war on the peninsula. The museum was built in order to collect and preserve historical relics and records related to war, including conflicts with other nations as well as internal strife, and to educate people on the subject with the aim of preventing future tragedies.

304

3. *The Thinker* (*Le Penseur*)	*The Thinker* is a bronze and marble statue created by French sculptor Auguste Rodin and housed in the collection of the Musée Rodin in Paris. The statue, which depicts a man deep in thought while meditating on the agony of the human condition, is regarded as a work of art that strongly expresses the image of human beings engaged in eternal contemplation.	309

12. Wine and Song

1. Hansan *sogokju*	Brewed in the township of Hansan-myeon, Hansan *sogokju*, which has been handed down for over 1,500 years, is one of the oldest traditional Korean alcohols. On July 3, 1979, it was designated as Intangible Cultural Property No. 3 of South Chungcheong-do Province. With its excellent flavor and aroma, Hansan *sogokju* has been the subject of many entertaining stories. In the Joseon Dynasty, a Confucian scholar on his way to the capital to take the *gwageo* (the highest level of state examination to recruit government officials) stopped at a tavern in Hansan. Captivated by the flavor of the tavern's homemade *sogokju*, he lost track of time and missed the test. In those days, *sogokju* was nicknamed "*anjeun baengi sul*" (after an outdated name for paraplegics) for the way that drinkers seemed unable to walk away from the taste of this alcohol. On the medicinal side, it is said to be good for preventing high blood pressure.	324
2. *nuruk*	*Nuruk* (*Aspergillus oryzae*) is a fungus used as a fermentation starter to convert starches to sugars. It was first grown in Korea before the Three Kingdoms period. The two main types of *nuruk* are *tteongnuruk*, grown from rice, and *heutim nuruk*, grown from wheat.	324
3. *godubap*	*Godubap* is rice that is hard-boiled until the grains turn hard and dry. The rice is washed and left to soak for a day. It is then drained and steam-cooked.	324
4. *gumeongtteok*	One of the starters used for alcohol, *gumeongtteok* is a variation of *gaetteok* in which holes are poked through the centers of the *tteok* patties. The patties are made by adding boiling water to rice powder and kneading it. *Gumeongtteok* was primarily used among wealthy families and the nobility. It can be stored for longer periods of times, even in the summer.	324
5. *songpyeon*	In contrast to *gamhyangju* or *hahyangju*, which are made from *gumeongtteok*, a *songpyeon* starter was used to make clear, refined alcohols. The *songpyeon* dough is much thinner than *gumeongtteok*.	324
6. *injeolmi*	*Injeolmi* came into use as an alcohol starter during the Joseon Dynasty, when rice cakes became more diverse in form and flavor. *Injeolmi*, which is excellent for achieving fermentation, is used to enhance the flavor of alcohol.	324
7. *gaetteok*	*Gaetteok* is a rice dough made from ground rice powder and shaped into flat patties. It is used for liquors like *dongjeongchun*, which are known for their aroma.	324
8. *beombeok*	Another type of alcohol starter, a variety of powdered grains are added to boiling water and mixed. It resembles undercooked porridge. It is used to make *banghyangju*, which has a strong aroma and high alcohol content.	324

9. *balhyoju* — Also known as brewed alcohol, *balhyoju* (fermented alcohol) has a low alcohol content of 1-18%. Unlike distilled liquors, 2-8% of the content is sugar, amino acids and fixed acids, which give it superior flavor and aroma. — 324

10. *jeongnyuju* — *Jeungnyuju* is distilled alcohol, like soju or whiskey, with a high alcohol content. — 324

11. *honseongju* — *Honseongju* is aged liquor to which sugar, honey or fruit juice has been added to sweeten the ethanol created in the distillation process. — 324

12. *iyangju* — Alcohol is brewed from *nuruk* then reused as a starter to create a high-quality liquor. — 324

13. Su Dongpo — Su Dongpo, also known as Su Shi, was a writer, poet, scholar and statesman from the Northern Song Dynasty in China. As one of the Eight Masters of the Tang and Song Dynasties, he had a profound understanding of literature and created a new school of poetry with his deeply philosophical works. His most memorable work was *The Red Cliffs*. — 335

13. *Hanok*

1. *gudeul* — Also known as *ondol*, *gudeul* refers to Korea's unique underfloor heating apparatus in which hot air from a stove or furnace travels beneath the floor to heat an entire room or house. Flat stones, called *gudeuljang* or *ondol*, installed beneath the floor were used to conduct heat: the fire would heat the first stone, which would heat the next stone in turn, warming the floor of the room in the process. Though a similar principle of underfloor heating has been used in northeast China and Mongolia, those countries differ from Korea in that it was only used to heat part of a room rather than the entire room. — 351

2. *maru* — A raised wooden floor found at the center of a traditional Korean house, *maru* is said to have been used as far back as the Three Kingdoms Period, but it was not fully developed until the Joseon Dynasty. One of the distinguishing features of the *maru* is the long wooden posts or stone pillars used to lift and support the floor. Akin to a porch or veranda, the *maru* opens onto the courtyard or rear garden, allowing in views of the outside and serving as a place for rest and relaxation. It also functions as a passageway, linking rooms to each other. A multifunctional space, the *maru* also prevents moisture from the ground from seeping into the house, blocks harsh sunlight in summer, and provides ventilation through both the front and back of the house. — 353

3. *yongmaru* — Identifiable as the white ridge along the top of a traditional Korean house, the *yongmaru* sits at the highest horizontal point at the very center of the roof and supports the rafters. — 361

4. *hyeonsuseon* — Known in English as a catenary, *hyeonsuseon* refers to the curve that is formed when a rope of even weight and thickness is attached at either end to two points of equal height, causing the center of the rope to sag due to gravity. — 361

5. *domoksu* — The chief or leader of a team of carpenters. — 361

Advisory Committee

Venerable Jeongnim, Gilsangsa Temple

Lee Hyo-jae, *Hanbok* Designer

Editorial Committee

Choe Kwang-shik, National Museum of Korea

Lee Won-bok, Arts and Sciences Research, National Museum of Korea

Park Hyeon-mo, Sejong State Administration Research Center

Kim Il-gwon, Professor of Folk Studies, The Academy of Korean Studies

Lee Sang-hae, Professor of Architecture, Sungkyunkwan University

Special thanks to:

Choi Yeong-gan, Seoji Chogatteul Restaurant

Hong Ssang-ri, Cheongmaesil Plum Farm

Kim Oe-sun, Culinary Researcher

Ahn Hwa-ja, Natural Dyes Expert

Jeon Yong-bok, Iwayama Lacquer Art Museum

Jan Yong-hun, Jangjibang Paper Mill

Venerable Hyeguk, Spiritual Director of Geumbong Seon (Zen) Center, Seokjongsa Temple

Venerable Daejung, Baekheungam Hermitage

Venerable Bulsan, Director of Seon (Zen) Center, Unbuam Hermitage

Park Dong-chun, Research Institute of East Asian Tea Culture

Shin Gwang-su, Shin Gwang-su's Tea Farm

Lee Jae-jong, Sanbaragi

Docheon Cheon Han-bong, Master potter

Lee Han-su, Mayor of Iksan

Lie Sang-bong, Designer

Park Rok-dam, Korea Traditional Liquor Institute

Ubong Yun Jin-cheol, *Pansori* Master

Chung Mi-sook, Korean Furniture Museum

Shin Yun-gyun, Director of Areumjigi Culture Keepers

Jeong Min-ja, Adviser of Areumjigi Culture Keepers

Cho Gi-sul, Director of the Hanok Division, Housing Board

Bae Yong Joon

Bae Yong Joon is one of East Asia's foremost actors and an ardent
supporter of intercultural communication and exchange. For Bae
Yong Joon, staying in conversation with our past is important for the
future of humanity, and this book is a creative and heartwarming
record of what he has gained from that conversation.

   Bae Yong Joon made his acting debut in 1994 on the KBS
television series, *Salut D'Amour* (*Love Greeting*), and rose to stardom
with his role in the 1995 series, *A Sunny Place of the Young.* Having
established his acting career through a number of movies and
television shows, Bae Yong Joon became an international megastar
with his role as Jun-sang on the 2002 series *Winter Sonata.*

   A Journey in Search of Korea's Beauty was a yearlong project that
Bae Yong Joon undertook in order to learn more about traditional
Korean culture from the unfledged yet earnest point of view of
one Korean, and to record in a down-to-earth way what he learned
and felt in the process. This book is intended not only for foreign
readers who would like to learn more about traditional Korean
culture but do not have easy access to it, but also for Korean
readers as well who are in search of this country's beauty.